[... After the Media]
News from the Slow-Fading Twentieth Century

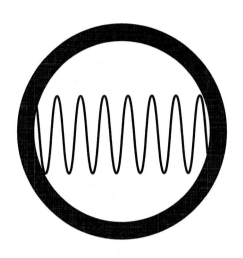

Siegfried Zielinski

Translated by Gloria Custance · Univocal

[... nach den Medien]
Nachrichten vom ausgehenden zwanzigsten Jahrhundert
by Siegfried Zielinski
© 2011 Merve Verlag Berlin

Translated by Gloria Custance
as *[... After the Media]*
News From the Slow-Fading Twentieth Century
First Edition
Minneapolis © 2013, Univocal Publishing

Published by Univocal
123 North 3rd Street, #202
Minneapolis, MN 55401

Thanks to Jon Thrower, Joe Hughes, and Gina Newman.
Designed & Printed by Jason Wagner

Distributed by the University of Minnesota Press

ISBN 9781937561161
Library of Congress Control Number 2013947974

Table of Contents

Preface

The question that has increasingly occupied my thoughts since the last *fin de siècle* is easy to phrase but difficult to answer: What would a praxis of research, artistic experimentation, and reflection on and with technological apparatuses and devices be like that amounts to more than just providing services for the media? And how can we avoid falling into the two traps of merely reviving the strong subject and once again propagating the sovereignty of the flesh?[1]

Future and past are identical, said Heidegger.[2] To seek answers to my question, or to be more precise: after refining and narrowing down my inquiry it seemed clear that I should go back to the early roots of thinking about media and how this evolved, and in the process investigate both the discursive establishment of the field as well as the energies, enthusiasms, and objects of curiosity with which I, too, was involved. What was it, exactly, that interested and excited us when, at the Technical University of Berlin within the milieus of the Institut für Sprache im technischen Zeitalter more than 40 years ago we turned our attention more and more toward the processes of machines, studied the inner structures of recording and playback devices, explored the possibilities of an editing table for creating a montage of the senses.

It was about understanding and laying open to view that which could be calculated, the scientific grammars and formalisms on the one hand, and on the other the relatively unbridled imagination; *poiesis* in the sense of

---

1 *Proud to be Flesh* is the title of *Mute* magazine's expansive *Anthology of Cultural Politics After the Net* (ed. by J.B. Slater and P. van Mourik Broekman, New York 2009).
2 Discussed in Elmar Holenstein's essay, "Von der Zukunft unserer Herkunft," in: *Perspektiven interkulturellen Philosophierens: Eine Bestandsaufnahme*. Festschrift für Franz Martin Wimmer (Vienna, 2013).

1

reactivating a synthesis of doing and of devising fantastic designs, and thus at the same time expanding the classical understanding of hermeneutics. Is it possible for grammatically organized systems of ordering and anarchic complexes of the imagination to work together? Or are they irresolvable antagonisms? Should they perhaps be conceived of as a non-trivial relation within interactions, including with the sciences?

Reasons, motives, and subjects for our intense curiosity abounded. The modes in which the Nazis had organized language and media manifestations as command structures was something we needed to understand. Many people had supported that murderous system of their own free will, and considerable numbers with great enthusiasm. In order to grasp how the battle for hearts and minds had been fought, I watched films like Veit Harlan's *Jud Süss* (1940) at least 70 or 80 times; both as an expensive 16 mm bootleg film copy from the USA on the institute's Steenbeck editing table, and as a ½ inch videotape on a heavy reel-to-reel video recorder. We wanted to know how the Nazi nightmare factory operated in the details of dramaturgy, *mis en scène*, dialog construction, camera work, use of music, costumes and make-up.

At that time the pronouncements of the powers on both sides of the Berlin Wall had again taken on the character of self-aggrandizing propaganda, and not only within the immediate area of political events. In the audiovisual media, which were becoming stronger all the time, mass-produced TV products assumed the role of advertising certain life-style concepts which were capable of integrating individuals, of promoting conformity to the programs of the power structures in the East and West. The first U.S. TV miniseries that ventured into controversial territory, which were actually early television auteur series, were the subjects of fascinating discourse analysis. The themes were political — *Roots: The Saga of an American Family* (1977) engaged with the identity and suffering of black Americans in conflict with whites, and *Holocaust,* the story of a German Jewish family, with the Fascist mass murder and persecution of Jews. In both cases, for the first time, important and disturbing historical subjects were dealt with in television miniseries that were entertaining and also quality productions.[3]

The arts also provided plenty of material for analytical treatment. An anarchic cornucopia of experimental films, radio plays, and videos were an invitation to expand the praxis of hermeneutics, which up to then had mainly been developed for literature. In the 1980s we had become so much a part of the techno-logical evolution ourselves that we wrote instruction manuals for food processors, electric shavers, and early office software like poetic texts. In return we got the first Unix computers at the Technical University Berlin and were able to use them for our experimental purposes.

From the outset, layers of time deeper than the present played an important role. In our quest for intellectual backup for the activities of "guerilla television," such as the Raindance Corporation propagated in 1970 and the architecture and design group Ant Farm brilliantly designed, we rediscovered the 1920s Arbeiter-Radio-Bewegung (Workers' Radio Movement) of the Weimar Republic and their forgotten and repressed media programs and expressions. We came across the radio transmitters of the resistance fighters, for example, the secret transmitter that electrical engineers built in the Buchenwald death camp which helped to liberate the prisoners in April 1945 before the SS were able to organize the "evacuation" that was actually planned as a death march.[4]

---

3   My first text published in the USA was on this subject: History as Entertainment and Provocation, in: *New German Critique* (Milwaukee, WI), No. 19/Winter 1980, trans. Gloria Custance.

4   See Hans-Joachim Hartung, *Signale durch den Todeszaun* (Signals through the death fence) (Berlin 1974).

These were very exciting research adventures. Through authors like Gotthold Ephraim Lessing and his introduction to the difference between painting and poetry in the famous *Laocoon* text of 1766 we gained the first concepts of time-based forms of expression and we learned to specify what media were before the media. With their marvelous archaeologies of film and the cinema, Friedrich von Zglinicki and C.W. Ceram already demonstrated in the 1950s and 1960s that we would have to excavate deeper than the nineteenth century if we wanted to reach the sources and complex developments of modern media.

We have now been working on this project for ten years. Under the operational neologism "variantology" we seek to develop in new ways what really interests us about media — as rich variants of relations between arts, technologies, and sciences. To date we have published five volumes on media before the media, from 2005 to 2011, to which artists, scholars, and scientists from over twenty countries of the old and new worlds have contributed. This research endeavor into the deep time of the contexts that interest us will culminate — for the time being — in 2014 with a conference in Amazonia with the title *Variantologia australis* (*Variantology of the South*). The conference will be dedicated to the communication and cultural techniques of indigenous peoples before the arrival of Europeans in their countries.

Because of the powers in play in our contemporary context, however, a scrutiny of the more recent past is also urgently indicated. That is how this book came to be written; as a contemporary essay and as a kind of act of intellectual liberation. None of my other books have engaged with such recent time dimensions. Thinking about media has only been a specific intellectual undertaking for a couple of decades. The essay is intended as a contribution to contemporaneity and as part of an ongoing work in progress. Immediately after the original German edition was published we launched a series of fortnightly events of discussions with protagonists of media thinking to keep the options for the future as open as possible.[5]

[... After the Media] is written from a European perspective, sometimes even from a Berlin perspective. This is partly due to the fact that we are at present engaged in a kind of "instant archaeology" to create an atlas of media thinking in the former capital of the Cold War. But I also think that comparable thematic genealogies need to be written by authors who bring in their own cultural and intellectual experiences and areas of competence, before we can bring them together at scales of greater dimensions and can explore and try out their compatibility in the long term.

From the perspective of the USA I have gleaned valuable ideas from contemporary thinkers such as Manuel Castells, Timothy Druckrey, and Avital Ronell, and from artists and writers like Perry Hoberman, Paul de Marinis, and Bruce Sterling, which appear indirectly in the text; to them I owe a debt of gratitude. I am also very grateful to Drew Burk and Jason Wagner, the courageous Editors at Univocal Publishing who have taken the risk of making my unwieldy *News from the Slow-Fading Twentieth Century* available to an American and international readership. My sincere thanks to Gloria Custance for the excellent translation, to Tom Lamberty for making publication of the German original edition possible with Merve publishers, and to Daniel Irrgang for all his help and work, especially with the illustrations.

Berlin, April 2013
Siegfried Zielinski

---

5 The website is bilingual (German/English): http://genealogy-of-media-thinking.net

Melatten-Friedhof Cologne, 2005 (Photograph: Pascal Fendrich / Nik Kern)

Introduction [The Argument]
The Media Have Become Superfluous

I.

The first decade of the twenty-first century was basically nothing more than an extension of what had gone before. When I began writing this book in the autumn of 2010, I had the feeling that we were still in the twentieth century. In the area of technology-mediated communication, there were scant grounds for speaking about the experience of a different historical quality. The first ten years after the zeroes rolled over to 2000 largely confronted us as the consequential fulfillment of processes that can be regarded as characteristic of the twentieth century: the implementation of a techno-scientific picture of the world as the determining worldview—despite the unfathomable catastrophes of Auschwitz, Hiroshima, and Nagasaki (which were also consequences of humankind's merciless measuring of the world); the enormous boost in standardization, both of technology itself as well as of the natural organisms processed by it; the expansion of the electronic control of technological conditions; the establishment of an aggressively advertised regime of media which offers to help the individual consumer cope with real-life deficits, breaks, and damages without going insane.

The beginning of the second decade of the new millennium was marked by an enormous discharge of the extreme tensions between nature and technology, which had been systematically cultivated in the twentieth century. In Japan of all places, whose population had already experienced the terrible destructive qualities of aggression-oriented nuclear technology first hand, a new nuclear catastrophe took place, with unforeseeable consequences. When one of the high security facilities collapses, known for allegedly producing the cleanest and most effective form of energy, it creates an uncontrollable maximum of lethal filth. What the monstrous power plants were actually built for, namely to generate energy, was brought to a standstill after nature massively intervened. The Japanese island of Honshu, including vast parts of the ocean in which it lies, was exposed to horrendous poisoning by radiation. The operators of the nuclear power station, and the politicians who shield them, have recklessly and with matchless arrogance played with the health of countless people for many generations to come. And they did not stop issuing statements about matters that lie well beyond their limited area of competence. The elaborated technological systems of communication perish in the face of the power that liars possess. Information does not happen.

A decade before the catastrophe in Japan, highly ideologized or bought suicide squads announced that the economic, political, and cultural order of the world, which the capitalistic West had established, would not last forever. The incredibly brutal and also desperate attacks on the World Trade Center in New York not only led to tight security measures as the normal state of affairs. For millions of young people in Africa and the Arabian Peninsula, this showed that using their bodies as weapons could trigger profound political shifts. Even though the price for this is very high indeed.

With propagandistic catchwords such as Twitter-, blog- or even Facebook-revolution (which from now on we will not use) at the beginning of the second decade of the twenty-first century, the international mediaocracy is suggesting to us that the world will now become entirely different because nearly everyone is able to exchange texts, sounds, and images with almost everyone else. In fact, commercial telematics are being used to organize rebellion against fossilized structures and brutal dictators with whom the affluent oil-dependent world had only recently done wonderful business. The message the insurgents have, though, is not immaterial. These young people have nothing to lose, except for their lives. With the entire dignity of powerlessness, they throw their bodies into the lethal interplay between different power constellations in the hope that those who recently had shamelessly applauded and supported dictators for egotistical reasons will now grant them their favor.

As a communicative system, globalism seems to work very well. Many want to be voluntarily included and respected within it, want to live like the Western and Northern Europeans, at least with regard to the constitution of their social and political orders and the level of their consumerism. The Internet, in its ambivalence as a techno-political tool for integrating the heterogeneous democracies and marketplaces and as adventure playground for delirious communications of extremely diverse kinds, is very hard to control and has established itself as the youngest mastermedium in history. In many regions of the Earth, millions of individuals have settled into the most impossible places. They have appropriated the new media and their cheap artifacts and have now themselves been appropriated by them with their promises. In this interaction, the potential of the media and its artifacts unfolds. Brecht's verdict from the late 1920s—that everybody now has the possibility to tell everybody anything, and immediately—is now an effect installed in everyday life.

The organization of life-threatening rebellion has become part of a process in which the utilization and provision of communicative services as a civil right are interconnected. Young people especially react to what kinds of notions of freedom, global brand-worlds, and popular culture are visible on the Internet. They want to participate in the redistribution of the world taking place at this moment. They also want to talk to everyone, travel everywhere, and buy everything. It was not a state, but the Hungarian multi-billionaire George Soros who managed to implement his idea of an Open Society all over the world, which is the name of his powerful foundation. As a result of highly successful speculations on the stock market, he is in a position to support processes for installing market-based and market-cultural ideas of freedom. It began in the 1990s in Eastern European countries; now the continuation of those developments has reached the Middle East and North Africa. The imaginary movement knows no boundaries because it is not primarily about territories or other physically experienceable qualities or about familiar political values. Openness and happiness are the objects of desire, and these are repeatedly cited by the individual protesters; nothing more, but also nothing less.

We are gradually becoming accustomed to paradoxical interaction processes. Crowded together in the telecommunicative networks are the most banal private things, the most hidden dirt, and the most desperate forms of prostitution in the dubious twilight of delirious publicity. However, when it comes to sensitive decisions and events that potentially affect existing power structures, they increasingly take place well away from this techno-communicative transparency. The only witnesses of the shooting of Osama Bin Laden are most likely the automatons of the killer commando themselves, and the only ones, who in the most direct sense of the word were actually allowed to be in the (recorded) picture, belong to the innermost circle of power at the White House.

We do not live in an Internet society, nor has the communicative action, which Jürgen Habermas once outlined as his utopia of an imaginary regency of enlightened actors, secretly taken over power.

The advanced level, the basic openness, and the existing wealth in the communication situation stand in diametrical opposition to the conditions of everyday life for the majority, in which there is a huge lack of basic necessities and any surplus that makes life worth living, and in which the murderous terrorizing of others is a daily ritual. In this sense, too, the communicative Nirvana of some is entirely detached from the real hell of many.

For the Orient (to which China and India also belong from a Hegelian perspective), a new century has long since begun. Furthermore, we are beginning to sense that the future constellations of a *mondiale* society are unimaginable without the countries of the African continent. The Japanese calendar scheme has begun a new era, given that coherence is imperative. Nevertheless, in the East a pronounced qualitative transition to the twenty-first century has not yet taken place. A strange lethargy and satisfaction with what exists holds sway. We first have to create new qualities with our own intellectual, political, and artistic activities, capable of stimulating or irritating us and others, otherwise they will never exist. If this is not done, new qualities will be forced upon us by others, something we should not accept.

II.

So that misunderstandings do not pile up during the course of my argument, an explanation right at the start is appropriate. I do not share the comfortable view that we no longer need a concept of what we term media or the media. Terms are the frameworks of abstraction, which we need for thinking and acting in ways that are interventions. The definitions that we make should satisfy two important criteria. They should be of a provisional character and should be open enough to allow further operations.

What I describe as media has developed into a heterogeneous, interdiscursive field. As a multifarious phenomenon, media process a variety of concrete, resistant artifacts, programs, and issues located between the arts, sciences, and technologies. These three meta-discourses form tension-fraught relationships with each other as well as with other discourses such as economics, law, and politics. These relationships are embedded in overarching *dispositifs*, to which so far mainly truth, knowledge, and sexuality belong. Many years after Michel Foucault's great work, this does not need to be repeated time and again; it is implicit throughout the entire presentation. If one thinks of a *dispositif* as something which is a given in a concrete situation and which fundamentally determines our behavior, it may be necessary to expand the above set of *dispositifs*; namely, by adding the concept of unconditional connectivity as a result of the idolization of technologically mediated dialogue. This remains to be seen.

III.

From time to time, a deep-time view of developments suggests that one should risk a quick look from a bird's eye view. Here one accepts, of course, that this perspective has the greatest possible distance from the viewed object of both photography and cinematography, and that this perspective is only possible to produce through artificial means, such as flight via airplanes. As an experiment, such a view can be helpful. With regard to history, it is informed by the interest in understanding the past not as a collection of retrievable facts but as a collection of possibilities.

Under the assumption that we are not only dealing with European Modernity but different competing Modernities which evolved at different times in different places, it makes sense to locate the development of the modern relations between the arts, sciences, and technologies at an earlier period and not in Europe. The Mesopotamia of the late eighth and early ninth century of our calendar is very suitable as an operational starting point. With regard to the last 1200 years, interesting and also quite regular fluctuations in the temperature of the relations between arts, sciences, and technologies can be observed. In the following these will be conventionalized.

With the invention of programmable universal musical automatons and a constant supply of energy to mechanical devices by the Banū Mūsā brothers, the House of Wisdom in Baghdad marked a strong increase in temperature in the early ninth century. During the turn of the ninth to the tenth century things slowly cooled down again. At the beginning of the eleventh century, relations heated up again enormously through the groundbreaking work on optics by Ibn al-Haitham. Devices such as the camera obscura were described exactly. Visual perceptions were rendered comprehensible as cases of mathematical-geometrical perspective and as a parallel activity of the brain. Above all a culture was established in which experiment was not only understood as an illustration of the correctness of an *a priori* hypothesis, but also as a process in which new knowledge could be gained. The development of the very rich Muslim automaton theater based on Alexandrian, Byzantine, and Greek traditions began in the new millennium with the *Book of Secrets* which the Andalusian engineer Ibn Khalaf al-Muradî wrote at the beginning of the eleventh century in Spanish Cordoba. With the compendium on theory and practice of the mechanical arts by the genius

Ibn al-Razzãz al-Jazarî, a Kurdish engineer from around the year 1200, this development reached its zenith.[6]

In the following centuries, the knowledge discovered and invented by Arabic scholars was enlarged upon, shamelessly exploited, and spread across Europe. Arab scholars' translations and adaptations of works from Ancient Greece, plus their own innovative additions, were translated into Latin, frequently without crediting the source, and then assimilated into Western knowledge. By the fifteenth century, the tensions and frictions intensified again enormously due to the protagonists of the second Renaissance, from Filippo Brunelleschi and Leonardo da Vinci to Alberti. During the second half of the sixteenth century, Giovanni Battista della Porta contributed to an enormous popularization of experimental and technical knowledge. In 1600, William Gilbert laid the foundations for a systematic conception of diverse magnetic phenomena prior to their emergence as electricity. This strange stuff on the borderline between materiality and immateriality, related to the Greek *nous* and at home in the imaginary ether, can at this point in time be considered as discovered.

During the developments in the run-up to the European enlightenment, alchemist and physicist Isaac Newton is an exceptional figure who does not fit in with the concept of the subsequent cooling down period. By comparison, Kepler, Galilei, Descartes, and Huygens were cooler, with primarily mathematical minds. They formulated the essential foundations of modern science and systematized the scattered, fragmented knowledge of the previous centuries. Athanasius Kircher, primarily a collector and a genial recycler of ideas, was a thinker who generalized the particular in the spirit of Catholic theology and natural philosophy, and in this specific sense was

6 See Zielinski and Fürlus (2010).

not only a polymath but also an early strategic media expert in the service of the Vatican.

Shortly before the turn of the nineteenth century, the formulated abstractions and separations under the sign of the new scientific rationalism caused the temperature to plummet in the relations that interest us here. Whereas for Julien Offray de La Mettrie in the 1730s bodies were eternally unorganized and uncontrollable, at a far remove from anything mechanical, in the writings of the Marquis de Sade lust became the object of a shameless and painful perversion of rationality. At the end of the eighteenth century, *Justine* and *Juliette* (1797–1801) formed the positive and negative poles of a morality that ran amok in quantifying the immeasurability of sexuality. "Something that is supposed to open the audience's eyes," commented Hans Blumenberg on the then flagging automaton culture of the Enlightenment, "now only induces the cheapest kind of stupefaction through effects whose mechanisms are concealed inside casings."[7] Exactly at the end of the century, in his 1799 *Hymns to the Night*, the Romantic poet Novalis lamented the passing of the gods: "Alone and lifeless stood Nature. It was bound with an iron chain by dry Number and rigid Measure. Like dust and air the immeasurable flowering of life crumbled into words obscure."[8]

A friend of Novalis', Johann Wilhelm Ritter, initiated a long heated-up phase concerning the relations between the arts, sciences, and technologies with his notion of electricity as a new *central phenomenon* that maintains everything in a perpetual state of tension and oscillation. This phase was the founding era of the new media, of the technical image, of sound recording, and of telematics.

---

7 Blumenberg (2009), p. 62.

8 *Novalis' ausgewählte Werke in drei Bänden*, ed. Wilhelm Bölsche (Leipzig: Max Hesse, n. d.), vol. 1, p. 23f.; online: Projekt Gutenberg, Hymn 5; trans. George MacDonald (http://www.george-macdonald.com/etexts/poems/hmn_to_the_night.html) modified by G.C.

The excitement about the media age lasted well into the twentieth century with its gigantic agglomerations and discharges, destructions and explosions, in which the media was already involved to a large extent. At the end of the century, the Internet seemed like a gentle dissolution of the concentrations—fascisms as Flusser termed them—which historically had been pent up for a long time. The digitally connected warehouse, with its seemingly infinite stock of images, texts, sounds, commodities, and services, offered the mobilized private users from Capetown to Copenhagen, Shanghai to Dublin all the possibilities of an up-to-date existence and state of the art cultural and technological sensibilities. For a great many people, social relationships would become primarily technology-based relationships. Henceforth, telecommunication would connect even more effectively and efficiently, but it would connect what is already deeply separated, as Guy Debord had announced in his *Society of the Spectacle* in 1967.

IV.

Now the media exist in superabundance, there is certainly no lack. For the thoroughly media-conditioned individuals media cannot possibly be the stuff that obsessions are made of any longer. What has turned into a given that is at one's disposal is now utilized and defended as property, but it is no longer a coveted object of desire. In this specific sense, the media have become superfluous. Through the monumental exertions of the twentieth century, they have also become time-worn.

An update of the promise that the media could create a different, even a better world seems laughable from the perspective of our experience with the technologically based democracies of markets. As an ersatz utopia, this promise appears to be obsolete in the formerly hegemonic regions of North America and Western and Northern Europe.

Now that it is possible to create a state with media, media are no longer any good for a revolution. Media are an indispensable component of functioning social hierarchies, both from the top down and the bottom up, of power and countervailing power. They have taken on a systemic character. Without media, nothing works anymore. Media's still surviving color supplements what we, in a careless generalization, continue to call a society. Media are an integral part of everyday coercive context, which is termed "practical constraints." As cultural techniques, which need to be learned for social fitness, they are at the greatest possible remove from what whips us into a state of excitement, induces aesthetic exultation, or triggers irritated thoughts.

At the same time, many universities have established courses in media design, media studies, and media management. Something that operates as an intricate, dynamic, and edgy complex between the discourses—that is, something which can only operate interdiscursively—has acquired a firm and fixed place in the academic landscape. This is reassuring and creates professorial chairs, upon which elements that were once anarchic can be pondered over and developed into knowledge for dominating and controlling. Colleges and academies founded specifically for the media proactively seek close relationships with the industries, manufacturers, and professional trade associations of design, orientation, and communication. In one of the myriad practice-oriented study courses of the late twentieth century, responsibility for a few weird television programs was sufficient qualification to be made a professor. A standard answer by many grammar school students to the question, what they would like to do in the future, jobwise, is "something or other to do with the media." If one spends hours a day in various connections to the technological worlds of communication anyway, then one might as well try to earn a living with it. Parents who, with the best intentions, want to give their children a safe future recommend them to train as a data processing services salesperson or as a communication designer, because if the kids put enough into the job they may reach the desirable position of a manager of a complex, the ramifications of which the parents themselves are unable to appreciate any longer.

"In a certain sense, we have transformed the entire world into a place, which is perfectly suited for analytical techniques." [9] Technology-based communication has superbly established itself. In such a clear cut situation —at least with regard to the media — it seems necessary to attempt to summarize, highlight certain points, and above all open up this familiar field for questions. How has the strategic option of the media developed over the last decades? What role did theory play in it? How did the current situation of stabilized boredom with respect to the media develop? Is it possible to at least sketch the contours of what quality may come afterwards?

The attempt to pursue these questions and to define them more precisely involves a certain risk. One has to reflect critically on how the main argument-configurations of various media discourses have developed in the past six to seven years. As I am involved in this process myself, this also implies that my own opinions must be called into question and should not be taken too seriously.

Detlef B. Linke, professor of clinical neurophysiology and neurosurgery rehabilitation, whose life was, with tragic irony, cut short in 2005 by a brain tumor, said that

---

9   De Landa (1997), p. 41.Meshworks, Hierarchies, and Interfaces in *War in the Age of Intelligent Machines*, Zone Books.

criticism is no longer effective because people are far too occupied with surviving the crisis. However, I am quite willing to accept its relative ineffectiveness, by which I also acknowledge my powerlessness. The position from which I believe it is still or is again possible to formulate criticism is located on the periphery, not in the center. This position can be found everywhere new ideas have been developed, before they are celebrated as fashions and trends in the metropolises and centers, before they have matured as products and are marketed as commodities or services. Let's take a chance and try to reactivate a profoundly dislocated point of view again.

1. Critique of the Strategic Generalization *the Media,* Their Provenance and Aims: An Unabashed *tour d'horizon*

To posit differences is simply an attempt to set one's thoughts in order. One distinction is essential for my following argument. I distinguish between two antithetical meta-concepts to apprehend what mediates between the one and the other; that "which consists of positing identity in opposition and opposition in identity,"[10] as Hegel describes the activity of electricity. The first concept brings together the instances and processes of mediation in the strategic concept of *the media;* it needs them as a generalization. The second concept operates with a loosely connected and fundamentally unclear multiplicity of technologies and artifacts of communication. In this case the objects of our curiosity — either singular or plural — are termed "media" and designated without the article. Hegel uses the term "media" to denote those phenomena "in which transparent media, various mutual positionings of reflecting surfaces and many further circumstances, produce an external difference in the appearance of light."[11]

The media refers to a specific historically and systematically deducible discourse, which has incorporated concrete entities. This discourse encompasses in principle the technical materials of communication, and at the same time instructions for their use. When we speak of "media," we are only citing an umbrella term for heterogeneous phenomena of a primarily technical nature. In the same way "wine" is both a collective name for an alcoholic beverage made of red or white grapes (as well as barbaric variants made from other fruits), and can also

---

10   G.W.F. Hegel. 1970. Hegel's *Philosophy of Nature,* ed. and trans. M.J. Petry, vol. 2, London: George Allen & Unwin, p. 168.

11   Ibid., p. 167.

be used for a particular wine that one has ordered to accompany dinner, perhaps an Amarone della Valpolicella.

The media are the result of work on generalizing that is powerful, virtuous for society, and in this sense geared toward virtuality. This work has its own history. *The media* have the character of a *dispositif* in the sense introduced by Michel Foucault — and following him, Giorgio Agamben. Their objectivations belong to the resources of knowledge and manifestation that structure power. *The media* are significantly involved in producing the cultural self, as well as co-constituting the sanctioned notions of the Other.

By contrast, for me individual media belong, wherever feasible, to the resistant particularities, to the free-floating singularities. Even so, they can also get dragged into the machinery of the systemic and thus also take on or be assigned a strategic character. This happens to machines as well as people and is, among other things, a question of time.

I hope that in the following miniature the distinction outlined above will become clearer. This brief genealogy of thinking about and conceiving media over the last sixty years or so is structured according to the caesuras that possess a certain authority or binding character for developments. In the sections of the book that constitute these caesuras, I attempt to show the salient positions and lines of argument that seem to me to be of particular interest for specific constellations in the past and for what is to come.

The selection is governed by my perspective, but it is not arbitrary. First, it incorporates figures from the history of how we have thought about media that have unjustly been marginalized and forgotten. Second — although this may appear paradoxical in the light of the preceding point — as a priority I discuss positions that were of special significance for my own intellectual development as a media researcher and collector of curiosities. In such a genealogy, continuity is impossible anyway.

The media become established as a specific interdiscursive field with a special claim to validity and power in the second half of the twentieth century. However, they develop such a strong presence during this period that the entire century appears to bask in their reflection.

Psychoanalysis and poetics are just two of the fields which, in the 1920s and 1930s, intensify their efforts to develop approaches that give a sharper profile to their diffuse fields of study and endow their elusive objects of study with the semblance of subjects amenable to scientific, that is, quantifiable methods, or even methods from engineering science. In the sector of communication via technical artifacts and systems, from the outset there is the intention of making operations and processes that are difficult to control more reliable, effective, and flexible, which were the frames of reference for these normative formulations to begin with anyway.

John von Neumann wrote his paper titled *Zur Theorie der Gesellschaftsspiele* [On the Theory of Games of Strategy] (1928) during his time at Berlin University. After emigrating to the United States, together with Oskar Morgenstern he applied the results of his previous mathematical analysis of games of chance with strict and not-so-strict rules to problems of capitalist economics. With the "minimax theorem" elaborated in von Neumann and Morgenstern's *Theory of Games and Economic Behavior* (1944), an attractive socio-psychological complex becomes the subject of cybernetic deliberations before these were even part of a defined field of study.

Cybernetics evolves as a discipline out of a fear of entropy and from the intention of using applied mathematics to describe what is difficult to calculate or predict, and to monitor it in tests, which at the same time extend the promise of controlling it. This is similar to the study of propaganda, which proceeds according to maxims that are comparable to those of cybernetics. In this field, formative evaluation means to organize process-es of expression, which at first glance appear opaque or disorderly, in such a way that within the economy of signs a foreseeable, i.e., calculable in advance, input–output relation can result. The analysis of propaganda, which goes hand in hand with its production, can be re-garded as one of the most important sources of the sys-tematic analysis of media phenomena. The concept of propaganda does not distinguish between the markets for politics or the markets for commodities. Viewed ge-nealogically, propaganda refers in equal measure to pro-moting ideologies and countries as well as things, ser-vices, and companies.

The political scientist and sociologist Harold Dwight Lasswell is an outstanding theoretician of propaganda as a necessary dimension of modern mass democracies if they are to function on a technocratic and scientific ba-sis. A prominent member of the Chicago School, Lasswell studies Freudian psychoanalysis in Berlin and writes his PhD thesis in 1927 on *Propaganda Technique in the World War*. In Lasswell's thesis German ideas, as outlined in works such as General Erich Ludendorff's *My War Mem-ories, 1914–1918* or *Karl Kerkhof's The War Against German Science* (1922), play a preeminent role. He regards such works as the most fruitful resources for his research into the characteristic traits of propagandist utterances and perception processes.

In the first half of the twentieth century Lasswell's position in investigating this form of communication is comparable to that of Jacques Ellul, author of *Propa-gandes* (1962), in the second half. The meta-theoretical premises of the two writers, however, are very different. Lasswell is a psychologically trained social scientist with an approach influenced by positivism. His credo is as fol-lows: if the masses want to be liberated from the iron chains of their existence, they must accept the new ones of precious metal. With this he offers a transition from propaganda research to applied social psychology.

In contrast, Jacques Ellul is a thinker well-versed in ideological critique. For Ellul, it is a foregone conclusion that propaganda is the rule in modern communications and not some extraordinary feature of politics. Propaganda must be approached within the framework of the constitutive terms and conditions of a "technological society." Therein it has the function of integrating what is unwieldy, what does not fit, into the technological world. Propaganda is an "effect" of technological society. Ellul ascribes an important role in this integration process to the "mass media of communication." With their own distinctive drawing power they ensure that individuals are transformed into a collective, a public, the masses.[12]

Anyone who desires to penetrate the market for theory must know how to formulate complex issues in short and pithy phrases which, ideally, lend themselves to formalization. Theoreticians, who invent such formulas, accept that for simplicity's sake such phrases will be used rather than the theoretical constructs on which they are founded. Lasswell's formula operates with interrogatives beginning with "W." The simple question is intended to express the essence of communication processes via technical means "Who says what in which channel to whom with what effect?" Here, the medium is still understood as an empty, neutral channel of transmission. The extreme reduction of complexity and sleekness of simple linearity, which are also the basis of all telematic processes, makes this phrase the instant formula of an emerging new field of research.

An entire branch of learning oriented on the social sciences and information theory will sprout from this formula. With his 1948 article, *A Mathematical Theory of Communication*, Claude Shannon supplies it with what

12 Ellul 1973, citations p. XVII and p. 104.

27

was then state-of-the-art information-technological know-how. His schematic diagram of any and every communication system is also composed of five elements and has a similar linearity to Lasswell's formula. It describes how a message, with as little loss of information as possible, can be transmitted effectively from its source to its destination, no matter whether the message source is a person speaking, a television tube, or a telegraph, and no matter whether the receiver is a person or an artifact.[13]

Together with Warren Weaver, Shannon poured his model into the mold of a simple function diagram. This formula is also used for purposes other than intended, for which the mathematician who invented it of course was not responsible: the model is adapted for psychology and other applications without any restraint, in spite of the fact that Shannon repeatedly insists that it describes a functionality in engineering science and not a cultural process.

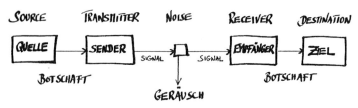

Technical communication as a simple directional event, after Shannon (1948) and Shannon and Weaver (1949).

With the observation, description, and the declared aim of more effective communication for the masses by technical means one can now acquire political merit and even earn money. This is an important step along the road to the means whereby technical communication is realized in taking on a strategic character. In the course of their propagation they will be called "mass communication," which literally means one transmitter simultaneously

13 Shannon (1948). See also in this connection Mc Quail and Windahl (1981).

serving a great number of receivers. Vilèm Flusser will call this kind of communication "fascist," because it implies an intense pooling and concentration of power.

HEIDEGGER
NIETZSCHE DERRIDA
ADORNO/HORKHEIMER BERGGRUEN
BATAILLE LÉVI-STRAUSS FOUCAULT
LACAN BRECHT TURING CAILLOIS ROTHKO AJEMIAN
BELLMER CAGE BACON
DE SAUSSURE
ORWELL MASSON MOLINIER MAKLÉS
BENJAMIN SCHRÖDINGER
— 1948 + McLUHAN
LASWELL KLOSSOWSKI
SHANNON ELLUL GIACOMETTI
WIENER WEAVER BARTHES
KLOSSOWSKI

- 1948 +

The concept of "mass communication media" endures for quite some time. It implies an audience that is passive, that is fed information and keeps quiet. Only during the 1960s does it give way to models predicated on active participants in the communication process. The *uses and gratifications approach*, developed mainly by Elihu Katz, introduces the figure of the user, who will become essential for telematic conditions. Yet already in the 1940s when the concept of mass communication was becoming established, Shannon and other mathematicians and engineers were working on more effective interpersonal, one-to-one communication, in network-like structures. Such systematic connections are already in existence in the technically elaborated form of telephony. During World War II, for example, technological efforts are already underway to solve communication problems, like the telephone queue that arise when lots of subscribers in the same community want to be put through to other subscribers at the same time.[14]

In 1948 telecommunication triumphs as a *dispositif*, which is of huge importance — at least for pop music culture. After successful experiments with electromagnetic pickups in the 1930s the first mass-produced, solid-body electric Fender guitar goes on the market. It is called Broadcaster, and is renamed Telecaster in 1950. Paradigmatically, the instrument simulates the core idea of technically based telecommunication. The message can be separated temporarily from the material body producing the message. The body of the electrically amplified guitar no longer needs a resonating chamber; it has been degraded to the level of a frying pan. The loudspeaker, whose membranes now vibrate and produce audible sound, is connected to the instrument by a cable. Whether the cable is two or 200,000 yards long is immaterial; the message can be heard at the location where it is received. The resonating chamber can be anywhere, provided the electrical connection works. A couple of decades later guitarists will play notes in Los Angeles that will be heard in a studio in London, for example. Instead of a cable the connection functions wirelessly.

With the trivial formulas of Lasswell and Shannon (trivial because they are one-dimensionally directional, i.e., without a feedback loop) we are traversing the immediate postwar years that are hugely important both for various arts and for science and technology. In the period around 1948 a mass of highly disparate works appear that are all very influential and each intervene in

---

14   See the informative outline for a dissertation at MIT in Boston, MA, by Leonard Kleinrock (1961) p. 4f.

their own way in the specific interplay of the technoid and the humanoid which is established in a third entity, *the media*. During the long years of Fascist terror, ideological pressures, and denial of artistic freedom much had remained pent up in intellectuals and artists, which is now unleashed. Some of the most important works had been created in the final years of the war, but only now see the light of day.

In 1946 and 1947 George Orwell writes his dark scenario of a future in which communications technology is the instrument enabling total control over society — *Nineteen Eighty-Four* — which is published in 1949. The writer and filmmaker Alain Robbe-Grillet, who at first works as a statistician after the war, writes his first novel *Un regicide* (*A regicide*) in 1948/1949 — against the true-to-life-representation ideology of realism and for the poetic autonomy of literature. A complete version of this experimental work will not be published until thirty years later.

From 1946 to 1948 John Cage composes the *Sonatas and Interludes* for prepared piano. Like a manual for a piece of technical equipment, Cage describes exactly what objects "of very different material" should be inserted where on which piano strings so that they "change the character of the notes entirely." Cage said he discovers his actual variants of prepared piano by experimenting with various materials and their arrangements.[15] Cage dedicates *Sonatas and Interludes* to friend and pianist Maro Ajemian who records it for the first time in 1948. In the same year Cage composes *"Dream."*

Jackson Pollock begins to produce his manic action paintings in 1947 which, unhampered by any constraints of figurative representation, unleash an archaic, delirious energy of color, line, dots, and material. The tiny sculptures that Alberto Giacometti made during World War II are now gradually allowed to assume larger dimensions.

---

15   John Cage, *Sonatas and Interludes*, in: Kostelanetz (1973) p. 107.

Attenuated figures gracefully stride or solemnly stand within exhibition spaces where visitors eye them eagerly as sculptural wonders. The Swiss master of designed empty space's quintet of awesome beauty, *La Place* (*City Square*) is created 1948/1949. At about the same time Francis Bacon begins to paint his bold, raw pictures with their metamorphosed, contorted, screaming faces which are exhibited for the first time in 1949. In the same year Mark(us) Rothko(witz), who comes of a Latvian-Jewish family, embarks on his radical large-format canvases with rectangles of color. They seem like alchemy transported into the sphere of art. At the same time, for a painter from a Jewish background, they seem to be the only possible artistic response to Auschwitz: abstraction as visual mise-en-scène of the absence of God and simultaneously the presence of God in the artist's genius and in the systematically formed material.

Hans Bellmer, who is originally from Katowice, studies engineering at the Technische Hochschule Berlin in the 1920s, which is not considered a university at this time in Germany because it does not have a philosophy department.[16] Bellmer begins his work as an artist among the circle of intellectuals connected with the left-wing publishers Malik Verlag, he is taught most notably by George Grosz. In 1933 Bellmer begins his curious Pygmalion Project. In his tiny dark apartment in Ehrenfelsstrasse 8, Berlin-Karlshorst, he constructs from wood and dark human hair a seductive doll "as non-compliance with German Fascism and the prospect of war. Cessation of all socially useful activities," Bellmer announces. The first version of the artificial being of 1934 contains a media apparatus. The doll's abdomen, which otherwise "has no function whatsoever," is an automatic

---

16 At the time of writing, the Technical University of Berlin is again reverting to vocational-oriented education. In the eyes of many politicians post-industrial society needs as little philosophical thought as industrial society did.

peep-show. Pushing a button on the left breast of the doll sets a rotating panorama of images in motion, and through its navel these shameless technically fabricated images are revealed to the voyeuristic gaze.

In 1948, after ten years of exile in Paris, Bellmer breaks his long silence (and puts an end to being ignored) by verbalizing his project in the brochure *Les jeux de la poupée* (*The Games of the Doll*), published by Heinz Berggruen in 1949 to support the impoverished artist. Bellmer's text focuses on the mechanics and ball joints of the kinetic artifact, whose origins he locates in the automatons of the Byzantine epoch and even in Judaic mysticism — "the apparatus resembles those censers that turn yet retain their equilibrium."[17] Already in the first sentences of the text, which was probably written before the outbreak of war, Bellmer gives a baffling interpretation of the survival strategy his project represents:

"Since games belong to the category of experimental poetry, toys can be regarded as 'poetic stimulators.' The best sort of game does not aim so much at a specific goal but draws its excitement from the thought of its own unforeseeable sequels — as if spurred on by an enticing promise. The best toy would therefore be one that is far removed from the lofty pedestal of some predetermined, unchanging function, but instead is as rich in chance and possibilities as the lowliest rag doll, which approaches its surroundings provocatively like a divining-rod in order to discern, here and there, the feverish responses to what is always awaited and everyone can repeat: The sudden images of the "YOU."[18]

17 Bellmer quoting Philo of Byzantium in: Hans Bellmer (2005), *The Doll*, trans. Malcolm Green, p. 61.

18 Hans Bellmer, Preface to *Les Jeux de la poupée / The Games of the Doll* [Paris 1949], in: Hans Bellmer (2005), *The Doll*, trans. Malcolm Green, p. 59. The French version of the text, which Bellmer wrote together with Nora Mitrani, does not contain the delightful expression "poetic stimulator." The otherwise excellent Special Issue *Obliques, numéro spécial Hans Bellmer* (see Bellmer 1975) unfortunately contains many errors in the German sections; see also Schade (1989), p. 19f.

The idea that the highest forms of play do not serve productivity but are a gratuitous activity associated with a state of exhilaration or delirium makes one think of other works. Johan Huizinga's *Homo ludens* of 1939, for example, and perhaps the most important book on game theory of the twentieth century, Roger Caillois' *Les jeux et les hommes*, published in 1958 by Gallimard. One also thinks of Ludwig Wittgenstein's nice association in his *Blue Book*: "*Compare: inventing a game – inventing a language – inventing a machine.*"[19]

Bellmer illustrates many of George Bataille's texts, including *Story of the Eye* (1928) and in large format *Madame Edwarda* (1941). In the 1930s Bataille develops his concept of an alternative economy of the "accursed share," which centers on the category of expenditure. Caillois works with Bataille in the anti-Fascist group Contre-Attaque, and in 1937 he begins working at the Collège de Sociologie. Walter Benjamin is an occasional guest there while he is still able to move about freely in his exile in Paris.

Joseph Schillinger finishes his master theory *The Mathematical Basis of the Arts* in 1942, shortly before his death. Although his bold propositions are published as a book in 1948, for a long time they are ignored by the arts and art theorists alike and are certainly not improved upon. Schillinger systematically investigates how mathematical logic enters aesthetic objectifications, why artistic devices such as mimicry or mimesis necessarily contain mathematical laws, and how in the course of future developments humans will derive their creativity directly from principles that can be mathematized: "With developments in the technique of handling material art media (special components) and the rhythm of the composition as a whole (general components: time, space), man is enabled to choose the desired product and allow the

---

19   Wittgenstein, *Zettel*, §326–7.

machine to do the rest; this is the rational and functional period of art creation."[20]

In 1948, a year after his appearance before the McCarthy House Committee on Un-American Activities, Bertolt Brecht publishes his revised and condensed instructions for dramatic art in the scientific age. He calls it *A Short Organum for the Theater*. In the title Brecht reestablishes a connection to the texts of Aristotle, whose aesthetics he had energetically opposed with his concept of Epic theater. With the Greek word "organum" Brecht emphasizes the toolbox-character of the work. It can be read as a manual for a new kind of art production — and not just for theater. For Brecht the *Short Organum* is a (self-) critical review of his reflections on the interaction between drama and poetry, science and scholarship, and society. It is a theoretical outline for practical interventions in the form of sagacious and quick-witted action in the aesthetic field.

> "I who am writing this write it on a machine which at the time of my birth was unknown. I travel in the new vehicles with a rapidity that my grandfather could not imagine […]. And I rise in the air: a thing that my father was unable to do. With my father I already spoke across the width of a continent, but it was together with my son that I first saw the moving pictures of the explosion at Hiroshima."[21]

The central idea of this toolbox is pleasurable learning and teaching through productions which at once interpret the world and are the world. "But science and art meet on this ground, that both are there to make men's life easier, the one setting out to maintain, the other to entertain us. In the age to come art will create entertainment from that new productivity which can so

---

20   Schlesinger (2003) p. 4f., quotation p. 5. Part 2 is devoted to the Theory of Regularity and Coordination, and Part 3 the Technology of Art Production.
21   *Brecht on Theatre. The Development of an Aesthetic*, ed. and trans. John Willett, Methuen: London, 1964, §16, p. 184.

greatly improve our maintenance, and in itself, if only it is left unshackled, may prove to be the greatest pleasure of them all."[22]

In 1948 Alan Turing writes his report "Intelligent Machinery" for Great Britain's National Physical Laboratory. The core of the report is a description of a thinking machine, which is not trivial but capable of learning. An obliging machine that simulates a child's mind which would then be subjected to a course of education where it would learn experience and knowledge and thus be enabled to reproduce and generate this in ever greater complexity without feeling any tiresome side-effects of hunger or desire.

To this day, Turing's idea of a machine that can think for us, and which possesses extensive operative abilities, is highly provocative. For Turing the prerequisite is an image of a human being who, with regard to thinking, already functions like a machine. "A man provided with paper, pencil, and eraser, and subject to strict discipline, is in effect a universal machine."[23] The highly organized part of thinking can be exported out of the biological hardware and implemented in a machine. This is the practical application of an idea that Ludwig Wittgenstein formulated succinctly in the early 1940s: "If calculation appears to us to be a mechanical activity, then the human being who performs this activity is a machine."[24]

Turing is an attentive and critical listener at Wittgenstein's Lectures on the Foundations of Mathematics.

---

22   Ibid., §20, p. 185.
23   (Turing 1948: 9.) Alan Turing, "Intelligent Machinery". National Physical Laboratory Report. In: B. Meltzer and D. Michie (eds.). 1969. *Machine Intelligence 5*. Edinburgh: Edinburgh University Press.
24   "Wenn uns das Rechnen als maschinelle Tätigkeit erscheint, so ist der *Mensch*, der die Tätigkeit ausführt, eine Maschine." Ludwig Wittgenstein, *Bemerkungen über die Grundlagen der Mathematik,* Teil IV, 1942–1944 [1953], Frankfurt/Main 1984, 234; English translation: eds. G.H. von Wright, R. Rhees, G.E.M. Anscombe, trans. G.E.M. Anscombe, *Remarks on the Foundations of Mathematics* [1956], revised edition, Cambridge MA, MIT Press, 1983.

What Turing means epistemologically by intelligence in his works remains unclear. Conceptual precision is not the center of his epistemological interest. He is not a philosopher but a mathematician and an engineer. And a heretic. He wants to provoke people into stepping out of their comfort zone, and he seeks a practical solution to the problem of the capability of thinking in other entities besides humans. It is for this reason that he develops the Imitation Game, a role playing game that is later named after him. The Turing Test shows that the performance of a machine expressed in language is in some measure comparable to the performance of a human expressed in language. A machine that can work as intelligently as a person and express itself can be called intelligent. It is becoming apparent that conceptions of intelligence are increasingly a problem of how language is viewed, and that the compilation of formalizable dimensions of intelligence has something to do with statistics:

> "I believe that in about fifty years' time it will be possible to programme computers, with a storage capacity of about 10^9, to make them play the imitation game so well that an average interrogator will not have more than 70 percent chance of making the right identification after five minutes of questioning. The original question, 'Can machines think?' I believe to be too meaningless to deserve discussion. Nevertheless I believe that at the end of the century the use of words and general educated opinion will have altered so much that one will be able to speak of machines thinking without expecting to be contradicted."[25]

Norbert Wiener's *Cybernetics,* with the explanatory subtitle *Or Control and Communication in the Animal and the Machine*, is published in 1948 in the USA and a few months later in German translation, and establishes the new discipline of controlling processes that are nonpredictable

---

25   A. Turing, (1950), "Computing Machinery and Intelligence," *Mind*, 59 (236): 433–60. The text also describes the Imitation Game; see also Link (2007).

or noncontrollable or difficult to predict or control. The idea of a thinking machine is also inherent in Wiener's cybernetics, as well as the uncertainty that has to be factored in at the interface of technoid and humanoid, when one attributes machines with the ability to think and allows for the mechanical dimensions of thought.

Erwin Schrödinger, mathematician and Nobel laureate in Physics (1933) who emigrated to Dublin, takes another direction in the first postwar years. In view of what the Nazis had done to and with technical rationality, and how the principles of nuclear physics have culminated in the atom bomb, Schrödinger returns to ancient thought, notably the Pre-Socratics and Democritus in particular. He explores the question of how the world was thought of at the time when the divisions that inform the modern view of the world did not yet exist: the division between subject and object, between mind and matter, between true and false.

Sigfried Giedion's critique of European modernity is elaborated in his superb opus *Mechanization Takes Command*. It will take German publishers over thirty years to bring out a German version of this influential work, which was originally published by Oxford University Press. Confidently and freely, *Mechanization Takes Command* crosses the disciplinary boundaries between art, science, and technology. It is an outstanding archaeology of the Modern era, long before this label existed for work in the field of cultural studies. The book's associative linkage of discourses that were previously conceived of as separate will become paradigmatic for processes characterized by cultural techniques. In Germany, authors such as Wolfgang Schivelbusch (*The Railway Journey: The Industrialization and Perception of Time and Space*) and Christoph Asendorf (*Batteries of Life: On the History of Things and Their Perception in Modernity*) later draw on Giedion's method and, in turn, influence an even younger generation of culture and media studies scholars.

A work like Giedion's has not yet been written for electronics. Perhaps it is only possible to think about heterogeneous connections as radically as Giedion did in retrospect. We have not yet left the period of electronics behind us like Giedion had left mechanics.

The title of Herbert Marshall McLuhan's *The Mechanical Bride* is a reference to Marcel Duchamp's *Le Grand Verre* or *The Bride Stripped Bare by Her Bachelors*, but the Canadian philosopher of communications theory is also well acquainted with the work of Sigfried Giedion. In his first book of short essays McLuhan analyzes individual phenomena of mass media communication like A.C. Nielsen's Audimeter, an electronic device for measuring broadcast audience data to compile statistics on audience listening, and later viewing habits. McLuhan approaches his subjects rather like an anthropologist as belonging to the phylum of techniques that can be used to observe life in primitive societies. His concept of "tribal man" also follows a cultural anthropological argument. The reception of electronic media brings people together, whereas that of traditional media, like the book, separates them. A central point, however, is the essay that gives the book its title, "The Mechanical Bride," in which McLuhan interprets the dominant pattern of the grammar of images in popular print media as rhetorical tropes of sex and technology. "'The walk,' 'the legs,' 'the body,' 'the hips,' 'the look,' 'the lips.' Did she fall off a wall? Call all the king's horses and men."[26]

While Norbert Wiener is puzzling out his cybernetics at MIT in sedate Cambridge, Massachusetts, two other intellectuals in their exile in California, the German-Jewish émigrés Theodor W. Adorno and Max Horkheimer, are deploring that technological rationality is already sliding into barbarism. The collection of essays,

---

26 McLuhan refers explicitly to Giedion in *The Mechanical Bride* (1951) in the essay on the Audimeter, p. 50; the following quotations are on p. 98.

Dialectic of Enlightenment describes this disaster; Adorno and Horkheimer assert that the instruments, which humankind had created to deal with and compensate for any inadequacies of the individual, have now assumed an independent existence and begun to strike back at their makers. The culture industry, in the form of the modern mass media, is now ruthlessly enforcing the idea of the — originally utopian — potential inherent in art; namely, to fuse (a) unrestrained subjectivity with (b) the notion of a common purpose, with the idea of a *communitas*, and occasionally even being able to reconcile the two. The first entity does not have to be called the individual, and above all the second does not have to be called society.

I have never understood why an unbridgeable epistemic gap should exist between this variant of Critical Theory, of "enlightenment as mass deception," and Jacques Lacan's idea of the imaginary as was later asserted in a conveniently post-structuralist manner. Lacan's lifeline of the psychological, which he throws between the symbolic and the real in order that those who are suffering as a result of the division do not have to go completely mad, is doubly encoded with salvation and punishment in a similarly tricky way as the institutions of the culture industry system are in Adorno and Horkheimer. Communication and communion have the same etymological root. We need the phenomena of the imaginary in order to come to terms in some measure with our shortcomings and our desires. We need the images to compensate for the fundamental impossibility of satisfying our appetites. In turn, the images punish us through their irresolvably illusory nature (*Schein*). "By repeatedly exposing the objects of desire, breasts beneath the sweater, the naked torso of the sporting hero, it merely goads the unsublimated anticipation of pleasure, which through the habit of denial has long since been

40

mutilated as masochism."[27] Adorno and Horkheimer are not psychoanalysts. Their object of investigation is not primarily the human mind. They are sociologists who argue philosophically. However, their analyses of completely normal paranoia — installed by commercial interests — do not lag behind those of Lacan, at least not in terms of their ready wit and accuracy.

The final version of the collection of essays *Dialectic of Enlightenment* by the founders of the Frankfurt Institute of Social Research appears in 1947; the revised version of Lacan's "Mirror Stage" in 1949. In the same year in France, Claude Lévi-Strauss publishes his grand-scale case for interpreting ethnological and mythological complexities as phenomena with recurring structural features. His book, *The Elementary Structures of Kinship*,[28] implicitly ennobles linguistics and makes it the leading discipline of the humanities. Of all the disciplines engaging with the social, only linguistics has the ability to conflate in the broadest sense diachronic and synchronic explanations of psychological objects. By adapting Ferdinand de Saussure's theory of language, as well as its further development by the Russian formalists and the Prague School, it became possible to investigate the rites or myths of Amazon Indios that had hitherto seemed impenetrable to scholars of modern civilization. The meaning of a linguistic or cultural sign could be deduced from the difference to other linguistic or cultural signs. It becomes functional. Lévi-Strauss' critique of the concept of incest in Sigmund Freud's *Totem and Taboo* is a tour de force. His interpretation of the incest taboo as the basis and motivation of cultural and economic exchange becomes the master-idea of a new understanding of research in the humanities.

27 Theodor W. Adorno and Max Horkheimer, (2007), *Dialectic of Enlightenment,* Stanford University Press, p. 111.

28 *Les structures élémentaire de la parenté*; English edition: *The Elementary Structures of Kinship*, ed. Rodney Needham, trans. J.H. Bell, J.R. von Sturmer, and Rodney Needham, 1969).

Quand on parle de la valeur d'un mot, on pense généra-
lement et avant tout à la propriété qu'il a de représenter
une idée, et c'est là en effet un des aspects de la valeur linguistique. Mais s'il en est ainsi, en quoi cette valeur diffère-
t-elle de ce qu'on appelle la *signification* ? Ces deux mots
seraient-ils synonymes ? Nous ne le croyons pas, bien que la
confusion soit facile, d'autant qu'elle est provoquée, moins
par l'analogie des termes que par la délicatesse de la distinction qu'ils marquent.

La valeur, prise dans son aspect conceptuel, est sans
doute un élément de la signification, et il est très difficile
de savoir comment celle-ci s'en distingue tout en étant sous
sa dépendance. Pourtant il est nécessaire de tirer au clair
cette question, sous peine de réduire la langue à une simple nomenclature (voir p. 97).

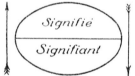

Prenons d'abord la signification telle qu'on se la représente
et telle que nous l'avons figurée
p. 99. Elle n'est, comme l'indi-
quent les flèches de la figure,
que la contre-partie de l'image auditive. Tout se passe

Fragment from one of several very influential books of the twentieth
century that did not appear under the names of those who wrote them:
Ferdinand de Saussure, *Cours de linguistique génerale* (1916), p. 158.

The psychoanalyst Lacan does not say a word about
Lévi-Strauss in his study of 1949. However, for the paranoia specialist the expansion of linguistic structuralism
as a kind of meta-concept for the investigation of psychological phenomena offers the chance of shedding
light on the obscure Freudian organization of the mass
of the unconscious ego through grammatical form. Other psychological remnants, which were hitherto not
accessible to scholarly research, are apprehended
through unremitting elucidation and the endless text.

I, myself, no longer speak, but the world uses me as a medium to articulate itself. The world speaks incessantly to me, through me to others, and through the others to me.

Only the permanently non-utterable and non-writable of the real stubbornly refuses to have any light shed on it, and as a result is circled around and venerated by the group of French master-thinkers like an idol. Bellmer, the obsessive from ultra-Catholic Katowice, the apostate Jesuit and ecstatic transvestite Pierre Molinier, and the artist and writer on literary, theological, and philosophical themes Pierre Klossowski become the uncrowned kings of the group's world of ideas with their endless erotic games involving bodies, dolls, and masks. From time to time some of them come together under the sign of Bataille's headless monster Acéphale in a secret society and a journal project of the same name. Lacan has an affair with the actress Sylvia Maklès, Bataille's wife, whom he subsequently marries. He buys the famous painting by Gustave Courbet, *L'origine du monde* (*The Origin of the World*) of 1866 from a decadent Hungarian aristocrat. Lacan asks André Masson, who in 1928 had illustrated Bataille's scandalous *History of the Eye*, to build a frame and draw another picture on it, covering the painting's detailed depiction of the pubic hair and genitals, and to conceal both pictures behind an opaque curtain.

After the proclamation by Nietzsche of the death of the Christian monotheistic God (a proclamation enthusiastically adopted by structurally oriented thinkers), not only a new father figure of psychoanalysis reigns with Lacan, but also thematically a new trinity, semantically not far from the old one: the imaginary, the real, the symbolic; Kronos, Kairos, Aion; God the Father, the incarnated Son of God, the Holy Ghost. Generalizing one could say: the trinity consisting of first, something that rules our lives; second, something that in its abstraction overflows far beyond life; third, something that as a special quality enters life and gives it rhythm. The triad is a persistent figure in Western discourse. Friedrich Kittler will also base his triptych of media devices, *Film, Gramophone, Typewriter*, on this ancient figure.

After Lacan split the ego into the I of the conscious imaginary (*moi*) and the real I (*je*) which cannot be consistent with its own reality, it is impossible to conceive of the contemporary subject as homogeneous any longer. It becomes out of sync, tact-less in the true sense of the term. What Lacan diagnoses as suffering in the paranoid mind, cultural criticism quickly generalizes into a fixed idea of all psychological relations. An absolute historical subject becomes inconceivable and is declared as something obscene. In opposition to the Marxist existentialist Jean-Paul Sartre and others who cling to the sovereign subject, a new generation of thinkers appears who combine structuralism, critique of power, Bataille's heterologies, the relative undogmatic Marxism of Althusser, which is influenced by Lacanian psychoanalysis, and Heidegger's philosophical thought into a "Gay Science" in the Nietzschean sense. From this they develop their own individual planets — Roland Barthes focuses on the arts, literature, and the signatures of the profane; Michel Foucault on history and power; Jacques Derrida on language and the text. With *Le gai savoir* in 1969, Jean-Luc Godard makes a nervous and colorful cinematographic tracing of these new and particular cultures of thought.

Barthes' short essays, published in 1957 under the title *Mythologies* are written between 1954 und 1956. With a similar approach to McLuhan's in his *Mechanical Bride*, in over fifty texts Barthes projects the concept of the myth onto surficial phenomena of contemporary mass culture: for example, a standard French dish "Steak and Fries," a stage show "Striptease," and a machine "The New Citroën." By looking closely at such familiar things they become alien. Like in Lévi-Strauss, but in reverse:

44

things from a foreign culture are experienced as alien, yet via structural analysis they are integrated in our own realm of intellectual experience. The starting point for each of Barthes' reflections is a fragment of media material that the author had fished out of the continually flowing production line of mass culture — a newspaper article or photo, a cinema film or theater performance, an exhibition. Critique of ideology and semiotic analysis amalgamate to form a fascinating compound in each vignette, and make *Mythologies* one of the most important books of semiotic literacy.[29]

Several months later another master text is published in Paris: Gilbert Simondon's *Du mode d'existence des objets techniques* (1958) (*On the Mode of Existence of Technological Objects,* 1980).[30] Although this text by the student of Canguilhem and Merleau-Ponty has an enormous influence on philosophy in postwar France, particularly on Gilles Deleuze, it is not available in German translation until 2012. Three paradigms in particular underpin Simondon's philosophical reflections on technology: technical objects like machines must be understood as heterogeneous constructions; technical objects have to be conceived in terms of ensembles; and technical objects are not fixed once and for all but are subject to continual change. In Deleuzian terms they are phenomena of becoming. Simondon's central idea that the machine is an alien which includes human elements, reveals an understanding of culture as a close-knit fabric of the human and the technological. These paradigms will later achieve particular prominence in Bruno Latour's and Bernard Stiegler's reflections on technology.

---

29 In 2010 Édition du Seuil released a large-format new edition of *Mythologies*, with photos and clippings from newspapers and magazines which vividly reconstructs Barthes' project.

30 *Die Existenzweise technischer Objekte,* trans. Michael Cuntz (Zurich 2012). In Germany Henning Schmidgen is one of the few commentators who has drawn attention to Simondon's work before.

AGAMBEN SIMONDON COHEN-SÉAT
GUATTARI TWOMBLY
LEBEL CHOTJEWITZ ROBBE-GRILLET
GENET QUENEAU ECO RESNAIS
GYSIN BURROUGHS
BALESTRINI BOMPIANI POP
REED SOMMERVILLE OLIVETTI KRAPP
BURRI FONTANA
WIENER — 1961+ PASOLINI GP ORRIDGE
MOLES
HÖLLERER KNILLI EISENREICH ADORNO
ZEMANEK SCHWITZKE MACIUNAS
CHOMSKY BENSE NORIS GENET
RAUSCHENBERG MEKAS KOUNELLIS LACAN

– 1961 +

Unsettling images appear in a few European cinemas
in the autumn of 1961. The two Alains, Robbe-Grillet
and Resnais, have completed *L'année dernière à Marienbad*
(*Last Year at Marienbad*), a *ciné-roman* with a very unusual structure. The classic linear form of narration is dis-
carded in favor of a horizontal, associative montage of
highly artificial narrative fragments. The tracking shots
and panning of the camera through the corridors and
rooms of the luxury hotel, the gestures of the protagonists, whom the authors call A, X, and Y, the voices of
actors and actresses whom one only sees in mirrors, the
illusionary profundity of the artificial dialog — everything is unusual and evidently out to reinvent cinema as
well as poetry. The film appears to have been shot with
mathematical and geometrical precision. The Paris intel-
ligentsia is in raptures. It was in Marienbad that Lacan
presented the first version of his Mirror Stage in 1936. In
1880 Nietzsche was there to recuperate in the Eremitage

but his health deteriorated dramatically and he was in a terrible mood for five weeks.

Sixteen years after the end of World War II, German tanks again roll through Berlin; this time against its own citizens in the Eastern part of the city. The acrimonious ideological and political struggles over the "right" consequences to be drawn from the twin disasters of Fascism and Stalinism culminate in the building of a wall, which will become much more than just an architectonic expression of the division of a city and a country. This edifice, which from the start had barbed wire and a lethal minefield, becomes the symbol of the Cold War; an emblem of the irreconcilability of the two worldviews of capitalism and socialism, which, as universalist principles, both press toward generalization. Language, in the broadest sense as everything that, following a grammar, articulates itself, becomes an important terrain for the hot and cold battles of the power-hungry know-it-alls. Once again, language is pervaded by propaganda and pathos-evoking formulas. Administrators threaten to dominate poetry with a heavy hand; culture brought within the sphere of administration, as Adorno never tires of criticizing.

This is the most significant reason — the impetus comes from external circumstances —why the decision is taken to found SPRITZ, the Institut für Sprache im Technischen Zeitalter (institute for language in the technological age). It is an initiative of Walter Höllerer, poet and professor of literature, in the year the Berlin Wall is built, at the Technical University Berlin, where the young Ludwig Wittgenstein had studied aeronautics before he moved to Manchester. "As of the 13th of August," writes Höllerer in the editorial of the first issue of the institute's journal of the same name, "the plan to publish this journal has become even more resolved. This date has once again demonstrated the dislocations that have been inflicted on contemporary language, the warping and masking of terms and of tone. At the same time these events have shown how difficult it is to respond to such a language and not lapse into invoking myths and mass suggestion." In a single sentence Höllerer formulates the program of the new institute's endeavor: "We are not going to plead the case for a 'language of technology' nor reduce language to its countable, mechanical principles, rather, language is to be investigated in terms of its necessary usage and resistance in a century that is influenced by technology."[31]

To this end, one needs to know exactly what technology is capable of. The close interplay between linguistics, computers, and electroacoustics, which is so characteristic for early communications research at the TU Berlin, is clearly demonstrated by the contributions in the first issue of SPRITZ. Heinz Zemanek's article focuses on the limitations of "automatic translation of language"; Herbert Eisenreich examines the "regularities of language and methods for opposing control of language"; and in an aside, with the journal's regular section devoted to "mass media" Höllerer heralds the later founding of the first media studies department at a German university — established in 1967 by his research assistant Friedrich Knilli. Knilli had studied mechanical engineering, psychology, and radio-semiotics (*Deutsche Lautsprecher*, 1970). In the mass media section of the first issue of SPRITZ, Helmut Krapp engages with the "contrasts between images and language," which in the age of the spread of the Internet remains an abiding theme; Heinz Schwitzke offers one of his many contributions to the "language of radio plays."

At the same time, a few hundred kilometers south-west of Berlin, Max Bense is working on what Höllerer excludes; namely, the "countable, mechanical principles" of language

---

31 W. Höllerer (1961), "Diese Zeitschrift hat ein Programm," in: *Sprache im technischen Zeitalter*, no. 1, p. 1f.

and its poetic concretions.[32] Let us briefly reconstruct how Bense has arrived at this.

In the 1930s Bense studied subjects in both the arts and sciences and received his doctorate for the dissertation "Quantenmechanik und Daseinsrelativität" ("Quantum Mechanics and Relativity of *Dasein*"). After the war he focuses on issues of poeto-logics.

Max Bense in the TV program *Kunst: Ein schwindendes Phänomen* (Art: A disappearing phenomenon), in the background is a work by Lucio Fontana, BR (Bayerischer Rundfunk — Bavarian Broadcasting), November 2, 1966. Photo © Paul Sessner.

---

32   When I asked Norbert Miller in 2010 again about the early relations between Höllerer's institute and the Stuttgart School, he brusquely assured me that the Berliners had had nothing to do with them.

"The world we live in is a technical world." This is the opening sentence, formulated with the precision of a Wittgenstein, of Max Bense's essay *"Technische Existenz" (Technical existence)*[33] *which had already been published in 1949. Five years later, Bense begins a series of monographs entitled Aesthetica, which investigate mathematical principles within the sphere of the arts. A few months before the launch of the new journal* Sprache im technischen Zeitalter at the Technical University of Berlin, Bense publishes a volume in his book series with the provocative title *Programmierung des Schönen (Programming beauty)*. Bense rediscovers Walter Benjamin and discusses him in conjunction with Wittgenstein as an early game theorist. Especially, however, he develops "a general theory of text and of text aesthetics," printed in a severe square format, which is up to date; that is, based on technical and information theory.

Referring to earlier critiques of civilization, Bense writes in the Preface to *Programmierung des Schönen*, "Civilization, as the supremely habitable sphere of this world which was made by ourselves is essentially based on *precision*." Our originality can only be de-ideologized and de-mythologized by "its dissolution in the finite steps of the production" of precision. "No mythology nor theology can put us in the relationship to technology that is adequate for existence,"[34] Bense has already noted in his *Technische Existenz*. He then associates the possibility of *programming beauty* with the idea of a new era of technology, which for him has already begun. The age of the classic, mechanical machine, which forced the old divisions, is over. The "trans-classic machine" of the electronic computer now makes it possible to reach "an understanding between technology and aesthetics." The concept of beauty is losing in substance, but gaining in

---

33 Bense (1998), p. 122, trans. G.C.
34 Ibid., p. 123.

function. On the basis of the thoroughgoing interplay of science and technology, of mathematics and information theory, one can now speak of an "artwork as a carrier of *aesthetic information*."[35]

In an obvious reference to Noam Chomsky's "generative grammar" from the mid 1960s, Bense calls the most advanced dimension of the new arts "generative aesthetics." By this term Bense understands "the aggregation of all operations, rules, and theorems [...] through whose application to many material elements, which can function as signs, aesthetic states (distributions and/or designs) can be produced intentionally and methodically."[36] At the end of a text written for *Bit International* magazine, which appeared from 1968 to 1972 in what was formerly Yugoslavia, Bense defines the idea of generative aesthetics with pragmatic clarity: "Its goal is to dismantle the process of producing art into *a finite number of constructive steps*. Thus it is a "definite" aesthetics. Ideally, it leads to the setting up of "programs," which serve to produce "aesthetic states" with the aid of *program-controlled* computers."[37]

Intimate connections between machines and organisms that are capable of thought are, at the beginning of the 1960s, by no means outlandish excursions into an imaginary future. On behalf of the U.S. *National Aeronautics and Space Administration* (*NASA*), psychiatrists, physiologists, narcotics specialists, programmers, and engineers work on hybrids of cybernetic machines and biological organisms, which over half a century ago are dubbed "cyborgs." The first cyborg was a laboratory rat with a tiny mechanical infusion pump implanted in its body.

---

35   Bense (1960), quotations pp. 10, 15, and 14, trans. G.C.

36   Bense (1965), pp. 11–13, trans. G.C.

37   Bense (1968), p. 81, which first appeared in *IBM-Nachrichten* 180, 1966, pp. 294–296; I am indebted to Margit Rosen for valuable information, trans. G.C.

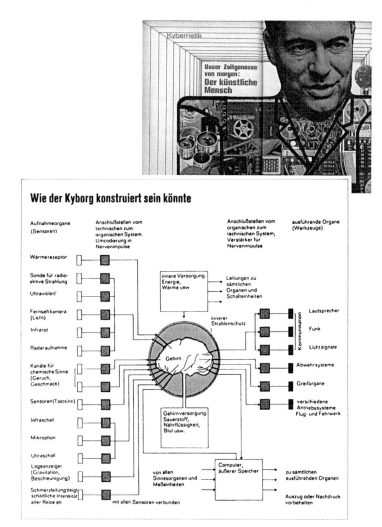

"Is the cyborg still a member of our society?" Source: The popular German magazine *Hobby. Das Magazin der Technik*, no. 22, 1970.

Intelligent machines hold out the promise that they will not make the same mistakes as the people who invented them. Artificial designs, exact sketches, defined rules and their precise execution do not only apparently compensate for the imperfections of nature, as Adorno and Horkheimer and Lacan each propagated in their own way. By these means the imperfections can be avoided or even overcome, at least in fields that are not averse to formalization. Machines and programs, which seem like signs of their intelligence, should at least get the chance to do everything better, including art and poetry.

The beginning of the 1960s is the stuff that dreams are made of for a part of the young Italian avant-garde. Pier Paolo Pasolini, who at this time has already been expelled from the Italian Communist Party, makes *Accatone* in 1961, his first social melodrama with an anti-social hero from the Roman suburbs; the writers Nanni Balestrini and Umberto Eco together with Alberto Noris, a doctor of engineering from International Business Machines Corporation (IBM), sit down at a large computer and generate the permutational poem *Tape Mark 1*. The title refers to the Automatic Sequence Controlled Calculator, a computer developed in 1943/1944 at Harvard University, and the computer using tubes that was built 1948/1949 at the University of Manchester — both were called Mark 1.[38]

The IBM 7070, for which Balestrini designed the poem out of units of existing literary phrases,[39] stands in the new computer center of the Cassa di Risparmio delle Provincie Lombarde bank in Milan. The three protagonists in front of — or rather in — the huge machine are wearing ties and conservative suits. The IBM 7070 was

---

38 On the Manchester Mark 1 see David Link (2006), p. 19f.

39 His sources were Michihito Hachiya's *Hiroshima Diary*, Paul Goldwin's *The Mystery of the Elevator*, and Lao Tzu's *Tao Te Ching*; see the *Almanacco Letterario Bompiani 1962* and our English translations in *Variantology 5* (Cologne 2011).

one of the electronic monsters that large banks used to do their routine accounting faster and more precisely. In the late 1950s, the Italian typewriter manufacturer Olivetti develops huge mainframe computers for offices and banks similar to those of IBM; however, the elegant Olivetti Elea 9003 remains just an intermezzo.[40] The experiments of the Italian avant-garde are performed on a machine from the USA. In Milan, Bompiani provided them with a publishing platform. The *Almanacchi letterari Bompiani* yearbooks of the early 1960s are compendia of a new aesthetic, poetic, and political feeling. The edition of 1963 with the title *Il messagio fotografico* (*The photographic message*) contains a brilliant analysis of journalism photos by Roland Barthes. The main focus of this edition is the structural interpretation of popular images, *La civiltà dell'immagine* (*The civilization of the image*) by Gilbert Cohen-Séat, an impressive heuristics for thinking the apparatus before the advent of Apparatus Theory, which has still not been translated into English or German from the original French. Valentino Bompiani is able to present as contributors Burri, Fontana, Kounellis, Lichtenstein, Rauschenberg, Twombly, and Warhol — a considerable section of the world's artistic avant-garde elite. Without resorting to any hierarchical ranking, the 1963 *Almanach* describes last year's output of Fluxus art, theater, cinema, and television, and meticulously lists the nuclear weapons tests carried out by France, the Soviet Union, and the U.S. from October 4, 1961 to September 25, 1962; a full dozen, that is, one nuclear explosion per month.

When Pasolini's film *Il Vangelo secondo Matteo* (*The Gospel According to St. Matthew*) reaches Italian cinemas in 1964, in which he gave Giorgio Agamben a part lasting a couple of seconds as Jesus' disciple Paul the Apostle,

---

40 On the development of complex computers within the Italian Olivetti company, which came to an end not least because of the death of Adriano Olivetti, see Parolini (2008). George Maciunas honored Olivetti in November 1962 with a Fluxus performance.

Balestrini was fabricating his permutation novel *Tristano*. Umberto Eco is still grateful to him for this today. Balestrini, who very reluctantly attended an engineering college but quickly dropped out,[41] impressively demonstrates how one can even generate new narrative literature from existing literary phrases using a clever algorithm in *Tristano*. Balestrini modestly calls the aesthetic product that can be created with the help of the machine an "aurina" or "auretta"; a cute little aura.[42]

The cofounder of the Gruppo '63 and Neoavanguardia does not succeed in producing a bestseller using this concept. With Antonio Negri and many others Balestrini is accused of armed subversion and involvement in the assassination of Aldo Moro. He escapes over the Alps to France on skis. There he meets Jean-Jaques Lebel and Félix Guatarri, among others, and he still lives there today, as well as in Rome. He knows Robbe-Grillet from the time of their collaboration on the literary journal *Il verri*. Almost half a century after the artist, who also produces visual text collages for galleries and museums in Dadaist manner, conceived his literary experiment Suhrkamp publishers print 2000 variants of his *Tristano* novel. Eco writes the introduction and, shortly before his death, Peter O. Chotjewitz translates the novel into German.[43]

41   Personal communication, November 2010.
42   Personal conversation in Rome, 4/8/2011.
43   Balestrini (2010). In Italy the experimental novel was rediscovered two years earlier. Il verri devoted a Special Issue to it with the title "attività combinatorie," see Balestrini (2008).

Nanni Balestrini (second from left) with Jean-Jacques Lebel, Giairo
Daghini, Jean-Paul de Gaudemar, Felix Guattari, Christian Descamps,
and Jean-Pierre Faye (from right to left) at the presentation of the
journal *Change International* in Paris 1983. Photo: personal archive of
N. Balestrini.

Raymond Queneau pursues primarily poetic goals in his
collection of permutationally modified sonnets *Cent mille
milliards de poèmes* (1961). The poems are cut into pieces
with one line per piece, and the reader can arrange them
in any order and produce a myriad of variants. However-
er, there is another permutational product whose reproduction entails a fair amount of effort. Balestrini's idea
is a mixture of technical utopia and radical democratic
market for culture. It propagates the concept of manufacturing processes being sped up and rendered more
effective by computers. Under the terms of the highly flexible, trans-classic machine (Bense), it should be
possible to control printing presses in such a way that
each copy of a book produced has different information
content. Not endless reproducibility of objects, which
the assembly line stands for, but the generation and
distribution of unique items with many variants: each

customer would receive their very own version of the novel. For each copy of the work printed, 200 of the novel's approximately 300 paragraphs would be combined in a different order. Originality is random. The user plays no part in this process, as will be later the case with the custom-made products that 3D printers connected to the Internet produce as printouts which are referred to as processed design. Every customer has their own text and can use it to create an *auretta*.

One can already imagine how book publishers might adapt this idea. Readers will select and put together texts from a commercial database according to need or as they see fit. After the texts have been printed out, each anthology will be given an individual cover with the reader's name on it as editor. In the early 1960s options did not play a determining role in the electronic department store. "Permutational art is imprinted on the technological era like a watermark," as Abraham A. Moles, associate of Bense and later friend of Vilém Flusser, at the end of his *First Manifesto of Permutational Art* points out emphatically.[44]

---

44 The short text was published in German as #8 in the legendary "Rot"-Reihe (Red Series) by K. Maier in Stuttgart (n.d.), edited by Max Bense and Elisabeth Walther; the quotation is on p. 21. At the end of the text the editors attach importance to stating that the text was produced "on an IBM Executive by Heidi Döhl." The gesture of laying open one's toolbox to public view is something that accompanies the avant-gardes of all the arts.

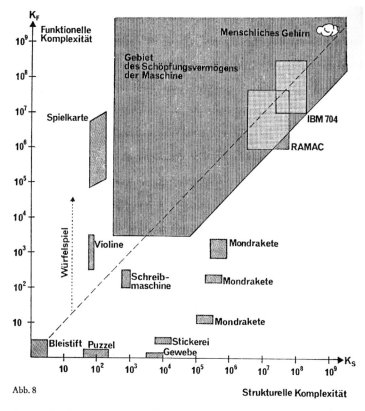

Abb. 8

Strukturelle Komplexität

Above the bisector toys and games, below technology perfected to the point of automation: "As the condition for complexity enabling possibilities of creative usage one lights on the following postulate: Functional complexity must outweigh structural complexity to a sufficiently strong degree." Moles (1971), p. 54.

Permutation, combinatorics, poetry from a machine; cutting up, taking apart, and putting together again, disregarding conventional rules of writing and purposeful breaches of the boundaries of genres: these were the gestures used to creatively attack the bourgeois tradition of the post-war manufacturing of culture. At the same time practitioners were working on generating a language that no longer had any need of an author in the classical sense: "Come to free the words / To free the words come / Free the words to come / The words come to free..."[45] $5 \times 4 \times 3 \times 2 \times 1$ permutations of these five short words give a total of 120 lines: a poem without an author, for even the first line was not written by the person who had the idea of generating the variants. From 1960–1962, Brion Gysin experiments in texts and images, often together with William S. Burroughs, with automatic combinations of found material. I AM THAT I AM and JUNK IS NO GOOD BABY, which Gysin programmed together with Ian Sommerville, who later became Burroughs' lover, are early examples of machine poetry with its own unique rhythm. The protagonists use computers as well as tape recorders for their performances. The permutation poems are also produced as tapes. The aggressively titled *Pistol Poem* was created at the time of Brion's collaboration with Burroughs in a cheap hotel in Paris, later famous as the Beat Hotel at No. 9 rue Gît-le-Cœur in the Saint Michel district. Commissioned by the BBC, *Pistol Poem* transforms the sound of gunshots, numbers, and scraps of words into an ecstatic, rhythmic chant. Gysin has cut up recorded material into tiny scraps and put them together again in rhythmic loops. Later, rock musicians like David Bowie, Genesis P. Orridge of Throbbing Gristle, Iggy Pop, Lou Reed, and bands like Cabaret Voltaire, are the biggest admirers of Gysin. In academic culture Gysin is still an outlaw. Like the gay artist and petty criminal Jean Genet, whom Gysin idolizes above all others. Jonas Mekas, an emigré from Lithuania who also uses cut & paste techniques in his cinematographic work, gives a public screening of Genet's banned film *Un chant d'amour* (1950) in New York in 1964. Mekas is arrested and put on trial.[46]

---

45   Brion Gysin (1987); see also Brion Gysin (2010).

46   Dwoskin (1975), p. 59; the author is a founding member of the London Filmmaker Coop.

You follow the red road to re
never strikes--The boy follwo
sky)--The air is motionless--
I am master of silence--My du
beyond the tomb and no comm
new noise--Sounds of cities i
ots confound all the plagues
that will send you everywhere
in a riot of perfumes
The up and pond smokes contin
The untimely sou
and our young misery--Oh that
from the south excited all th
the dried fields--The city wi
us far out along the roads--
of my childhood,my summer da
white ray falling from high
and language are reduced to
howling in the mud of the st
e along invisible rails
in the gorges--Bachantes o
howls--And i impatient to ri
slope angels whirl woolen ro
Revolving the rushing hum of
perfumed and blue below--I e
the steeples and the domes o
like a God with huge blue ey
ogs--A breath disperses the
s days and the seasons the
st against the silk of sea

Waste Land and other poems
own them all--I have gone a
in shirt sleeves leaning
us and we drown--Thou has
another country and besid
any a one has failed--
A Greek was murdered
smoky days--and newspaper
uttered rooms--Thou has
er diner sleep dreaming on
ain--Money in furs--The boa
Countess passed on until
d monkeys-- and a glass
t month--bin gar kunt kein
you fell free--The dead tre
I will show you fear in
wo wellest du?--Living or d
--"Here,said she "is your
that were his eyes--Sm
do not find the Hanged Man
ght death had undone so man
of nine--Hypocrite lecteur
ou thinking of?-- What thin
e his eyes-- Hurry up pleas
make yourself a bit smart
ood night sweet ladies--It'
Winter evening behind the
he waters-- Plebas the
e the id that walks beside y
s in the violet light--

Cut-up from *The Third Mind* (1965), at the bottom right are the
signatures of the authors Burroughs and Gysin (Paris 1986).

During this time, Oswald Wiener, the Austrian counterpart of the American Beat Generation writers, is working for the queen of Italian typewriter manufacturers in the data processing section. It is the phase in which Olivetti is developing the Elea 9000 series. From 1962 to 1967, Wiener writes most of his novel fragments *Die Verbesserung von Mitteleuropa* (*The improvement of Central Europe*), which are published by Rowohlt Verlag for the first time in 1969. In Particular his *Bio-Adapter*, which Rowohlt includes as an appendix to the novel, deserves to be rediscovered, in connection with contemporary theories of the interface. Wiener's programmable "pleasure suit" as a "complete solution for all problems of the world," is basically an ideal interface which no longer requires any media at all as a prerequisite for communicating with the world. The "liberation from philosophy through technology," Wiener proclaims, is "the opportunity of our century," and naturally, like Moles and others in this period, everything is written in Brechtian epic style without any capital letters whatsoever, as seemed fitting for the typewriter. The merry bourgeois anarchy of Viennese Actionism, in which the sex drive often hijacked the brain, is not enough for Wiener. He also sees in the new, intelligent machines the possibility of overcoming the clumsy concept of the humanoid. Wiener's "pleasure suit" is the complete opposite of the armor that envelops Lacan's split "I" after the mirror-stage. The Bio-Adapter is a paradise machine; the armor is an interface with the everyday hell of life.

> "In the opinion of the designer of the bio-adapter only the unit human-adapter can stand firm when challenged by responsible anthropological criticism, and, in addition, will for the first time satisfy the healthy and heroic ideal of a *homo sapiens* that rules the cosmos; on the one hand, by draining the cosmos, and on the other by liquidating *homo sapiens*. Human beings, when out of their adapters are exposed, nervously activated

61

and badly equipped (language, logic, mental capacity, sensory organs, tools) lumps of slime, shaking with fear of life and petrified by fear of death. When they put on their bio-complement, however, they become masterful entities who have no need of the cosmos or of coping with it, because in the hierarchy of conceivable significances they rank spectacularly above it."[47]

The year that *Bio-Adapter* is published both the Unix operating system and C programming language become available as information processing options. The U.S. government sets up an elitist network of their Advanced Research Projects Agency. ARPANET becomes the technical and political basis of a paradoxical form of technology-based communication: it is supposed to be extremely secure, reliable, and completely open at one and the same time. To begin with, the four nodes of the network are developed and run by the research facilities that are most involved in armaments R&D: the University of California, Santa Barbara (UCSB), the University of California, Los Angeles (UCLA), the Stanford Research Institute (SRI), and the University of Utah.

In 1967 at a conference on weights and measures in Switzerland, the second is redefined as a duration of 9,192,631,770 periods of the radiation corresponding to the transition between the two hyperfine levels of the ground state of the caesium-133 atom at a temperature of 0 K. The unit of time is definitely removed from cosmology with this, but also from what is accessible to human perception.

---

47 "Wiener, Appendix A, der Bioadapter, (prospectus 1965/66), (not revised)," in Wiener (1969), p. CLXXV.

Foucault LÉVI-STRAUSS BRECHT ALTHUSSER
SARTRE
CHAPSAL BLANCHOT BENJAMIN PLATON
LACAN BATAILLE DERRIDA HEATH BAEZ KUENTZEL
LIBESKIND DEBORD ECO NETZSCHE
KRISTEVA DYLAN HEATH
BACHTIN LOTMAN EISENSTEIN BURDON
GREIMAS HALL BARTHES BELLOUR
CHA — 1968 + DEBRAY
STING
KLAUS METZ ROPOHL SCHOLEM
ZOHN
REISS KNILLI KITTLER GOODARD
SPIESS AHRENDT YOUNGBLOOD
HOGGART HÖBER NADER WENDERS LUHMANN MULVEY
WILLIAMS THOMPSON HOOD GODARD
JONES FREUD COMOLLI de LAURETIS
BAUDRY SOLLERS PLEYNET MORRISON
HUSSERL WOLLEN

– 1968 +

Monsieur Foucault, "when did you stop believing in meaning?" Madeleine Chapsal asks the 38-year old phi-losopher during an interview in May 1966 in Paris. In that year Foucault is teaching in North Africa; *Les mots et les choses* (*The Order of Things*) appeared which suddenly makes Foucault an object of "mondaine curiosity"[48] for Paris intellectuals. Foucault's answer to Chapsal: "The point of rupture was the day when Levi-Strauss for soci-eties and Lacan for the unconscious showed us that the *meaning* was probably no more than a surface effect, a mirroring, a foam; and that what deeply ran through us, what was there before we were, what sustained us in time and in space was the *system*."[49]

48 Agamben, "Der Autor als Geste," in: Agamben (2005), p. 57.

49 Quoted in Howard Richards, *Foucault and the Future: A Philosophical Proposal for Social Democracy*, Chp. 5, Early Middle Foucault (1964–1969), http://howardrichards.org/peace/content/view/72/100/ accessed 10/15/2012.

Foucault radicalizes the thoughts of the masters in the French post-war think tank by projecting them at the same time onto the construction of history, onto the historical process. In a harsh manner he opposes the ideas of humanism that are permeated by the notion of the sovereign historical subject which have dominated historiography for so long. Along with Georges Bataille he shares the unsuccessful, yet wonderfully squandering endeavor of breaking out of triumphant subjectivity, both in the spoken and the written word. In the first years of this published debate his most prominent opponent is Jean-Paul Sartre. Foucault's criticism culminates in the formulation that for the Structuralists the individual does not think, but is thought, and for the Structural linguists the individual does not speak itself, but is spoken through the system of language.

Methodologically, Foucault's thinking no longer permits a homogeneous concept of truth. He does not invent any philosophical category that would be suitable to replace the vanished god of idealist philosophy. He is a historian who argues incisively and philosophically, and borrows concepts from various authors. He takes his genealogy almost word for word from Nietzsche; he borrows transgression and heterology from Bataille, from which he derives his own concept of heterotopia; in the interaction with Bataille he uses Blanchot to sharpen his understanding of sovereignty; the system and the structure, respectively, he adapts from Lèvi-Strauss. His revival of the term "discourse" is unconventional and original, which in the scientific tradition stood for the production of objective truths. If one goes through the Foucauldian analysis of a phenomenon, what remains in the end is only the will to objective truth that is inscribed in the discourse and its presentation techniques. Closely linked to Foucauldian discourse analysis are his strategic concepts of "archive" and "archaeology." In Foucault's later work, archaeology is increasingly replaced by the unbridled and methodologically more open tactic of genealogy.

Closely associated with Foucault and the unremitting philosophical endeavor directed against Western European logocentrism and its truths that construct consciousness is Jacques Derrida, who was born in Algeria. However, Derrida's practice of searching for truth is not to work through history, but to interpret literature, particularly as written texts. A year later, in 1967, Derrida's *Of Grammatology* appears and has a similar spectacular impact as Foucault's *The Order of Things*. Both are works that cannot accept the tyranny of the normative, the established hierarchies and alienations. For Derrida this concerns everything that can be said, and especially everything that can be written. Jürgen Habermas describes *Of Grammatology* as the endeavor to found a science of writing; whereas Heidegger was content with characterizing language as something akin to the House of Being, Derrida begins with a systematic study of language in the shape of literature.

The meanings of linguistic expressions for the philosophically arguing philologist are not fixed, but are constructed anew, and possibly differently, with each utterance, each act of writing, and each time a text is read. This is the starting point of what Derrida calls "deconstruction." This should not be misunderstood as a philosophical category, he stressed repeatedly, deconstruction describes the practice of perpetual shifts in meaning that occurs through speaking and writing, which is conscious of the differential character of linguistic sign production and continually demonstrates this. In deconstructive writing and deconstructive reading every text unfolds as a specific production of difference, which in the case of these active shifts Derrida wishes to see written as *différance*; in the spoken word, however, the two cannot be distinguished.

Obviously, neither Foucault nor Derrida are media theorists. Technical media and their metaphors as installed discursive practices are implicit constituents and frequently the objects of their thinking, however, these are not their explicit or even an especially attractive, focused field of research. Their tools of heuristics and theory, however, are avidly adapted and used to analyze media phenomena. Foucault's panoramic view, for example "panopticism," as a specific form of *supervision* which he gained from analyzing Jeremy Bentham's enlightened concept for a prison, becomes a paradigmatic character for a plethora of studies that engage with seeing organized by technical means. A similar thing happens to Derrida's concept of deconstruction. It is adapted as an aesthetic tactic in painting, film, or electronic video, but most of all in architecture. Daniel Libeskind's Holocaust Museum Berlin, for example, is regarded as an outstanding memorialization of one of the most attractive operative notions in aesthetics of the second half of the twentieth century.

Another seminal publication that appears the year before the watershed of 1968 is a harsh, poetic, and analytical continuation of the critique of capitalism through the critique of mass communication and its subjective effects. Guy Debord, self-proclaimed leader of the Paris Situationists publishes his essay *La société du spectacle* (*The Society of the Spectacle*), written in the breathless style of a pamphlet. The text appeared in November 1967; six years later it was also the soundtrack of a furious film montage of the same name. *The Order of Things, On Grammatology,* and *The Society of the Spectacle* are the trinity that no critical thinker can ignore in the following decades.

Dissection and articulation — with this pair of terms, whose components mesh like the gears of a machine, Roland Barthes describes the "structuralist activity." In this way he succinctly generalized the practice of an entire generation of philology and linguistics students and professors. Twenty years later, Friedrich Kittler alludes implicitly to this, in language that owes a certain debt to Lacan, when he defines a basic characteristic of film: "Chopping or *cutting* in the *real*, *fusion* or flow in the imaginary — the entire history of cinema research revolves only around this paradox." The splitting up of media activities in dissecting something and (re)articulating something, which Kittler borrows from the Structuralist activity, pervades his analyses of material in *Gramophone, Film, Typewriter*.[50] It also describes the basic operation of montage.

"Love is just a four letter word," writes Bob Dylan sometime around 1965, and Joan Baez makes it into a hit. The semiotically trained 1968 generation learns and teaches that in a linguistically structured world everything visible and audible consists of signs, and that under these systems of ordering the familiar relations between the psychological, which signifies, and that which is signified, have run into trouble. Semiotics becomes a fashionable subject with pretensions to being a meta-discipline, which is also eminently suitable for critiquing the ideologies circulating between the East and the West. Everything which appears in the form of established orders of expression — architecture and urban planning, a Volkswagen car, music, paintings, a cheap novel, a fashion show, comics, legal practice, or erotica insofar as it is formulated — becomes an object of the avid attentions of specialists for signs and their orders. The international stars of semiotics or semiology, the more posh name it sometimes gives itself, are gathered together in a 1977 anthology under one publisher's roof, although their approaches diverge considerably: Michail Bachtin, Umberto Eco, Algirdas J. Greimas, Julia Kristeva, and

---

50   Kittler (1986), quotation p. 122.

Jurij M. Lotman.[51] Even in the philosophy department of East Berlin's Humboldt University the Marxist semiotician Georg Klaus ensured that the power of ideological words is negotiated at the level of the international debate from the perspective of "real Socialism," but nevertheless with a whole lot of utopian potential for those who cringe at official jargon.

At this time two sensational experiences are of special importance for my studies. My first media studies seminar with Friedrich Knilli in 1973 at the Technical University Berlin is unforgettable. Already in the corridor to the seminar room at 135 Strasse des 17. Juni one could hear the sounds of inordinately ecstatic moaning. I opened the door and found about a dozen young intellectuals, male and female, sitting around a black-and-white VDU connected to a Bell & Howell KV-360, a ½ inch reel-to-reel video recorder, which was playing a pornographic, staged sex act. The students glanced back and forth at the screen and their notes in which they were carefully recording the characteristics of the pornographic shots, scenes, and sequences. If my memory serves me correctly, the seminar was called "Analysis of Commercial Porn Films and Spaghetti Westerns." (The seminar room was quite close to the lecture theater which today contains the Frauenhofer Institute's wave field synthesis system with 2700 loudspeakers on 832 independent channels). A short time later, I had the opportunity of speaking to an author whom only few people know by name. Heinz Werner Höber was one of the inventors of the fictional character of FBI agent Jerry Cotton, who in his snazzy red E-type Jaguar hunts down evil wrong-doers on the streets of Manhattan, often for days and nights on end, and then after a shower and a couple of fried eggs is ready for the next round of good deeds. Höber

---

51 See *Textsemiotik als Ideologiekritik* (1977) (Semiotic textual analysis as ideological criticism); the texts were written almost without exception in the 1960s.

lived in the West Berlin quarter around Potsdamer Strasse and Bülow Strasse which in the 1970s was an exciting mix of media firms, brothels, and bars. Around the corner were progressive publishers like Volker Spiess and Rotbuch, Wim Wenders' production company Road Movies, and Kommedia, the first book shop in Berlin to specialize in media literature. It was fascinating to listen to the pulp fiction writer's dry account of how he redrew the character over and over again, together with his faithful side-kick Phil Decker, based on a specific set of attributes, motives, and conflicts in ever new permutational variants; sometimes even writing two novelettes a week. For the film versions starring George Nader, Höber received a couple hundred Deutschmarks. At that time Höber had never set foot in Manhattan; he couldn't afford it. His meticulous descriptions were written with the help of city maps and postcards. Accuracy of detail but disregard of the bigger picture is a significant feature of formula fiction. In addition to Höber, there were dozens of other authors churning out these novels who contributed to the enormous success of the series. In the meantime the Jerry Cotton books have been translated into many languages and by now have reached a total circulation of around a billion.

Christian Metz takes Structuralist semiology to extremes for cinema, which in the 1960s is one of the last refuges for anarchic characters. His schema of a grand syntagmatic category of narrative film[52] offers inexhaustible material for seminars and tutorials in the early years of film and media studies. It should help to detect patterns and regularities in the vast diversity of syntactic constructions of film narratives. The categories for the various qualities of narrative conditions — from the autonomous shot to more complex syntagmas — are projected onto the multitudes of filmic realities ad nauseam.

---

52   Published first in France in Metz (1966); English edition: *Language and Cinema* (1974), trans. Donna Jean Umiker-Sebeok, The Hague: Mouton.

Everyone has to know this set of tools as the self-evident basics of film analysis with its dimensions and perspectives of shots, camera axes and camera movements, and the various indexical characteristics of sound. To have a command of the language of film seriously impresses one's fellow students tasked with a comparative analysis of the Italian journeys of Goethe and Heine. Someone who has finally understood that, for instance, one of the many concepts of film montage in Eisenstein's *October* (1927) is a special case of an "achronical syntagma," namely, a "bracket syntagma" within the framework of conventional narrative conditions of film, certainly knows a thing or two. In this case the bracket syntagma refers to the close semantic proximity of different images and shots and is close to Eisenstein's intellectual montage.

Film analysis becomes a competency just as twenty years later programming becomes a cultural technique that has to be acquired when the universal electronic control machines establish themselves. To my knowledge, the earliest German publication on *Einführung in die Film- und Fernsehanalyse* (*Introduction to film and TV analysis*) has the subtitle "An ABC for Viewers." It is a matter of learning a new language. The glaring discrepancy between the agitational approach of the handbook directed at a mass audience and the extremely cumbersome semiological and ideology-critical jargon it is written in, the authors — Friedrich Knilli and Erwin Reiss — attempt to compensate with sharply defined, rather pornographic drawings by Karin Reiss. Extreme academicism and objects of trash culture go together perfectly.[53]

A university in one of the most important cities of the Industrial revolution in England's West Midlands whose heyday was over, becomes the nucleus of a new field of research in which such combinations of extremes are

---

53   The book was published by Anabas (Steinbach 1971).

met head-on as challenges. The Birmingham Centre for Contemporary Cultural Studies provides all the concepts that lead later to the arbitrarily expanded and socially empty cultural studies that will spread all over the globe. Initiated and accompanied by seminal studies from Richard Hoggart (*The Uses of Literacy*, 1957), Raymond Williams (*Culture and Society*, 1958; *The Long Revolution*, 1961), and the Marxist historian and sociologist Edward P. Thompson (*The Making of the English Working Class*, 1963), bourgeois academic discourse is thrown open to admit the poets and playwrights of factories and work benches, for phenomena of other cultures including the indigenous sub-cultures, for products of radio and television, and even for early variants of rock music. The particular use of media products by those who essentially produce the wealth of society but at the same time have the smallest share in it, attracts attention. The previous ontological distinction between highbrow and lowbrow culture is declared to no longer be the crucial factor. Williams, in particular, develops an operational concept of culture that even for today's techno avant-garde has lost none of its edge.

For Williams, culture does not have a delimited sphere of reality with clearly defined objects, such as outstanding aesthetic achievements in the past, rather he understands it as a system with relationship quality between conditions of life, day-to-day activities, and actual development of the individual. As relationship quality and as expression of changing ways of life, culture is characterized by interaction and process.[54]

In his historic *Television: Technology and Cultural Form*[55] Williams attempts, at a very early stage, to clarify a debate that continues to the present day. It concerns the

---

54   I discuss Williams' concept of culture at some length in Zielinski (2010), Chp. II, p. 43f.

55   London: Fontana, 1974

question of how, basically, the relationship of technology and culture should be conceived. He distinguishes between two main interpretations, referring to them as "technological determinism" on the one hand and "symptomatic technology" on the other. In the first view technology is held to be a commanding determinant. Along with the steam engine, the automobile, and nuclear power, television for example, has created modern humans and their characteristics. Writing machines not only write down thoughts, they also significantly contribute to them — the technological *a priori*, as Kittler will call it years later. The second view of technology as a symptom emphasizes the accidental nature of technical innovations. Here the determinants are located in different elements of social development, for example, in economics or politics, which singularly or together determine the model society. Technology becomes a mediating by-product: "Television, like any other technology, becomes available as an element or a medium in a process of change that is in any case occurring or about to occur."[56]

On the one hand a belief in progress fixated on technical devices, and on the other social thought that does not revolve around them — the British cultural studies scholar proposes a third path: the interdependence of cultural and technological developments. Thus the tedious question about what came first, the chicken or the egg, is replaced by far more interesting questions about how the discursive fields of technology and culture mesh together in practical cases, and how they intersect and interweave as fields of human activity. Whatever is processed by technology and culture is informed by the one and the other.

Fortified by English translations of Critical Theory texts by Frankfurt School authors, texts by Walter

---

56 Williams [1974] (2003), London: Routledge Classics, pp. 5–6.

Benjamin, Bertolt Brecht, Roland Barthes, and Pier Paolo Pasolini[57] as well as the intensive reception of French semiology and Althusser's Marxism, cultural studies develops as a colorful and vital field of cultural and media discourse in Birmingham. With cultural studies a new type of intellectual appears on the scene. The lectures of Jamaica-born cultural theorist Stuart Hall are powerful and infectious theory-reggae, which sounds out the boundary between a talk and a performance on the academic stage. Stephen Heath spins and weaves Raymond Williams' thought into a filigree, difficult to decode but highly stimulating fabric of apparatus heuristics and critique of culture and technology. It is not easy to assess at which points Régis Debray's "mediology" goes beyond these insights and findings of the 1960s and early 1970s; for this reason I shall not describe his work of the 1990s. Especially since cultural studies has spawned a plethora of studies on mediological facts and processes in the sense used by Debray, which still await discovery as valuable approaches for further research.

In Berlin's academic scene it is not until the end of the 1970s that a new scholarly journal with the programmatic title *Wechselwirkung: Technik, Naturwissenschaft, Gesellschaft* (*Interdependency: technology, science, society*) is founded. The editorial board is a dedicated group of scientists, computer scientists, and mathematicians who work in the Mehringhof alternative cultural center in Kreuzberg's Gneisenaustrasse. With great precision the philosopher of technology Günther Ropohl formulates the notion of interdependency in his 1979 book *Eine Systemtheorie der Technik* (*A systems theory of technology*), which also contains a brilliant critique of

---

57   Besides Hannah Arendt and Harry Zohn, the left-wing Scottish writer Stuart Hood also worked as a translator on the system for decoding Enigma messages. Hood had an affair with Renée Goddard, the daughter of Werner Scholem, brought Brecht, among others, to London and had a lasting influence on independent art cinema in Europe.

73

the putative systems-theoretical approach of Bielefeld's star of sociology, Niklas Luhmann. Even Ropohl's formulations correspond to those of the cultural studies protagonists, although at that time he is not aware of their work. "Technology encompasses the concrete artifacts, their development and utilization, whereby the utilization of technical constructs can also serve to bring forth new artifacts […]. Thus nature, the individual, and society equally impose the conditions to which technology is subject, as to how they are exposed to the consequences of technology." The idea of interdependency enables one to effectively combat "those trivial points of view that hold 'technology to be either an unproblematic result or vice versa an unproblematic determinant' of non-technological phenomena."[58]

In 1968 Godard shoots *One Plus One*, which will be his last cinematographic film for over a decade. Like many Fluxus, action artists, and other artists, Godard turns his attention to electronic video, which is easier to operate and offers more autonomy for the user. He exhausts its potential both politically and aesthetically. This is the time when Gene Youngblood is working on a superb book in California that describes the manifold possibilities of a cinema expanded by electronics and the computer. In terms of media material Godard's *One Plus One* already oscillates on the threshold between film and video. It centers on the Rolling Stones recording *Sympathy for the Devil* in London's Olympic Studios. Brian Jones, who plays one of the decade's greatest guitar riffs on *Little Red Rooster*, is still alive. Interwoven in this filmic document of the studio recording of a song are agitprop elements such as statements by Black Panther activists and a porno seller reading from Hitler's *Mein Kampf*. The film composition is extremely fragmentary.

---

58   Ropohl (1979), quotations p. 69, 43f. trans. G. Custance. The quote within the quote is P. Weingart on the historical function of technology (1976).

The narrative style is aggressive, in spite of the Stones' calm and concentrated improvisations in the studio. The boundaries between documentary and fiction have completely disintegrated. There is no unified subject of the narrative, but different irreconcilable points of view. Godard works increasingly on producing films with explicitly political subjects and also on declaring his own practice as political; this includes the dramaturgy of filmmaking. Cinema should damn well reflect on the conditions of its own production, which are deeply embedded in existing power structures.

Brian Jones, Rolling Stones guitarist (left) and Jean-Luc Godard during the filming of *Sympathy for the Devil / One Plus One* 1968 in the Olympic Studios London on 7/30/1968. The following year Jones died at the age of 27. Photo: Keystone Features © Hulton Archive, Getty Images.

In Paris a debate is sparked by ideas from artistic film practice and published under the far too cumbersome name of "apparatus theory" in the magazine *Tel Quel*. With regard to cinema theory the protagonists are the professional dentist and novelist Jean-Louis Baudry, the writer and editor Marcelin Pleynet, and the filmmaker and theorist Jean-Louis Comolli, who chiefly writes for the *Cahiers du cinéma*, the journal that taught Godard film criticism. (Other members of the loosely connected group around *Tel Quel* are Derrida, Kristeva, and Philippe Sollers). Their essays, couched in language that is very *dense* and abstruse, nevertheless have a clear focus. They adumbrate an ideological and aesthetic critique of power *as* critique of technology. With different accentuations they boldly integrate heterogeneous theoretical borrowings into a heuristics of film and media that has not been thought of before: the Marxist critic of ideology and apparatuses Althusser, the psychoanalysis of Freud and Lacan, the phenomenology of Husserl (Heidegger comes a bit later), and, whenever needed, classic philosophers like Plato with his famous allegory of the cave.

Their core approach can be paraphrased thus: technology is not reflected as incidental, but as essential for the realization of the aesthetic work as well as its perception. The idea of Nietzsche's, that our writing instruments contribute to our thoughts, which has considerable popularity in post-Structuralist media theory and achieves great prominence in the Federal Republic of Germany in the 1980s, is discussed here as indispensable reflection on the technical conditions that bring forth aesthetic objects. Likewise, the concept of *dispositif*, which is explicitly included in the title of Baudry's 1975 essay on the impression of reality in the cinema but already plays an important role in his essay on "The Ideological Effects of the Basic [Cinematographic] Apparatus" of 1970.[59]

---

59 One reason why we translated Baudry's essay "Effets ideologique — produits par l'appareil du base" into German was that Alan Williams, who translated the text into English, transformed the term *dispositif*, which later made such an important career in Foucault's writings, into "technical arrangement" and similar words. See our translation, authorized by J.L. Baudry: "Ideologische Effekte — erzeugt vom Basisapparat, trans. Gloria Custance and Siegfried Zielinski, in: Eikon (Vienna), no. 5, 1993, 36–43. In the American translation "cinematographic" is already juxtaposed with "apparatus" in the title which ensures a focus that Baudry did not intend at all.

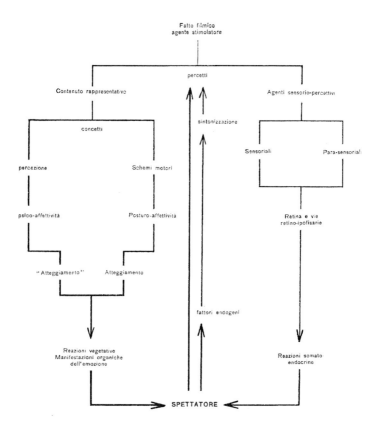

PROIEZIONE CINEMATOGRAFICA

Atto percettivo
(Modalità patogeniche)

Fatto filmico
agente stimolatore

percetti

Contenuto rappresentativo   Agenti sensorio-percettivi

concetti

sintonizzazione

percezione   Schemi motori   Sensoriali   Para-sensoriali

psico-affettività   Posturo-affettività   Retina e vie retino-ipofisarie

"Atteggiamento"   Atteggiamento

fattori endogeni

Reazioni vegetative
Manifestazioni organiche
dell'emozione   Reazioni somato-endocrine

SPETTATORE

Apparatus theory before there were apparatus theorists: Gilbert Cohen-Séat's diagram of film perception in the cinema; "The pathogenic modalities of visual forms of communication include complex factors"; between the "cinematographic projection," "the act of perceiving," and the "filmic fact as stimulus" (above), there unfolds for the "spectator" (below) a structure of representations, fine-tuning, perceptions, affects, sensorial and para-sensorial percptions. vegetative and "somatic and endocrine responses," as well as "organic manifestations of feelings." *Almanacco letterario Bompiani* 1963, p. 141.

In rock music, Jim Morrison sees to the popularization of instant psychoanalysis with the famous oedipal lines "Father – yes, son? – I want to kill you! Mother ... I want to ... fuck you!" in his 1967 song *The End*. In 1971 he is buried in Paris. In the mid 1970s psychoanalysis has long been an integral part of film and media theory discourse in France. The high point of this theoretical tradition is the essay *The Imaginary Signifier* by Metz. It will take over twenty years for the German academic publication machine to release a German translation.[60]

In countries influenced by Anglo-American traditions translations appear faster. Two legendary anthologies of texts by the protagonists of apparatus theory are released by two women, the Italian culture and gender theory scholar Theresa de Lauretis and the Korean artist and theorist Theresa Hak Kyung Cha.

De Lauretis' anthology is very much in the tradition of cultural studies. Among others, she works with Steven Heath, one of Raymond Williams' heirs. Cha's anthology is oriented more toward psychoanalysis and aesthetic practice. She is a writer, filmmaker, photographer, and also studies in Paris with Raymond Bellour, Thierry Kuntzel, and Christian Metz, thus she is well acquainted with the authors of the apparatus debate.[61] In her Paris period, Cha authors theoretical works on video and film, *Vidéoème*, for example, a Structuralist dissection of text in the image, as Godard likes to practice in his films, and *Permutations*, a filmic anagram of the head of her sister. Cha was only 31 when she died. In 1982 she was

60 On this section see Baudry (1975) and Metz (1975). The second more well known text by Baudry appeared together with Metz's essay in a Special Issue of *Communications* (1975) titled *Psychanalyse et cinéma*, published by Centre d'études transdisciplinaires of the Ecole des hautes études en sciences sociales in Paris. As social sciences, Soziology, Anthropology and Semiology were integrated in the Special Issue. It also includes contributions by Kristeva, Guattari, Bellour, and Barthes (with his legendary text Text *En sortant du cinéma / Upon Leaving the Movie Theater*).
61 On Cha see the fine catalog by Lewallen (2001).

murdered on a New York street. At the time she was working on a critique of commercial propaganda and a project on hands in Western painting.

The hands of the apparatus theorist and artist Theresa Hak Kyung Cha at the typewriter in 1979. Photo: James Cha, Lewallen, 2001.

For the development of feminist film theories and practices, the heuristics of the apparatus debate are of major importance. The argument is compelling: if the ideology of bourgeois society, which is basically patriarchal, inscribes itself in the *dispositifs* and technical systems with which, for example, films are made, then this means that the world of apparatus is male-coded. With her essay *Visual Pleasure and Narrative Cinema* (1975), the British filmmaker Laura Mulvey puts the entire situation in a nutshell for a whole generation of women artists and theorists: men are the active agents and organizers of the gaze, whereas women have to suffer the male gaze; their status is that of objects of desire.

Put pragmatically in terms of cinema — the woman is in the image, on the screen; the man stands behind the camera and directs. Interposed between the woman and the man is the recording apparatus. With Peter Wollen, Laura Mulvey made the filmic version of this theoretical concept from psychoanalysis and feminism, *Riddles of the Sphinx* (1977).

– 1974 –

The notion that human existence oscillates between being at least partly co-conditioned by technology on the one side and a manufactured appearance (*Schein*) that is completely artificial on the other has been a prominent feature of artistic production with and through media since the 1960s. Godard makes his computer film *Alphaville* already in 1965. This filmic criticism of the ubiquitous mega-machine, a dystopia of George Orwell's that has become a reality, needs stark counterweights within the film. Eddy Constantine, an actor with a strong physical presence plays the male lead Lemmy Caution, and Godard's wife, Anna Karina, embodies the entirely Other of unsettling emotions, seduction, and love. With *Alphaville*, Godard reacts to the private and public installation of the huge mainframe computers from IBM whose involvement in the murderous machinery of the Nazis is only known at this time to a handful of alert historians.[62] And he also reacts to urban developments in Paris, parts of which seem like an architectonic enforcement of the circular consistency concept that is implicit in cybernetics as a social technique. Jaques Tati needs three years, from 1964 to 1967, to realize this ingeniously in his film *Playtime* as a scenario set in the present. Stanley Kubrick's *Space Odyssey* is released in 1968.

The West German companion piece to *Alphaville*, important scenes of which are also shot in Paris, is released in 1973. *Welt am Draht* (*World on a Wire*), Rainer Werner Fassbinder's two-part TV film, is based on a science fiction novel by Daniel Francis Galouye, titled *Simulacron-3*.[63] Again, the lead actor is distinguished by his strong physical presence.[64] The German macho-star Klaus Löwitsch plays a computer engineer who is not merely battling against one machine, but against a pervasive techno-substance which appears to have generated everybody. Everyone is caught in this matrix and views each other as capable of anything; there is no mutual trust. In the end the computer engineer also turns out to be a machine whose intelligence is so highly developed that he also has emotions and is capable of feeling pity. Fassbinder delves a little deeper into the

---

62 Edwin Black's book on the role of IBM in the German Holocaust was only published in 2001.

63 The original title was *Counterfeit World* (1964); the corruption of the lovely term "simulacrum" from the poetic and philosophical arsenal of the Ancient Greek Atomists is clearly not only the prerogative of Baudrillard.

64 Fassbinder acknowledges his fellow director in France and his filmic work by a brief guest appearance of Eddie Constantine.

techno-imaginary than Godard; the real seems to have disappeared completely in the film, and love is "colder than death" (*Liebe — kälter als der Tod;* Love is Colder Than Death) as another film of 1969 by the German master of melodrama is called.

Various reconnaissance of artistic production operating under the conditions of informatics aesthetics have long been conducted in other parts of the world. In 1973, Iraqi Mahmoud Sabri quotes Brecht's dictum that the barbarians have their art and we have to create another, and with his Quantum Realism creates a program for an art that he considers appropriate for the technological and atomic age. For Sabri, with the splitting and combining of atoms, humankind has entered the third phase of civilization, after the phases of hunter-gatherers and agriculture. Conceptually, this new art direction is determined by the interchangeability of mass and energy and its subject is the representation of atomic processes. Sabri creates a new language consisting of 92 atoms/units and a color alphabet; he seeks to integrate Marx and Einstein in his conception and challenges the new civilization with the task of creating nature anew.[65]

In the second half of the 1960s post-war West German capitalism, which has prospered almost entirely without restraint for fifteen years, goes into deep recession. The West German Republic is severely shaken by both economic and political events. In the steel sector alone 10% of the workforce is made redundant. It has become evident that mining and heavy industry, up to then stable pillars of prosperity, will not be economically valuable forever. The sacred cow of "growth" shows itself to be highly vulnerable and unreliable in its dynamics. Thus, in the early 1970s, there is an immense political drive to change the structure and content of industry and to put it on a new, or at least expanded base. Electronic technologies are

---

65 Sabri (1973).

entering the international markets with artifacts and systems of information technology, data processing, and communications. Their development promises a new, post-industrial economy and a revolution that will be awesome, in which no blood will be spilled and nobody will get their hands dirty. Technology-based services are synonymous with speed, cleanliness, efficiency, predictable reliability, and more intensive social interaction.

Zbigniew Kazimierz Brzeziński, head of the Institute on Communist Affairs of New York's Columbia University and in the mid 1970s Jimmy Carter's National Security Advisor, coins a strategic neologism in 1969: the *Technetronic Era*. "The post-industrial society is becoming a 'technetronic' society: a society that is shaped culturally, psychologically, socially and economically by the impact of technology and electronics — particularly in the area of computers and communications."[66] By conflating technology and electronics Brzeziński identifies not only the massive shifts within the USA, but also a paradigm shift within the geopolitics of the planet. On the way from the age of industrial production to the age of electronic communication technologies, a "global" even "planetary" community is emerging. On the basis of telematic information that is all linked, the course of history is no longer determined by ideologies that aggressively try to beat the daylights out of each other; rather; it is determined by the community of advanced countries in agreement with each other (by which Brzeziński means first and foremost the USA, Western Europe, and in third place, Japan). The new community of the technetronic era will be ruled by a knowledgeable elite, who will also shape future universities. This elite will guarantee perfect communicative structures as well as the optimal governance of what has previously not been adequately under control.

---

66   Brzeziński (1969), p. 10.

"The product of Television, Commercial Television, is the Audience.
Television delivers people to an advertiser. […]
Mass media means that a medium can deliver masses of people.
Commercial television delivers 20 million people a minute.
In commercial broadcasting the viewer pays for the privilege of having himself sold.
It is the consumer who is consumed.
You are the product of t.v.
You are delivered to the advertiser who is the customer.
He consumes you. […]
The NEW MEDIA STATE is predicated on media control. […]
POPULAR ENTERTAINMENT IS BASICALLY PROPAGANDA FOR THE STATUS QUO.
Control over broadcasting is an exercise in controlling society.
[…]
The NEW MEDIA STATE is dependent on propaganda for its existence. […]
Every dollar spent by the television industry in physical equipment needed to send a message to you is matched by forty dollars spent by you to receive it.
You pay the money to allow someone else to make the choice.
You are consumed.
You are the product of television.
Television delivers people."

In 1973 Richard Serra and Carlotta Fay Schoolman make the ultimate video on commercial television, which is heralded as a license to print money and as a new master medium. It is called *Television Delivers People* and consists of a simple text in white letters that slowly scrolls down before a blue background to a Muzak soundtrack. The excerpt above shows approximately half of the video's text.

While the hippie movement is engaged in trying out practical combinations of cybernetic thought, Zen philosophy, individual creativity, and alternative lifestyles that refuse to contribute to mass production (which keeps them extremely busy), in the first half of the 1970s the systemically important functions of the media are elaborated and examined in detail from every angle for a possible technological future. In the Federal Republic of Germany the messages from the helmsman in the USA, Brzeziński, which Norbert Wiener has also studied in detail as well as Daniel Bell's early texts on the *Post-industrial Society* and the gender debate, arrive with a slight delay. Here the expansion of the classic telephone network to include data, text, and image communication plays a seminal role. The state-owned Deutsche Bundespost (German federal post office), successor to the Reichspost (German imperial post office) and still heavily informed by its bureaucratic traditions, begins a technological and political offensive. This behemoth is forced to work on dismantling itself; there is no other option. The foundations are laid for the later German Telecom. Private entrepreneurs, who are looking for investment opportunities and innovations, enter the market. Communication is declared to be a public and a commercial service.

In 1974 the Federal German government sets up a commission of experts to analyze the structure of contemporary telecommunications and possible future scenarios of technical communications. The lavishly funded group is known under the abbreviation KtK (Kommission für den Ausbau des technischen Kommunikationswesens — Commission for the Development of Technical Systems of Communication). Already in early 1976, the commission publishes its findings and proposals, a set of documents comprising a report and eight volumes of appendices. It gives a practical lesson in new terminology and with an obscene pairing signals the direction which developments will take: the envisaged expansion of the telecommunications system of the Federal Republic of Germany will be "economically rational and socially desirable," opines the Federal Minister of the Post and Telecommunication Systems, Kurt Gscheidle, in the preface with a personal and dynamic flourish. To maintain a constant balance between the rational and the desirable will become the central discursive field of media politics.

Based on 24,500 data stations that are registered as connected by the end of 1974 in the Federal Republic, the KtK formulates pragmatically in F 18 (F for Finding): "Meeting the requirements for data communication services is necessary for both the economy and the administration. This has positive social effects." This leads to Recommendation No. 3: "It is recommended that the telex and data network being introduced at the moment in view of the increasing need for data communication be extended without delay." In F 24 to F 26 the new forms of written telecommunications and telecopying are propagated for companies and public authorities; in F 27 electronic letter delivery is introduced. Technical monstrosities like *Bildschirmtext* (screen text), which is transmitted via the telephone network, are described and installed shortly afterwards as a trial.

A considerable proportion of the KtK's findings and recommendations concern the expansion of radio through broadband communication, as well as cable and satellite services. In the years that follow this is what mainly draws the fire of media critics. The report on telecommunications, however, distinctly centers on the new networks, which are clearly conceptualized strategically. In a special section on the systematics of forms of telecommunication, the term "communicaton" is explicitly used from the outset in the sense of interactive dialog and as a particular case of "human–machine communication" and "machine–human communication."

Twenty years later, lengthy media studies applications to the German Research Foundation are required to obtain grants to elucidate the relations between analog and digital. In 1976 the KtK only needs two sentences: "The s i g n a l is the representation of the message by physical quantities, for example, the chronological sequence of a voltage or current. The signal is d i g i t a l when it only consists in symbols, i.e., it is encoded, and a n a l o g when the parameter of the signal is modified by a continual function."

The concepts are circumscribed in veritable gargantuan ensembles of signifiers that in the 1990s will be briefly and concisely consolidated by way of the Internet. To integrate the various services and functions one needs "a great many connections, i.e., a t e l e c o m m u n i c a t i o n s n e t w o r k …. Such networks have, for example, star-shaped, meshed, or compound structures…. The aggregation of the various telecommunication networks and the forms of telecommunication realized within them can be termed a t e l e c o m m u n i c a t i o n s s y s t e m." And in the following sentence another term is introduced as a matter of course, which will play a determining role in media theory in the 1990s: "In a system of this type, commensurate with the many forms of telecommunication, there are many i n t e r f a c e s (*Schnittstellen*) of a technical, operational, and organizational/financial variety."[67]

These technopolitics with a state-funded, post-capitalistic impetus directly precedes a culture of debate in communication and media theory that is pledged to a critique of political economy. To varying degrees, the 1960s are informed by philology, poetics, and linguistics; the first half of the 1970s in Western Europe is

---

67   All quotations are from the *Telekommunikationsbericht* (1976); p. III, 4, 21, 23. The emphases (italics) follow the original. Translation from the German by G.C.

determined on a metatheoretical level by variants of the sociology of communications and the critique of ideology. This is accompanied by fierce battles about ideological positions among the weak Left.

Hans Magnus Enzensberger is so bored by all of this that for a time he occupies himself obsessively with computers, invents a German poetry machine, and makes an attempt at stimulating a new techno-culture in artistic literature with the slogan "Poetry programmers of the world unite!" His 6 KB program of 1974 is very modest, but not the perspective that Enzensberger threw open: "Poetry automata of a higher order far exceed the capabilities of any writer. They can only be realized by a team consisting of linguists, programmers, and poets."[68]

Among the theory protagonists is the Munich sociologist Horst Holzer. As a result of an ugly *Berufsverbot*[69] (professional ban) campaign against all the civil services, including teachers and university teaching staff, Holzer is barred from teaching in Bremen because he is a communist. The leadership of Munich University, where Holzer had taught, orders that all the works he has authored be removed from the university library, a measure that we students brand a cold book burning. *Gescheiterte Aufklärung?* (*Failed enlightenment?*) is the title of Holzer's 1971 book in which he places Critical Theory on the agenda again and sharpens its arguments for a contemporary critique of television; his *Kommunikationssoziologie* (*Sociology of Communication*) is published in 1973. The texts by Franz Dröge from Bremen are written from more of an educational sociology perspective.

---

68   Enzensberger (2000), p. 64 and 63.
69   On January 28, 1972, West German Chancellor Willy Brandt and the premiers of the states instituted the so-called *Radikalenerlass* (Anti-Radical Decree). Under this law, people who were considered to have radical views, especially if they were members of such parties, could be forbidden to work as civil servants (*Beamter*), which includes a variety of public sector occupations such as teaching. The decree was a declared response to terrorism by the Red Army Faction. Wikipedia, accessed 11/2/2012.

His *Wissen ohne Bewusstsein* (*Knowledge without consciousness*) of 1972, handily shortened to WoB for agitation purposes, vies with those of the Munich sociologist Holzer for the correct interpretation of Marxian criticism of political economy as applied to the current situation. They both agree, however, as did many other contemporary intellectuals, that "materialist communications studies" are tasked with comprehending "the media as instruments for organizing class action."[70]

The leading figures in early communications and media discourse are Marxists. The team of writers Götz Dahlmüller, Wulf D. Hund, and Helmut Kommer write a *Politische Fernsehfibel* (*Political TV primer*), which provides "material about class communication" parallel to the KtK in 1974. The Berlin philologists, semioticians, and cultural critics around the engineer and radio theoretician Friedrich Knilli subject *Die Unterhaltung der deutschen Fernsehfamilie* (1971) (The entertainment of the German TV family) and above all the filmic products of trash culture to ideological criticism. They also supply most of the members of a "Working Group on the Mass Media," which is initiated by the art society Neue Gesellschaft für Bildende Kunst (NGBK) to organize a media-critical discourse in public exhibitions. At that time the NGBK has premises at the Hardenbergstrasse no. 9 and belongs to the joint campus of the Technical University Berlin and the Hochschule der Künste (University of the Arts). The project "Television — A Class Medium" is presented in the summer of 1973, and receives generous financial support from the lottery fund Deutschen Klassenlotterie Berlin. The centerpiece of this agitprop show is a poster that illustrates the "economic level" of the situation. Here one learns, among other things, to distinguish between a "means of communication capitalist" (Kommunikationsmittelkapitalist — KMK) and a

---

70 Dröge (1972), p. 194.

"communications capitalist" (Kommunikationskapitalisten — KOK). KMKs mean the electrical companies that manufacture the appliances and hardware and produce the technical infrastructure. KOKs produce the software, films and television programs that are made by commercial companies as opposed to the state broadcasters. They are the main generators in the exchange process of money (Geld — G) and the communication/message (Kommunikat — KO).[71]

---

71 The catalog *Klassenmedium Fernsehen* (1973) had a copy of the poster in reduced format as an insert.

Ökonomie-Ebene

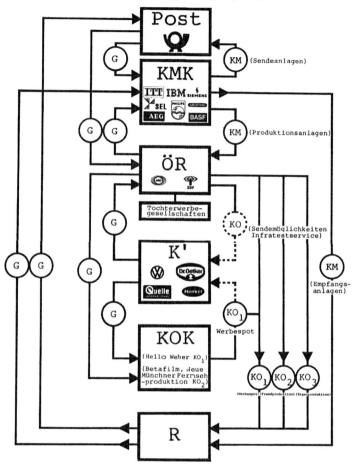

KMK=Kommunikationsmittelkapitalist
ÖR=öffentlich-rechtliche Anstalt
 K'=beliebiger Kapitalist
KOK=Kommunikatskapitalist

R=Rezipient (Fernsehzuschauer)
KM=Kommunikationsmittel
KO=Kommunikat
G = Geld

KLASSENMEDIUM FERNSEHEN

NEUE GESELLSCHAFT FÜR BILDENDE KUNST E. V.

ARBEITSGRUPPE MASSENMEDIEN

Enclosure of the catalog *Klassenmedium Fernsehen* (NGBK Berlin 1973); some of the words in Courier font have been slightly enlarged.

Media theory becomes identical to social theory irrespective of the microcosm it engages with thematically, whether in-depth analysis of a commercial for *Iglo* fish sticks, the interpretation of TV news reporting during the Vietnam War, the analysis of new technical artifacts, or the macro-analysis of complex political communication processes such as election campaigns. With this, media theory achieves a high level of generalization as cultural theory or even political theory, because equating media theory with social theory assumes that *the media* are constitutive for the social coexistence of individuals.

That the media are held in high esteem ideologically may be one reason why the major publishing houses willingly provide access to their printing presses and distribution systems for works of media criticism that were difficult to understand without first attending courses on Marx's *Capital*, Hegel, or Adorno. The German publishing house S. Fischer Verlag prints three legendary, cheaply licensed volumes of essays and excerpts from monographs on *Massenkommunikationsforschung* (*Mass communications research*). The first volume alone sells 25,000 copies in 1972/73; 425 pages for a mere DM 6.80. The second volume appears in 1973 with the title *Konsumtion* (Consumption), has 500 pages, and costs one Deutschmark more. It contains Hans-Magnus Enzensberger's *Baukasten zu einer Theorie der Medien* (Construction kit for a media theory), the materialist organon for the new generation of radio and video guerillas in the Western republics. The third volume in the S. Fischer series appears in 1977 and focuses on analysis of individual media products. Hanser Verlag publishing house even dedicates its own paperback series, with bright yellow covers, to *Kommunikationsforschung* (*Communications research*). From a formal point of view, Helmut H. Diederich's slim volume *Konzentration in den Massenmedien* (Concentration in the mass media) of 1973 represents the high point of the series. With the volume comes a loose insert, a folded poster in DIN A3 format printed on phosphorescent green paper, which for a time graces the walls of young critical media researchers, and represents a guide through the organized media forces of the early 1970s. The philosophical theory forges of the Marxists also eventually engage with the new subjects that are becoming trendy. *Massen/Medien/Politik* (*Masses/media/politics*) is the title of the tenth special issue of the journal *Das Argument*, mainly edited by August Soppe and published under editor in chief Wolfgang Fritz Haug. The vignette on the cover shows a target behind which people are seen going about their daily business — open season has been declared on them.

The appetite for new communications and media theory material was huge. At the Technical University Berlin the first course in media studies is developed. At various West German universities, for example, Marburg, autonomous working groups or reading courses are set up in which participants learn how power relations can be read as media relations, and which structures and patterns prevail in the seemingly unstructured and anarchic material. In the Marburg German department Günther Giesenfeld works on film analysis that can be automated with the aid of a computer. Jörg-Jochen Berns begins his adventurous excursions into the media history of the early Modern period, which is not yet called media archaeology. The working groups are organized by the students themselves, despite the opposition of a number of professors and lecturers who twenty years later are prominent surfers on the third wave of the media theory boom.

In the 1970s the political world of the poets and thinkers has nothing to do with that of installers and drivers. These are two cultures that are drifting apart and shun contact with each other. The bottom line of the KtK's recommendations is effective support of the "means of communication capitalists," whom left-wing intellectuals despise, of course. To implement the recommendations effectively and smoothly, one does not require experts in the critique of the political economy of the media or semiologically formulated Marxian ideology criticism. One needs electrical engineering technicians, engineers, computer scientists, and specialists in propaganda of all kinds.[72] However, when there are attempts at connecting the two opposing cultures, the results are often very bizarre. The specialty of the young TV professional Horst Königstein, a NDR (North German Broadcasting) public broadcaster in the 1970s, who naturally is viewed as a representative of the ruling establishment, gives interviews that are wholly at odds with the declared educational mission of the public broadcasting authorities. Königstein takes rock musicians, like Frank Zappa, Ringo Starr, or Pete Townsend from The Who, by surprise, confronting them with long exegeses informed by Adorno's cultural theory or critique of ideology. To the questions at the end of his monolog the interviewees can only respond with a weary "yes" or "no," utter amazement, or by demonstratively nodding off.

In the 1980s Federal Republic of Germany, the next generation of theorists tend to distance themselves from those who had prepared the media-theoretical terrain in the departments of philosophy. The "old school" seem too self-congratulatory with their leftist aspirations, too stilted with their semiology, too pedagogic, too involved in literary studies, and are ideologically and philosophically passé. The next generation of theorists want

---

72 At the Technical University Berlin we reacted in our own way to these requirements rather late, but in the early 1980s we began to test instructions for technical appliances and software packages or simply rewrote them. In this way we received the first UNIX computer from Siemens in return for our working group rewriting the manual for the office software in such a way that secretaries could understand and use them.

nothing to do with all of that at the onset of the decade of the postmodern. Other commitments count now. Critique of power is now spelled directly as critique of technology and aesthetic rationality. When these are directed at political constellations, it is befitting that one cites the historian of the system, the grandiose transgressor and radical actionist of truth Foucault. The majority no longer even know Althusser, who was an influential mentor for theorists of the techno-imaginary like Abraham Moles. This is not only due to Althusser's illness or that he stays in a psychiatric facility for years after having strangled his wife. His concept of ideological state apparatuses (ISAs) with its imaginary qualities, however, has become of seminal importance to the thinkers interested in the conditioning of politics and art via apparatus. It is the result of Althusser's attempt to think Marx and Engels together with Lacan. For Althusser, ideology also materializes in technical artifacts and arrays which makes his view relevant for media theory. With a curt gesture Heiner Müller dismisses the now superfluous left-wing state theorist in 1981 with the short essay "Mich interessiert der Fall Althusser..." (I am interested in the Althusser case...).[73] With this statement, Müller evinces his interest in Althusser as a psycho-pathological subject, and not in his political and philosophical ideas. Today a new reception of Althusser is already on the horizon. French political thinkers who have recently become known, like Badiou or Rancière, studied with Althusser.

In the Federal Republic of Germany, Jürgen Habermas undertakes the mammoth endeavor of understanding the drifting-apart of the technocratic cultures on the one side and aristocratic humanism on the other from a fundamental perspective of the Enlightenment and the philosophy of the subject. His differentiation between

---

73 In *Alternative*, no. 137, "Louis Althusser. Frühe Schriften zu Kunst und Literatur," Berlin 1981.

success-oriented purposive-rational action and under-standing-oriented communicative action has a theoret-ical half-life that carries over into the telematic constel-lations of today. "Instrumental actions can be connected with and subordinated to social interactions of a different type — for example, as the 'task elements' of social roles; strategic actions are social actions by themselves. By contrast, I shall speak of *communicative* action whenever the actions of the agents involved are coordinated not through egocentric calculations of success but through acts of reaching understanding." In the utopian dimen-sion of his concept, Habermas sketches a form of insti-tuting a community that has unjustly been consigned to de-membering (*entinnern*): "In communicative action participants are not primarily oriented to their own indi-vidual successes; they pursue their individual goals un-der the condition that they can harmonize their plans of action *on the basis of common situation definitions.*"[74]

That which is termed collaborative action in the new technological networks could not be defined any better. In the German studies departments of 1970s Feder-al Germany, the majority of professors are still preach-ing the absolute sanctity of the classical literary canon and stipulating the appropriate theories and methods to study it. Although it assembles a fair amount of irritating intellectual energy, the anthology *Ansichten einer künfti-gen Germanistik* (*Views of future German studies*) (1969) has as little impact on the institutions as *Neue Ansichten einer künftigen Germanistik* (*New views of future German studies*) (1973) four years later. In the latter volume there are contributions by the young professor of literature Gert Mattenklott, whose lectures in Marburg are veritable holy gatherings for sensitive rebels from the new Ger-man philology; by the 26-year-old doctoral student Peter Sloterdijk; by 25-year-old Hans Ulrich Gumbrecht who

---

74 Habermas (1984), vol. 1, pp. 285–286.

has already obtained a doctorate; and by Friedrich Knilli and some of his collaborators and students from the Media Studies department of the Technical University Berlin. Because institutions change so slowly, ten years later in West Germany Friedrich Kittler requires more than a dozen referees before his *Habilitation* thesis on the media conditionality and permeation of literature by the media is finally accepted in Orwell's year: *Aufschreibesysteme 1800/1900* (1984) (*Discourse Networks 1800/1900,* Stanford 1990).

– 1984 +

Out of cultural pessimism, one can either submit to or confront as a challenge the idea of total visual control that Orwell outlines with his telescreen novel *Nineteen Eighty-Four*. The Korean musician and artist Nam June Paik, who teaches at the art academy in Düsseldorf, chooses the second option. At a gigantic happening which takes place on different continents and is broadcast on television in Asia, Europe, and the USA on New Year's Eve, artists such as Joseph Beuys, John Cage, and Laurie Anderson welcome the new year of 1984 *online*. Their anarchic presentations cut the ground from under the feet of the notion that cultural processes can be totally controlled. They play around with chance, disruptions, sudden events, deviations, grammatically non-determinable tears, and laughter.

A few months after this show, which Paik calls "Art for 25 Million People," news of a spectacular exhibition in the Paris Beaubourg begins to leak across borders. The exhibition *Les Immatériaux* is scheduled to open in early 1985. A prominent contemporary intellectual, Jean-François Lyotard, has developed the concept for it in an article of the same name. A few years earlier Lyotard had presented culture-philosophical thought in Europe with a new concept that will influence the entire 1980s and early 1990s: postmodern. In 1979 Lyotard publishes his study *La condition postmoderne* (*The Postmodern Condition*). The work had been commissioned by the *Council* of *Universities* in *Québec, Canada.*

The five fields of *Les Immatériaux*'s exhibition structure reflect Lasswell's formula in a particular way, says Lyotard of his concept. Starting from the word stem of "matter," *mât,* the "operational structure" of his work approach breaks down as follows:

- "the material is the (substantial) vehicle of the message;
- the *materiel* is the equipment that enables the message to be realized, transmitted, and received;
- 'maternity' is the function of the sender of the message;
- the matter of the message is its referent (what the message is about);
- the matrix is the code of the message."[75]

The exhibition, which is realized in collaboration with the Centre de Création Industrielle, is organized following these five dimensions of *mât.* That physical work is being increasingly replaced by new technology is only its most obvious theme. In the exhibition space, darkened because of the many projections, the idea is floating around that everything which is still called "reality," is becoming intangible. The "immaterial" describes "a structure in which the conventional opposition between mind and matter no longer has any place," as Lyotard expresses it in a radio conversation with Jacques Derrida in October 1984.[76]

At this time the book *Zur Geschichte des Körpers* (*History of the body*) edited by Dietmar Kamper and Volker Rittner, which is intended to help ground a new anthropology, is already eight years old. In Germany, it is

---

75 Lyotard (1985a), p. 82; trans. G.C.

76 Ibid., p. 23.

above all Kamper who sees to it that under postmodern conditions, not only contemporary thought but also thematizing the body remain on the agenda. He links the two in a playful way and persistently introduces them into the debate about the new subjectivity. I have always understood thematizing the body in a double sense: as an activity closely bound up with the sensuality of the one who thinks, and also as a materialist reference to the dependence of all expressions of thought on the (media) bodies through which they are articulated.

The five-point operational structure for Lyotard's Paris exhibition. Sketch with (in the original) colored felt-tip pen. Source: *Les Immatériaux* (Paris 1985b), from the section entitled "Album."

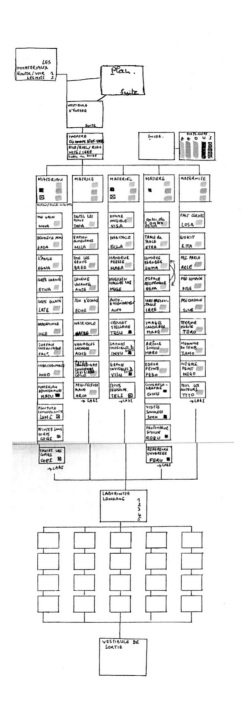

"Self-reassurance, in which the self with all its historical connotations is exorcised" — Kamper can also be programmatic which is why he is sometimes referred to as the guru of a new movement. As early as 1978 in an essay on "Maske, Schminke, Mimikry" ("Mask, Makeup, Mimicry"), he gives a succinct summation of the search for an identity project, which contemporary philosophemes, naturally, still revolve around:

> "The principle of hope is growing steadily weaker in the grand alternative plan. The endeavors for a better world that target the entirety have entered a phase of self-paralysis. Evidently it will be necessary to go back to strategies that enter into a pact with things that are also proscribed in anti-bourgeois projects ... : all that is dazzling, colorful, multifarious, concrete, non-generalizable; that is, incapable of being rationalized or controlled."[77]

At the end of the pamphlet from which the above quotation is taken, an author appears who is virtually unknown in Germany at this time. Paul Virilio contributes an early text that is translated from the French especially for *Mask, Makeup, Mimicry* on the "Ästhetik des Verschwindens" ("The Aesthetics of Disappearance"). A year later he turns up again in the first issue of a new journal, *Zeitschrift für Verkehrswissenschaft* (*Magazine for Trafficking*), published by Merve in Berlin with the intriguing main title *Tumult*. With his text "Der Urfall" [Accidens originale] (*The Original Accident*) it becomes clear that Virilio is a thinker to whom the rhetorical figure of the apocalypse is a sincere Christian concern. The nuclear accidents that happened at the end of the 1970s are for him "a dress rehearsal, the simulation of the Day of Judgement."[78] The editorial board of *Tumult*, who liberate communication from the suspicion of utopian

---

77 Kamper (1978), n.p. The quotation is also from this publication. My thanks to Claudia Schink.

78 *Tumult 1* (Berlin 1979), p. 82.

notions à la Habermas and hand it over to the insecurity of turbulent conditions, includes Frank Böckelmann, Walther Seitter, and Hans-Peter Gente; collaborators in France are Baudrillard and Foucault, among others.

Dietmar Kamper, qualified physical education teacher, sociologist, anthropologist and above all unfailing initiator of adventurous thinking, moves in 1979 from Marburg to the Free University Berlin. Kamper takes the name of his new university seriously, and in the sociology department creates a valuable space for speculation, fantasy, and critical thinking after the Critical Theory of the Frankfurt School, beyond any rigid rules or ideological prescriptions. For West Berlin, Kamper is a living connection to contemporary French intellectuals. At his invitation in June 1982, Derrida attends a seminar at the Free University that Kamper leads together with the philosopher Jacob Taubes. In a lecture lasting one and a half hours, Derrida analyzes Franz Kafka's parable "Before the Law," which is contained in his novel *The Trial*. Derrida points out that not only the person summoned to a court stands before the law but also the doorkeeper, who is not a victim but a perpetrator, an executor of the law; he is a medium in the direct sense of the word as he stands exactly midway between the law and the man from the countryside.

Kamper is always provocative, but in a gentle way. He favors the technique of the T'ai Chi martial artist; by cleverly yielding he will most likely win because he transforms the force expended by an aggressively attacking opponent into his own strong defense. In the 1980s and 1990s Kamper is one of Berlin's chief intellectual attractions. He draws the attention of the craziest thinkers and gives them the assurance that with him anyone can think or say anything. A spectacular high point of his work in Berlin is the 1998 "Foucault Tribunal on the State of Psychiatry" held at the Volksbühne theater with the title "Macht Wahn Sinn" (literally: force madness sense; but also does madness make sense). Kamper initiates the event together with Gerburg Treusch-Dieter and Wolf-Dieter Narr. In the context of the tribunal, which takes place in part under tumultuous conditions with over 1000 participants, the Free University gets a temporary Chair for Madness. In a spectacular action the Karl Bonhoeffer psychiatric unit is renamed Lady Diana Clinic — particularly due to the involvement of Bonhoeffer in the Nazi forced sterilization campaigns among psychiatric patients.[79]

---

79 *Die Irren-Offensive, Zeitschrift von Ver-rückten gegen Psychiatrie* (Berlin) (Offensive of the Psychotics. Journal by the insane against psychiatry) devoted Issue no. 8 (1999) to the Foucault Tribunal.

Die Irren-Offensive, Zeitschrift von Ver-rückten gegen Psychiatrie (Berlin) — Offensive of the Psychotics. Journal by the insane against psychiatry. Cover, No. 8 (1999).

The concept "postmodern" serves to mark the insuperable break in history which humankind has got itself into with its enlightened thinking and action: the inhuman catastrophes of Auschwitz and Hiroshima. With this rupture, modern science, according to some thinkers, has definitively compromised itself. The cognizing subject with his/her aspiration of generating true knowledge and being historically sovereign has disintegrated and is obsolete. With the rediscovery of Nietzsche the possibility of a "gay science" is celebrated: a philosophical thought that is danceable.

When the postmodern is at the height of its boom in the 1980s, artists, critics, and philosophers of culture react with this buzzword to the deep uncertainty they feel at being confronted with the penetration of electronic and digital technologies into all walks of life. Everything that is classed as being downstream of identifying with the material, seems beyond remedy. All juggling with figures inevitably ends up at the dead-end of the zero dimension of the algorithmic construction of the world. The complete disintegration of everything corporeal into abstraction from which there is no escape, is the result that is propagated. "Neither cancer nor Aids are the scourges of the present," says Kamper in a 1989 interview, trenchantly characterizing this worldview, "we are dying an audiovisual death, drowning in a sea of images without having experienced life, or grasped what sensuality is with our own bodies."[80] "Too many images — we have to take action!" is the title of an essay[81] citing Godard in which we focus on his *Histoir(e)s de cinéma* that at the twentieth *fin de siècle* looked back on a century of film.

A paradox: on the one hand Kamper feels genuine disgust for the media of technical sounds and images,

---

80   Kamper (1989), p. 31.
81   Zielinski (1992b). The original version of the essay I coauthored with Nils Röller. It was published as "Cogito ergo Video" in the Austrian avant-garde journal *Blimp* (Graz: no. 21, 1992).

particularly for their stagings. "Enough to make you go deaf and blind," he often remarks. Yet on the other hand he is always at the forefront where the menetekel of the twentieth *fin de siècle* is an issue — at the foundation of the Bildo-Akademie, the first private academy for studying media design in Berlin, which cleverly also offers seminars on boxing and drumming; on the meticulous analysis of Hitchcock's films using Lacanian psychoanalytic methods; on the philosophical interpretation of classic paintings at the Berlin Academy of Arts; and a wealth of symposia which are devoted to the criticism of technical images and their ubiquitous electronic presence.

Dietmar Kamper

Die (Hab)acht Devisen des Essays III

1. Gegen das Imaginäre hilft nur die Einbildungskraft. Nicht die Ver-
   nunft, nicht der Verstand. Sie allein erreicht den Glutkern des
   menschlichen Wesens und ist von daher mit allem Lebendigen ver-
   wandt. Sie ist der Kairos, die Zeit der Intimität.

2. Die Einbildungskraft ist Abkömmling der Erde, nicht der Sonne. Sie
   stammt aus der Hölle und aus dem Garten Eden. Es gibt zwei Formen:
   eine "imaginación mortificada" und eine "imaginación vivente". Man
   kann sie nur an ihren Früchten unterscheiden: die eine verurteilt
   zum Tode, die andere ruft ins Leben.

3. Man muß phantasieren auf Teufel komm raus und um Gottes Willen.
   Weitergehen als Freud! Alles, was aus der Dunkelheit des Körpers
   ans Licht kommt, hat seine eigene Logik. Träumerei zeichnet die
   äußersten Grenzen des Geistes. So träumt die Gattung sich selbst.

4. Wie das Zaubern kann man es nicht wollen. Dem infantilen Omnipo-
   tenzwahn ist ein erfahrbarer Riegel vorgeschoben. Die Einbildungskraft funktioniert erst jenseits der Barriere der Macht. In der
   Entkrampfung der Angst, welche die Bilder der Geburt und des
   Todes nährt.

5. Die daraus sich ergebende Fraktalität der geistigen Welt gilt in
   jeder Richtung. Je origineller im einzelnen, desto vielfältiger im
   ganzen. Negativ formuliert ist es die Unabschließbarkeit. Urteil
   und Schluß als Weltbeziehungen sind diskreditiert.

6. Keine Alternative mehr! Im Schutt des Sowohl/Als auch und des Weder/
   Noch nach Anfängen einer gleitenden Logik der Steigerung suchen!
   Alles, was übersetzbar ist, übersetzen in ein: "Je mehr/desto mehr."
   Den Jubel über die Intensität des Intimen zurückhalten!

7. Der Weg in das Körperwissen, in die Weisheit der Erde ist ein
   geheimer Gang. Er verläuft unterirdisch. Man kann ihn nur von Stufe
   zu Stufe begehen, und nur nach Prämissen, die erst die jeweiligen
   Stufen bereitstellen. Keine Chance für Überflieger.

8. "Sterblichkeit" als Devise ist keine Konzession, sondern eine
   Offerte. Sie verdankt sich einer untergegangenen Welt der Souverä-
   nität, der Gabe, des Geschenks, des Überflusses. Sie überschreitet
   sowohl die Alternative von Opfer und Massaker als auch die von
   Opfer und Verzicht.

Tansan 28.März 1993   D.

In 1989 Kamper is involved in the early German publication of *Zur Archäologie der Medien* which contains a late review of McLuhan's *Understanding Media*; the book had appeared in Germany twenty years earlier, in 1968, and was seized upon by the '68 generation. The review is by Norbert Bolz, a short and brilliantly written text with which he makes his debut in academic media discourse. A few years later McLuhan's metaphor of *The Gutenberg Galaxy* is the nucleus for a significant work written by Nobert Bolz, an occasional collaborator of Kamper's as well as for a short time the philosopher Jacob Taubes. With *The Media Is the Massage*, which the Canadian McLuhan develops with the designer Quentin Fiore, becomes the charismatic international pop star of the culture and media theory scene. Nam June Paik calls him "the cool essayist" and "hippie Joyceist." The mass media queue up for the dedicated Catholic and avid image-despiser to appear on their shows. With McLuhan as yardstick with regard to degree of attention, after the turn of the century Bolz becomes a socially conservative star of applied media studies as a consultant. In the media themselves, which he regards as long since dehumanized, Bolz seems to feel most comfortable; by the fake fireside of a late-night ZDF talk show or in Sloterdijk's and Rüdiger Safranski's TV panel where philosophy is staged as a spectacle.

In the 1990s Bolz works mainly in Essen, not very far from the concrete pile of the Ruhr University Bochum, where Kittler teaches and conducts research until he takes a position in Berlin. Also in Bochum starting in 1974, West Germany's youngest humanities professor, Hans Ulrich Gumbrecht, is already teaching his students the new direction of an expanded understanding of literature. As professor of Romance languages and comparative literature in the 1980s, Gumbrecht organizes exciting excursions with his colleague K. Ludwig Pfeiffer from English studies into the milder constellations and climate regions of existing socialism in which Kittler also participates. At the Inter-University Center Dubrovnik they organize a series of meetings which explore interesting and effective alternatives to classic hermeneutics for literary studies.

At this time Croatia has already been a favorite destination of the technophiliac avant-garde from Western metropolises for twenty years. Beginning in 1961, exhibitions and symposia take place under the title *New Tendencies* to explore algorithmic and permutational principles in the arts and poetry in the Croatian capital of Zagreb. Supported by the U.S. computer industry, the scene's protagonists from Paris, Milan, Vienna, Hamburg, Munich, and other cities are invited to attend; they include Marc Adrian, Herbert W. Franke, Abraham A. Moles, artists of the Zero group — Mack, Piene, and Ücker — and even the anarchist and protagonist of generic arts, Dieter Roth, who in the 1960s also experiments with permutational geometrical patterns. An introductory compendium volume, *Apparative Kunst (Apparatus art)*, of 1973 brings together many of the artists' approaches for German readers.[82]

At their meetings in Yugoslavia, Gumbrecht and Pfeiffer promote two theoretical focuses in particular. They view a modernized variant of structuralism as essential and at the same time its expansion into sociological systems theory, as developed by Niklas Luhmann. The knowledge about technology-conditioned production and reception of literature which has been circulating in Germany, England, France, and Italy since the early 1960s is more heterogeneous. Everything is collected here that promises to draw attention to the imaginary program of an understanding of literature affected by technology, from Maturana's constructivism to Virilio's dromology.

---

82 Edited by Franke and Gottfried Jäger in the *DuMont Dokumente* series.

110

However, in Dubrovnik no special attention is paid to the experimental approaches implemented in Höllerer's lab at the TU Berlin, the propositions of the Bense school on programmed aesthetics, or the projects of the literary avant-garde in Italy and Austria, the heuristics of the apparatus theorists from Paris, or the founders of Cultural Studies in Birmingham. Yet these were all robust prerequisites (from a literary studies point of view) for debating non-meaningful preconditions of literary meaning production. When the nearly 1000-page omnibus volume *Materialität der Kommunikation* (*Materiality of Communication*) appears in 1988, the initiators are hailed as pioneers of topical issues; issues that had in fact been circulating for a quarter of a century in humanities circles in Europe, the USA, and Canada. Years later Pfeiffer reflects on the specific materiality of communicative processes as a variant of *Medienanthropologie* (*Media Anthropology*), which is already very familiar to us as the idea of a different contemporary thinker, namely, Dietmar Kamper.

After many failed attempts at gaining recognition, Vilèm Flusser eventually becomes a charismatic theory star of the 1980s.[83] Today he is one of the thinkers whose ideas are most exploited, particularly by protagonists of art and cultural studies. The term "technical image," which he uses to refer to all visual expressions, from photography to synthetic computer images, and which is now used to substantiate research projects worth millions, is one of his original concepts from the 1980s; Other concepts such as "techno-aesthetics" and his notion of projection as a theory and practice of design formed by the abstraction of numbers being carried over into the concretion of the perceptible. For Flusser the

---

83 For details of his journalistic career see the Afterword by Silvia Wagnermaier in Flusser (2008).

new technical images are "a mode of expressing thoughts They are not copies. They are projections, models."[84]

Abraham Moles says that Flusser's work is "philosophical fiction."[85] The title of his essay refers specifically to Flusser's scientific tale about the *Vampyrotheutis Infernalis* and with this characterization, Moles includes Flusser among the ranks of the classic poet-philosophers. Throughout history such thinkers have always found it difficult to gain recognition in established academic disciplines while at the same time influencing them enormously. Moles' label of philosophical fiction also vividly pinpoints a characteristic energy driving Flusser's oeuvre and success. Originally from Prague, the cultural anthropologist and critic stages philosophical thought, and performs it like an actor who convincingly plays the part of a philosopher. He forms mental images of philosophy and performs them impressively through various discourses on stages — from academies to community colleges, from São Paulo to the provincial backwaters in France and Germany.

In general, Flusser avoids explicit references to *the media*, because he feels that both in the singular and the plural, the words are a travesty of the Latin *medius* and he therefore detests them on that account alone. However, here Flusser overlooks an important nuance because in theological treatises written in Latin one finds the term medium standing for an agency or means, and in the correct Latin plural, as in *media salutis,* media stand for healing substances and means of grace and are thus in close semantic proximity to the imaginary as a lifeline for the suffering mind. Cinema exists so that we don't go mad, as Godard expressed it in his own inimical fashion. In his best-known monograph, *Für eine Philosophie der*

84 Flusser in an interview with Miklòs Péternàk, Osnabrück 1991; included in Flusser (2010).
85 Moles (1988).

Photographie (*Towards a Philosophy of Photography*), his first book published in Germany, in 1983, Flusser discusses in depth the reciprocal relationship between technology and aesthetics using the example of a specific array of apparatus, which on account of its special technical nature, namely, the automatic ability to reproduce objects in a technical image, is often referred to as the first new medium — precisely photography. Flusser's central proposition, that "the categories of the apparatus" rely on the "cultural condition" and "filter" it, is familiar both from French apparatus heuristics and the debate in German on "apparatus art" a good decade before. However, Flusser sets a new emphasis by using terminology that points far beyond any individual medium: "the freedom of the photographer remains a programmed freedom. While the functioning apparatus functions according to the intention of the photographer, this intention functions as a function of the program of the apparatus."[86]

Flusser is clearly working toward a theory of apparatus, but then abandons this direction like he has done with several others. In his highly idiosyncratic interpretation of philosophical phenomenology he is in the best sense a superficial thinker. He is not one of those thinkers who laboriously get to the bottom of things and think them through to the end; instead, Flusser is like someone who kicks a ball and starts it rolling. Notwithstanding, in the 1980s the concept of the apparatus features very prominently in his argumentation. He uses it as a third instance, as an intermediary between human and machine — thus definitely in the sense of a third entity, a medium — and at the same time in contradistinction to the concept of an instrument or tool. In the use of tools the human is the constant and the tool is the variable. In the world of machines, however, the machine is the constant and the human is the variable. In the case of

---

86   Flusser (1983), pp. 32-33.

apparatus, which Flusser understands as a complex construct consisting of various machines and which therefore approximates to the concept of the *dispositif* and Deleuze's definition of apparatus, it is a matter of an "intrinsic correlation of functions:" the apparatus does what the human wants it to do, and the human can only want what the apparatus is able to do.[87]

Due to his pronounced interest in the resistance of individual technologies and their particular materiality, after his *Aufschreibesysteme* (*Discourse Networks 1800 / 1900*) (1984), Kittler discusses technical particularities of aesthetic expression: *Gramophone, Film, Typewriter* (1986). After all the trouble over his *Habilitation* the book is a liberating release and sets a trend in media theory, like Avital Ronell's *The Telephone Book* shortly afterwards,[88] whom the Berlin *Tageszeitung* newspaper affectionately names "deconstruction bitch." Discourse analysis presents itself as a closely synchronized, associative switch-gear between the fields of literary criticism and critique of technology, psychoanalysis, philosophy and philology, pop music, and natural science. With regard to media apparatuses, this is what practitioners figured Foucault might have meant by "interdiscursive analysis," and moreover, in an inimitable and breathless style which will be constitutive of Kittler's approach in the next two decades — more like a complex song than the epic form.

The technical *a priori* of everything in the way of expressions in signs that is making the rounds, including artistic expressions, becomes one of Kittler's theoretical trademarks as well as construing all communications

---

87 Rough translation from a letter of Flusser's to the editor of the journal *Leonardo* (MIT Press), which is undated; however, research in the Flusser Archive indicates it must have been written in Spring 1986. My thanks to Rodrigo Maltez Novaes.
88   First published in the USA in 1989, the German translation appeared in 2001 also with Brinkmann & Bose publishers and with a cover design similar to Kittler's book.

technology from constellations of war. McLuhan's opinion, that each (new) medium contains other (older) media — and in this sense the media are the message — again becomes popular in academe.

With the computer as "universal machine," in the years after his apparatus triad of an audio, a visual, and a writing machine, Kittler establishes a generalization that goes back to the mathematician Alan Turing. For humanities scholars this generalization is powerful enough to finally give them something to combat the impractical eclecticism of naive techno-adepts. In the 1990s and the early years of the following decade, however, Kittler abandons the generalization in favor of the concept of the vowel alphabet as the original generator of all aesthetic texts. He connects mathematics to the sensuality of Ancient Greek love poetry, and creates a mixture that is unique in theory. Thematically, the only contemporary parallel is formulated by Alain Badiou, for the first time in 1992 in Ljubljana and published in 1996 as a revised version of his lecture on Lacan's "challenges of philosophy": "The reference to mathematics arises at precisely the point where the issue is to make truth, which does not know itself, accessible to knowledge." In four propositions Badiou summarizes the procedure that negotiates between "love and mathematics":

1. "There is truth that is irreducible to knowledge.
2. Knowledge about truth is possible.
3. The real ideal of such knowledge is mathematical.
4. The procedure performed by truth on being is called love."[89]

The same applies to Kittler as to all the other complex positions briefly described here: his media-theoretical conception cannot be reduced to any one concept; rather, it is necessary to identify several that follow each other in dynamic sequence and are in a

---

89   Badiou and Rancière (1996) p. 61; trans. from the German G.C.

relationship of tension with each other. The paradigm of the military, that Kittler developed following Virilio's lead for telematic media, gains a completely different meaning in the context of short-distance media like writing love-poems or singing love-songs. Kittler's media theory is above all else a specific intellectual *activity* that is very close to Foucault's concept of truth.

In the second half of the 1980s, media theory is ushered in by Flusser and Kittler in the Federal Republic of Germany, and the early 1990s are one of the most exciting periods in the theoretical debate about the so difficult to define third entity situated between the concreteness of what is alive and the abstractions of the logos and technology. The number of interesting contributions to the debate from ever more disciplines rises exponentially. Sybille Krämer opens the doors of academic philosophy to the *Symbolischen Maschinen* (*Symbolic machines*) (1988), and more and more disciplines interrogate their discourses as to the conditionality of media influence. And the young media theorists' appetite for exceptional and unusual suggestions is voracious.

Otto E. Rössler, doctor of medicine, biochemist, chaos theoretician, and theoretical physicist, exerts great fascination with his ideas of radical micro-constructivism within which the experienceable world attains the status of an interface. His endophysics establishes the concept of the observer within the universe, which complements traditional "exophysics" with its observer outside. The endophysical participating observer, who significantly affects the processes in which he/she is integrated, becomes the paradigm of a type of artistic theory and practice that focuses on processual qualities and interaction. The world is consistent, but consistently new in every single moment. This is Rössler's challenge to science, which sees itself as responsible for describing and interpreting natural processes on both a macro and a

116

micro scale. Rössler himself has not only accepted this challenge, he lives it with dignity as a thinker quietly dancing at the boundary.

Hans Belting vacates the Federal Republic's most prestigious Chair of Art History at the conservative Ludwig Maximilians University Munich and embarks on the adventure of building a new college, the Staatliche Hochschule für Gestaltung Karlsruhe (Karlsruhe University of Arts and Design), with a focus on the interaction of arts and technologies. For Belting, this means subjecting art history and art theory to a radical rethinking in terms of technical media. Fundamental questions concerning the status of the image, the observer, and the gaze become central issues for him. Partly due to his friendship with Kamper, anthropology begins to exert a strong influence on his conceptions of the visual arts and their concepts of perception. His publications, which are devoted to a systematic analysis of the image, make Belting an early protagonist of the new direction of *image science* in an international context. With his elegant and insistent figures of thought, Belting, however, refrains from any gesture of a post hoc incorporation of the new image phenomena in the hegemonial pretensions of his home discipline.

From brain research and its history come Olaf Breidbach, Hinderk M. Emrich, Detlef. B. Linke, and Gottfried Mayer-Kress. They provide access to the microcosm of the psychological activities of the individual spanning calculating reason and limitless fantasy. Problems at the external interface between humans and machines become comprehensible as dramas inside the head. Mayer-Kress, for example, later works on the enormous adaptive flexibility of the dolphin brain. During his research he teaches the cetaceans to play with computers. This research reveals the self-aggrandizing presumption of humans as absurd, and shakes up an important element of the much-vaunted unique position of *homo sapiens*. Detlef. B. Linke, a specialist for neurophys-iology and neurosurgical rehabilitation, energetically de-fends the freedom of human thought against the apparatus fetishists of Artificial Intelligence. His studies on the rela-tionship between art and the brain combine exact scientif-ic and philosophical arguments with admirable clarity and elegance. This also applies to Emrich, a psychiatrist and philosophically trained psychoanalyst who specializes in issues which lie at the heart of human–machine relations relevant to art: synesthesia, dialectics of remembering and forgetting, and the capabilities of internal dreaming ma-chinery as the most powerful of these systems, which we shall not be able to control on any permanent basis.

From Paris, more and more fragments on *Capitalism and Schizophrenia* from Deleuze and Guattari's *Mille plateaux* (*A Thousand Plateaus*) become known to the public, including to those who cannot read the original French version, [90] which is not available in German translation until 1992. Their second conglomeration of texts and continuation of *Anti-Oedipus* operates very close to all the issues that inter-est the media gang. The intellectual oscillations between philosophy, critique of power, poetry, and psychoanalysis determine, up to and including terminology, experimen-tal practices and media-theoretical positions that operate with multifarious constitutions of subject, non-hierarchi-cal orders, and the greatest possible openness of dynamic relations, particularly with regard to communicative con-tacts established by technological means.

An especially important figure from Deleuze and Guattari's texts is the rhizome: the stem of a plant that is not vertical, but horizontal, and with a massive system of roots. The rhizome replaces the rigid hierarchies of the *structure* with a supple organic term, under a single banner capable of uniting the new networkers. Antonin Artaud's notion of a body without organs and many

---

90 The original appeared in 1980.

other mutually exclusive concepts of apparatus and machines, among which the war machine makes the most successful career, inscribe themselves in the indexes of advanced art and media theories as well as the associated practices without *the media* being made explicit at all. As an ardent philosopher of a particular medium, the cinema, in the 1980s the Godard-specialist Deleuze publishes one of the most important theoretical works. In *Cinéma 1. L'image-mouvement* (*Cinema 1: The Movement Image*) and *Cinéma 2. L'image-temps* (*Cinema 1: The Time-Image*) Deleuze developed a specific philosophical philology for the time-based form of expression of cinema. Within his oeuvre, it can only be compared to Deleuze's fantastic book, on the master of figurative movement in painting, Francis Bacon (*Francis Bacon: The Logic of Sensation*).

The fascinating studies of Michel Serres are also infused with questions concerning communicative exchanges and the third entity, which is so difficult to define, but without seeking explicitly to be media theory. Serres consistently takes up the cross-sectoral standpoints of science historian and historian of civilizations in order to discuss the translation of accounts between the one and the other within a broader perspective. His five books centering on the extremely complex figure of the Greek god *Hermès* (*I: La communication; II: L'interférence; III: La traduction; IV: La distribution; V: Le passage du nord-ouest)*, published in France from 1968 to 1980, are only available in German translation in the early 1990s, in the midst of the Internet euphoria, where at first they remain on the bookshelves like radiant fossils from another era. And in spite of the fact that they are eminently suitable for navigating the fundamental issues of technology-based communication — but not, however, as manuals. "Let us imagine a net-like diagram that is drawn in a representation space." This is the first sentence of the Introduction to *Hermès I* of 1968 before Serres expounds his discussion of the correlation between mathematics and Greek mythology. The book ends with one of the most wonderful remarks that I know in the many theories of communication: "Laughter is the human phenomenon of communication ... which accompanies all communication at the feast; its sound never ceases to be heard at the table of the gods."[91]

Virilio and Baudrillard, whose reception peaks in West Germany in the 1980s, are not very interested in individual media. In *War and Cinema*, Virilio is not primarily interested in film, its aesthetics, its language, or even looking at and listening to any examples of feature or documentary films. Rather, it is the comparison of structural and ethical attributes of film production with those of war that commands his attention. His associative linking of Etienne-Jules Marey's chronophotographic gun with the "revolving gun" of Samuel Colt, which culminates in the conceptual synthesis of shooting pictures, is irrelevant from the point of view of the history of technology.[92] As an adaptation of Roland Barthes' idea about the basic characteristics of structuralistic activities for the production of technical images, however, this hypothesis influences entire cohorts of media researchers, particularly those who are fascinated by the notion of war as the father of all (technical communication) things. Virilio's *War and Cinema: The Logistics of Perception*, which builds on this, attains paradigmatic status.

As an architect and urbanist, Virilio's principle interest is the radical change in the perception of space and time that technologies of acceleration bring about and which leads to an *Aesthetics of Disappearance*. Movement drives the event. The "art of the instrument panel" has developed into a "seventh art" as a more radical version

91   Serres, May 1967, quoted here from Serres (1991), p. 9 and 345; trans. from German by G.C.
92   See Zielinski (1993), p. 40 and 43.

of film. In his "dromoscopy" or "dromology," Virilio's position is essentially a deterministic view of the relationship between technology and culture. He regards all culture as an effect of technology. He maintains this position even though it possibly leads to ultimateness. Virilio generalizes Hannah Arendt's observation with reference to Auschwitz, that progress and catastrophe are two sides of the same coin, as an experience of the world that as a principle is inclined toward catastrophe. Or, to put it plainly, Virilio follows a profoundly religious view of technology/media that centers on the apocalypse. His tenet concerning the production and distribution of images at the speed of light leads Virilio to propose the hypothesis of "Polar Inertia," into which we all inevitably fall because of continual acceleration brought about by technology.[93]

Baudrillard only develops a special interest in media practice on two occasions. In a brilliant early essay he analyzes graffiti in the New York subway as an anarchic *Insurrection of Signs* protesting against social emptiness; his "Kool Killer"[94] essay renders media research a pleasurable and playful experience for many young intellectuals. Second, at the end of his life Baudrillard thematizes photography explicitly with reference to his own aesthetic practice. In 2004, the Fridericianum museum in Kassel devotes an exhibition and catalog *Die Abwesenheit der Welt* (*The absence of the world*) to this aspect of his oeuvre.

Baudrillard's intellectual endeavors are first and foremost considered as both continuing and advancing Marxian analysis of the commodity, and above all of commodity fetishism, in a situation in which remnants of reality are subject to thorough-going simulation. Through linking Marx and de Saussure,

---

93   See especially the catalog for the Paris exhibition that Virilio conceived for Fondation Cartier after the attack on the World Trade Center in NewYork: Virilio (2002). For various key terms see Virilio (1980), p. 135ff.

94   See Baudrillard's essay "Kool Killer or The Insurrection of Signs" *Symbolic Exchange and Death*. Sage Publications (1993), p. 76.

Baudrillard sees in the exchange of goods in late capitalism that exchange value and use value have entered into an arbitrary relationship similar to the signifier and the signified as the two sides of the sign in structural linguistics. Under the force of the signifier, the signified starts to flounder; exchange value is realized in interaction with other exchange values and not with reference to use value, which is doomed to disappear.

His concept of a simulacrum, a borrowing from the philosophy of the Greek atomists, notably Lucretius, clearly tends toward the negative and like a menetekel replaces a potential media theory. As with the apocalypse or polar inertia in Virilio, Baudrillard's simulacrum fulfills the function of a category of The End. However, at the same time it is entangled in its own paradox: it only functions because silently it presupposes something simulated, something epistemologically different to a simulacrum. Turning a simulation into concrete, formed material, for example, as Flusser conceives it, is not possible for Baudrillard to imagine. Nevertheless, he makes it abundantly clear in every sentence he writes that from now on one can no longer speak simply of real and false, true and untrue, as properties of reality. This methodological skepticism is hugely productive and helpful.

A 1987 electronic essay by the British filmmaker Geoff Dunlop brings the two Frenchmen, who had vitalized and shaped the discourse in Western Europe, together in an imaginary meeting. *L'objet d'art à l'âge éléctronique* is commissioned by the new experimental television broadcaster La SEPT, which later becomes the cultural channel ARTE. Dunlop's video film is a tribute to Walter Benjamin's famous *Work of Art* essay, fifty years after its publication. Dunlop's main tool is the recently developed, staggeringly expensive image processing machine Paintbox. Professional users could use Paintbox to intervene in the surface structures of electronic images and modify them. Dunlop assigns a specific aesthetic existence to each of the protagonists of apocalypse-influenced media theories with a light touch. Baudrillard is gradually painted over while speaking in a threatening voice about the domination of the simulacra. Virilio's half-length portrait slowly turns into a mug shot while he faces *Der Riese* (*The Giant*) by Michael Klier and talks about steadily increasing control via ubiquitous surveillance cameras. The theme of Klier's 1983 video film is a radical look at how the panoramic view became established in Western European cities before the Orwellian year of 1984. The video consists entirely of "found" footage from surveillance cameras.

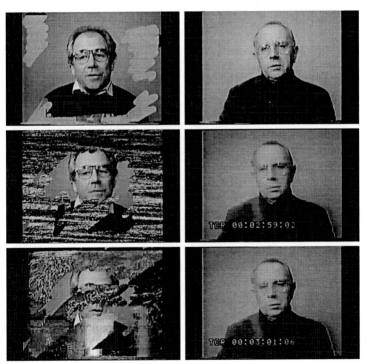

Stills from Geoff Dunlop's *L'objet d'art à l'âge éléctronique*, Illuminations, London 1987.

123

2. In Praise of What Is Not Systemic about the Arts: For a *cultura experimentalis*

Operational Anthropology

For the purposes of experimental usability during the transition from what is past to what could be future, the last two centuries have brought forth two anthropological designs that are especially outstanding. Both concepts have their origins in Eastern Europe. One was developed by Vilém Flusser, cultural critic from Prague, in the 1980s, and the other by the Silesian physicochemist Johann Wilhelm Ritter 180 years before that.

Flusser's operational anthropology follows a compelling idea which describes an ellipsoid movement that is dynamized by a magical concept of time. The cultural ability of an individual to apprehend the world initially takes the route of increasing abstraction of the reality of the lifeworld that is experienced. This is a concept from Husserl's phenomenology that Flusser is fond of using. When the apex of abstraction is reached, the act of projection opens up the possibility of a new design of the world. From out of the abstraction, or to put it better: through and via the abstraction, the individual is able to redesign his or herself in the direction of Otherness in a dialog with science and technology.

Civilization passes through five different phases during this process. The first phase is the four-dimensionality of the lived experience of reality — three dimensions of space and one of time. In the second phase, experience is reduced to the inoperative object of three-dimensional reality, to the monumental. Humans build dwellings for protection; that is, for self-preservation in their limited lifespans, and sculptures for eternity. The quality of the third phase is defined by the two-dimensional image. The conscious individual, who is aware of living in freedom, steps back from the object and draws or paints what they desire on the wall: to study it, to hunt it more effectively, to possess it, or to kill it more efficiently. In the fourth phase history begins. This phase is bound to the one-dimensionality of the text, which as a principle is aligned linearly. In the interpretation by Flusser, an iconoclast and believer in writing, it is this quality that empowers humans to approach images in a detached way and to criticize their magic. The medium in which this is done is writing. At this point of civilization's development there is a turn, which Flusser sees as dramatic. The period of post-history (*post-histoire*) begins. Flusser ascribes to the zero-dimension, as emptied of abstraction, a possibility to develop positively. In the number, in the mathematical formula, in the algorithmic command, the level has been reached that can no longer expand, a tabula rasa from which a new reality becomes possible, at least provisionally as a draft. Consequently, this new reality, which is in the process of becoming, is a hybrid, comprising experience of life and of machines.

On March 28,1806, the thirty-year-old Ritter put forward his view to the Bavarian Academy of Sciences in Munich. In his presentation titled "Physics as Art: An Attempt to Interpret the Tendency of Physics from Its History,"[95] in the space of one printed page he outlines the previous history of the arts as a specific, positive anthropology. It has four different stages. The most important point of reference for Ritter in this outline is human activity.

In its four-dimensionality of time and space, architecture/urban construction attempts to shape and immortalize human deeds in monumental form. In three-dimensional sculpture the actor seeks to embody his or

---

95   Reprinted in Ritter (1984), pp. 288–320, quotation p. 310; English edition of some of Ritter's texts: *Key Texts of Johann Wilhelm Ritter* (1776–1810) on the Science and Art of Nature, (2010), trans. and essays by Jocelyn Holland, Leiden, Boston, MA: Brill.

herself directly as an individual. Painting once again delegates the necessity of acting to people, because the flatness of images, which Ritter refers to as *halber Raum* (half-space), compels the observer to supplement this visual information with the imagination. So far, the arts have only addressed the eye. They show what has been, they live off the past, and are therefore arts of memory. Ritter summarizes his first three stages with an idea that is indebted to Lucretius and his poem about atoms, *De rerum natura*: "The purpose of art: To render present what is absent [...] Monument. The beloved, however, is more than her image."[96] It is only with music that history changes its tendency. Sound draws the activity of people into the artistic act; it is in music that the act first becomes directly present. What follows can only be achieved by physics; namely, the (re-)production of consonance between the inner and external nature of humans, the identity of nature and action, of living and enjoying the latter. For Ritter this is the highest art, which he is confident a future physics is capable of realizing, if it does not wish to forfeit its deeper meaning as a science.[97]

Both Ritter's and Flusser's concepts are not teleological — which is unusual for an anthropological perspective — nor are they apocalyptic. They offer opportunities for development toward a future which is open. They do not seek to be in the right, but rather to encourage actors to continue to work on the project of bringing about change in what already exists.

Motivated by the concepts of Ritter and Flusser, around ten years ago I began to work with an anthropology that is also to be understood as operational. Through engaging with the history of the special frictions between the arts, sciences, and technologies, this anthropology seeks

---

96   Ibid. (1984), p. 256.
97   Ibid., p. 317f.; see also the dissertation by Wolfgang Hartwig (1955), especially pp. 70–83; and Zielinski, *Deep Time of the Media* (Cambridge, MA 2006), pp. 177–182.

to keep open the possibilities of being active for the time to come — for scientists and artists as well as engineers who are deeply committed to a culture of experimenting, in the broadest possible sense.

In this approach the complexity of the relations between the autonomous fields of knowledge and work of art, science, and technology is highly reduced. I subsume them here briefly under the different historical qualities in the relationship between art and media. In this context, art specifically means art as an experimental aesthetic praxis which engages with science and technology. Otherwise the qualities of the relations, which are the issue here, would not make sense.

I differentiate between four relational qualities: art *before the* media, art *with* media, art *through* media, and art *after the* media. As with the phases and stages of Flusser and Ritter, these qualities should not be understood as a chronological sequence, but as differently weighted priorities in the deep time structure that interests us here. Historically, the qualities overlap and in part run parallel. The second and third relational qualities are the easiest to grasp.

Art *with* media reflects on the multifarious artistic utilization of insights achieved by mathematics, arithmetic, and geometry, their application in mechanics, acoustics, and optics, and the pressure resulting from this utilization that pushes toward the realization of artifacts and technical systems for communicating, teaching, illusionizing, shocking, entertaining, and proselytizing. Art *with* media implies an instrumental relationship between the intention of an expression and its technical realization. In the relational quality of art *with* media, flat or curved mirrors, pipes, funnels, rollers, magnetic telex machines, and mechanical combinatory systems serve as prostheses for the genesis of art, but are not an essential precondition for art to exist. These artifacts expand artistic praxis, can potentially make it more effective, but they do not renew it.

128

In a narrower historical perspective, this quality originally evolved in Europe during the geometrization of seeing and the mathematization of the image in the Golden Age of Arab-Islamic science cultures of the ninth to the eleventh century. It develops further in the Second Renaissance, which is how we understand the European movement from medieval to modern times. With innumerable models for cryptography and steganography, as well as elaborately staged spaces for technical images, it continues in the sixteenth century, and celebrates its first high points with concepts for automated musical composition, the sequencing of harmonious melodies, and the invention of a great number of visual special effects in the seventeenth century. Basically, all mechanical, optical, and acoustic innovations and inventions that followed in the eighteenth and nineteenth centuries — the founding years of the new media — use this instrumental relational quality. After World War II, it again becomes effective as a declared and demonstrative distancing from a dependency, which art could now enter into with the media that have become strategic. This particularly applies to the telematic means of communication.

Art *through* media means that the artistic process is essentially realized by *going through* a technical medium or array of technical media. This finally becomes possible with the advent of the artificial generation of electricity. In the Age of Enlightenment, forces of nature like electrical storms are tamed by technology. With the discovery of the physical and chemical principles of electricity in the eighteenth century a very rich culture of experimentation developed from London and Paris to St. Petersburg. Applications of science are demonstrated at spectacular performances in which weak electric current is sent through the bodies of heavy monks or lightweight boys and girls floating in the air. Salon experiments, like those in the 1730s by the German physicist

Georg Matthias Bose where visitors were greeted by an electrified beauty standing on an insulated stool so they could partake in the sensational experience of an electric kiss (of Venus), are already invitations to the guests to actively participate, which is precondition for realizing such performative installations. With diverse models of *tableaux magiques*, upon which electrical sparks describe awe-inspiring figures, devices are created for instruction and entertainment that generate images in a new modus; namely, in the modus of time.[98] The figures only become visible, or palpable to the touch, when the current is on. Such time-images are already in existence when other experimenters begin to write external reality onto light-sensitive paper using light. And with the electrical cures of Franz Anton Mesmer and other electro-medics at the end of the eighteenth century archaic forms of a *psychopathia medialis* appear, which as contemporaries we see develop throughout the twentieth century.

With his idea of a perpetually vibrating and oscillating cosmos, on a micro and a macro scale, Ritter is the one who not only theoretically formulates the relational quality of art *through* media early on, but also lives it by making his own body his laboratory and using his extremities and other body parts as conductors and indicators of electric current. Ritter's last, unrealized, book project is *The Theory of Glowing*. By comparison, the approaches used in the twentieth century to realize art through electricity, after the establishment of electronics as master technology, seem very disciplined, and appear subordinated to a strategic concept. However, they are endowed with new strength and expanded activities by the algorithmic machines.

---

98 In the early cabinets of physics these magic tablets were used to visualize the effects of electricity in dark rooms at popular demonstrations; cf. the detailed and illustrated account in: Louis Figuier, *La Machine Électrique, Le Paratonnerre, La Pile de Volta, L'électromagnetisme* (Paris, 1868), p. 485ff.

At the beginning of the third millennium CE the mechanical, electrical, and electronic media, with and through which art is produced, distributed, and perceived, are taken for granted. They are a part of everyday experience, like a faucet that one turns on and off at will without thinking much about where the content comes from, what is in it, and how it is disposed of after use.[99] The generations of scientists, artists, and engineers that are now learning, studying, testing, researching, organizing, and leading have been socialized to a greater or lesser extent by their experience with technical media, and the youngest have grown up with them. They are termed "digital natives." The media no longer represent any particular attraction for them.

With regard to the arts, the strategy of the early 1990s has worked. Media art becomes established, across the board and across cultures. It is integrated in public spaces, on bank premises as well as in private collections; on the gigantic facades of the high-rise buildings in Shanghai's new business quarter Pudong as well as in the exclusive shopping malls of Dubai or Qatar. Even Scandinavian, British, and the occasional German TV crime series seem today to be more influenced by the techniques and effects of video art rather than by narrators of gripping stories. The moans and groans that media arts are not well established in public and private spaces are mostly heard from people who have so far missed out on getting their fair share.

Art *after* the media does not refer to experimental praxis that dispenses entirely with technical media; this is no longer feasible either in applied science, cultural studies, or the arts. Rather, this relational quality draws attention to the fact that what we are looking for is an art of experimenting, which does not require media as a legitimation

---

99 This comparison was made already in 1956 by Günther Anders in his book *Die Antiquiertheit des Menschen* [*The Outdatedness of Human Beings*], (Munich: C.H. Beck, 1980). See particularly the section "Die Welt als Phantom und Matrize" [The World as a Phantom and a Matrix], pp. 97–211.

or as a special sensation any longer, but at the same time does not close its eyes, ears, and mind to the media. Just how art *after* the media will develop is, at the beginning of the third millennium, already foreseeable, but not yet a foregone conclusion. My anthropology, too, represents a modest attempt to interpret the tendency of art from its history, as Ritter formulated it for physics — as what was for him the all-encompassing science of life.

Before the ideas, concepts, and notions exist that push relentlessly forward to become the generalization *the media*, denoting a special area of theory and praxis, art does not get by without media. The devices for encryption and decryption of secret ciphers in the fifteenth century or the optical instruments (re)invented by Giovan Battista della Porta in the sixteenth century, the Monochord with which Robert Fludd wants to tune the beginning seventeenth century to celestial harmony, or the musical composition automaton for home use in well-to-do households constructed by Athanasius Kircher at the Jesuit College in Rome, are preceded by many centuries of research, speculation, cognition, and model development that do not inevitably have to culminate in the particular, concrete inventions of the pre-Modern period. In the two and a half thousand years between 800 BCE and 1700 CE, a multitude of optical, acoustic, magnetic, combinatorial, and algorithmic sensations were developed, which are only subsumed under the umbrella term of media because of the coercion exerted by the context of our contemporary perspective. In their own time the artifacts did not press forward in the direction of such a generalization, nor had they any need of it.

The modular grids and strings the ancient Egyptians used to calculate and construct the ideal body proportions for their sculptures of the gods,[100] from which the Pythagoreans likely derived their geometry-based concept

---

100   In this context see Albert Presas i Puig (2004).

of harmony, the shadow optics of the Chinese Mohists of over 2300 years ago and their sketched idea for a *camera obscura*, the automaton theater of *Philo* of Byzantium or Heron of Alexandria in the third century BCE and first century CE, which in turn correspond wonderfully with the mechanical and pneumatic/hydraulic devices of the engineer Ibn al-Razāz al-Jazarī from Kurdistan in the late twelfth century, the optical experiments of the Chinese astronomer Shen Kua with the projection of flying birds and racing clouds in eleventh-century China: singular and isolated sensations such as these from the deep strata of history I term technology and science-receptive art phenomena *before the* media. For an anarchaeology that is interested in the creations and developments of technical seeing, hearing, and combining, its iridescent diversity is among the most fascinating of the historical relational qualities. Of the four relational qualities described it is the one that is most relevant for the future as an open field which we wish to, and can, cocreate.

The concept of the deep time of a variantological relationship between arts, sciences, and technologies requires a specific attitude toward the past. The concept is not so much interested to what, allegedly, actually has been. This is dealt with by armies of historiographers and curators of archives. We are much more curious about what else might have been. If I am looking to extract options from the future, then I have to grant the past the right to exist in the subjunctive.

Over the last ten years we have interpreted past constellations at length and in depth. Here I shall concentrate on the challenge of sketching the options for future action. As the most important premise — analogously to the critique of theory becoming strategic — I focus on the establishment of media art after World War II. This means discussing the relations between art with and through media which have now become conventions. I shall do this through specific examples. Particular attention will be paid to an artist and intellectual who has not only played a defining role in shaping the past fifty years, but who has been successful to a large extent in preserving the breakup of what is systemically necessary as culture.

Nam June Paik

Occasionally Flusser also resorts to malapropisms of Latin terms, for example, when he rails against something or somebody vehemently. In a short passage from one of his last lectures in Bochum, which Kittler had invited him to give, Flusser talks about the experimental video center The Kitchen in New York. There he had met "a Korean by the name of Nam June Paik." Flusser says he is a "totally crazy illetterate," that is, a "dumb cluck" averse to reading and writing. This man Paik is to philosophy what he, Flusser, is to judo, namely, a disaster. At the same time the cultural critic from Prague, who fights his entire life for recognition as a philosopher, says the Korean artist is a "video person of genius."[101]

We are interested here in how Paik actually expresses himself in language. But first the epistemic core of Flusser's comparison needs to be highlighted. From Flusser's point of view (an intellectual who primarily expresses himself through writing and speaking), literary ability in the broadest sense, the power of abstraction, belongs to philosophy and finds its highest ennoblement in a finely honed concept. By contrast, an artist of genius can exhaust all possibilities of the particularity of the concrete. The artist is responsible for individual events and sensations, not for generalizations.

---

101 Flusser (2008), quotations p. 184.

This juxtapositioning has frequently been discussed and refuted with regard to art. There is no doubt that images and sounds also possess a high epistemic value and can take on a conceptual character, and just like words — including words that sound complicated — can be stupid and meaningless. Ninety years ago Sergei Eisenstein, following Lev Kuleshov, constructed his concept of dialectical film editing substantially on the generalizability of pictorial expressions; this was both a theory and concrete cinema practice. With regard to artistic processes, which have arisen with and through media, any split into language's capabilities for critique and philosophy on the one side, and the magic and seductive power of the pictorial and visual on the other, is totally questionable. These artistic practices arise and develop under the tension that exists with the hegemonial apparatuses of expression. They understand themselves as a critique of dominant concepts, or at least as figures of intentional deviation from them. And precisely because these artistic practices arose in close proximity to power, that is, to the strategic commissioning of the media, they are particularly challenged by critical reflection and theory and yet capable of both.

Obviously, John Cage did not invent silence, but he was the composer who attempted to give it a form, and as a musician he interpreted it in the unique piece *4'33*. Cage gave silence, as the absence of intentionally produced sounds, a conceptual meaning within a complex relational structure of theological, mythological, philosophical, and aesthetic reflection. These are the elements that compose Cage's microuniverse. The different dimensions of his practiced *Weltanschauung* could only be separated and isolated at the price of destroying it.

From 1959 Wolf Vostell assigns to his transforming, permutational, and interpretive practice in relation to the presence and representational status of mass media-produced images the concept of *dé-coll/age* and propagates it

135

as "events for millions." With regard to the technically produced imaginary he does the same as what Derrida will later do to texts and language with deconstruction. The technical image is not something objective nor is it a true given, that — once it has been created — is unchangeable. With the appropriate instruments to intervene it is subject to permanent change, which obviously includes reinterpretations. Vostell likes to play with the etymological oscillations of the word *décollage* and connects the concept with a gesture of getting going, of casting off from something tightly joined together, for example, glued.

In 1967 Peter Weibel performs *Synthesis zweier Sequentieller Maschinen* on the streets of Vienna. The performance is a dialog of the artist with a tape recorder. When Weibel starts the machine he says "On!" to which the tape recorder responds with a prerecorded "Off!" Weibel then turns the machine, which has now assumed the character of a player, off, says "On!" again, presses the start button once more, the tape recorder answers again, and so on until either the person operating the machine collapses from exhaustion or the machine gives up the ghost — as in fact happens during an early performance of the work. Human and machine are coupled in a circular, totally conclusive relationship, and at the same time stand in competition with each other. When one or other of the systems makes an error or gives up, the dramatic game ends. *Synthesis* can certainly be interpreted as a reaction to Claude Shannon's information theory and to aspects of Norbert Wiener's cybernetics. Weibel engaged with the work of both Shannon and Wiener long before the German scene latched onto them in the 1980s. Weibel's performance, however, does not react to a theory of the digital, for this does not yet exist in connection with aesthetic processes. Weibel formulates the two states from whose endless sequence and fast alternation future artistic production will be generated to a large degree;

he formulates them with art's very own resources — aesthetic ones. In terms of art, Weibel anticipates something. His performance is not an art of recollection.

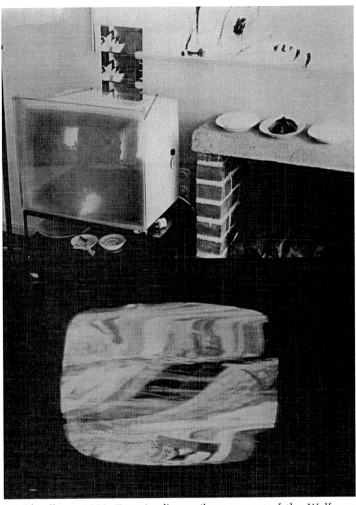

TV-dé-coll/age 1959. Top: Appliance (here as part of the Wolfgang Hahn Collection), Bottom: electronic *decollage*; in: *Wolf Vostell elektronisch*, Neue Galerie im Alten Kurhaus (Aachen 1970).

And when Friederike Pezold stages videographic ana-
grams of her body as signs of her very own writing she
is not illustrating a theory of gender relations, which
does not yet exist in an elaborated form. Instead, she is
implicitly reacting to Laura Mulvey, and at an early point
encourages feminist art and media theory to see women
not merely as an object in the image, that is, in the perspective of a victim, but to conceive the body electrically
as possessing two poles — as a force that both attracts
and resists. Pezold takes up a theoretical position and
a practical one. During an exhibition in Munich's Len-
bachhaus art museum she inspired Frieda Grafe, West
Germany's *grande dame* of film criticism, to write a fine
text. It is a lucid demonstration of how aesthetic practice
at that time was very much interwoven with theories
informed by psychoanalysis, and also shows the strong
influence that the gesture of consistently personal and
artistic image-making exerted on the culture of cinema:

> "The new images demand a new gaze. Standing in
> front of F.P.'s pictures one regains one's visual sense.
> The contemplative gaze turns into the drive to see.
> It is as though the gaze changes its morphology and
> after recognition has taken place, learns to feel again.
> It becomes tactile. It takes a new direction: no longer
> merely reacting to external stimuli, but accommodating
> an internal rhythm. It becomes an impression that
> avows its commitment to matter, which is its bearer."[102]

Interventionary Thinking

At first sight it does not appear to make sense to characterize Paik's activities in the first twenty years of his
artistic production with a rather cumbersome term of
Bertolt Brecht's. The German theater specialist and poet
is no longer alive when Paik begins to study in Munich

---

102   Grafe (1976), p. 125.

138

again. And in Japan Paik, had not studied the composer Hanns Eisler for his first degree but Arnold Schönberg, whose music invariably made Brecht go to sleep, as he noted in his *Arbeitsjournal* (work journal) written during his exile in California. The wild ideas and artistic processes of the Korean émigré to the West are too contrary to the rigorous epic verdicts of the German socialist whose general orientation is toward the East, who with *Me-Ti. Buch der Wendungen* (*Me-Ti. Book of changes*)[103] produced one of his finest texts. However, a closer look reveals that there are congenial complements. Provided that — in the sense intended by Fernando Pessoa — one thinks the merchant and the anarchist all at once; provided one is seeking to comprehend the persons dialectically:

"Let us therefore cause general dismay by revoking our decision to emigrate from the realm of the merely enjoyable, and even more general dismay by announcing our decision to take up lodging there. Let us treat the theatre as a place of entertainment, as is proper in an aesthetic discussion, and try to discover which type of entertainment suits us best!"[104]

Paik is completely serious about his art and studies while at the same time being aware that in the second half of the twentieth century he is living in a developed *Society of the Spectacle*, as the Situationist Guy Debord characterizes the postindustrial communal forms of the capitalist West in 1967. Paik has a very close relationship with electronic folklore, with spectacular events in the age of ubiquitous cameras, monitors, microphones and loudspeakers. He is quite prepared to push the spectacular over into slapstick humor, for example, by

---

103 Brecht, *Gesammelte Werke*, vol. 18, *Me-Ti Buch der Wendungen* (Frankfurt a. M. 1967). It is a striking phenomenon that many European avant-garde artists and intellectuals turn to worldviews from the far East— from Eisenstein to Brecht, from Cage to Vostell.
104 Brecht (1964), *Brecht on Theatre*, Prologue to "A Short Organum for the Theatre," p. 180.

"mooning" the audience of a concert, by taking a violin for a walk on a leash along the street to the great amusement of passersby, or by working with blatantly sexist gestures. In the Fluxus publication *The Monthly Review of the University for Avant-Garde Hinduism* he notes in verse form in the spring of 1963 "wer liefert was? / who supplies what? / qui peu livrer quoi? / As Spiegle Co. in Chicago or Neckermann Versand in Frankfurt / FLUXUS macht es möglich / Wir liefern Musik, / [...] or arm-pit hair of a Chicagoan negro prostitute / etc."[105]

Paik built his first robot *K 456* as a "surprise in a matter of seconds,[106] as a minimal sensational event in road traffic. He styles it as a rickety automaton with gendered features: a white cap and a pair of rubber falsies. His *Young Penis Symphony* (1962) calls for ten young men, one after the other, to stick their penises through a huge white band of paper "stretched across the whole stage mouth, from the ceiling to the floor" at the audience thus writing a notation consisting of erections.[107] The appearances with his muse and long-term musical accompanist, Charlotte Moorman, who topless, or with a bra made of transparent monitors, bows the clothed or naked chest of Paik or a gigantic model penis instead of her cello, even ending one time with the police arresting the pair. On the one hand this is intentional — to become better known and to provoke one's own social class — and on the other hand gestures such as these also tap into cultural practices that we associate with knee-slapping jokes and slapstick. The petit bourgeois knows best how to provoke other petit bourgeois, as Hans-Magnus Enzensberger says in a sarcastic text written for *Kursbuch 45* magazine: "The *bohème* was recruited in the main from the petit bourgeoisie, whose specialty was to scare other

---

105   Hendricks (1988), p. 426.
106   "sekundenschnelle Überraschung;" *Nam June Paik Werke 1946–1976, Musik-Fluxus-Video*, Kölnischer Kunstverein, Cologne 1977, p. 93.
107   Paik (1977). p. 47.

members of the petit bourgeoisie." Brecht, who hailed from the deeply provincial Augsburg, was also a past master of such tactics.

In his performances Paik demonstrates the experiment as an invasive culture of intervening in what is intact, harmonious, established. The sounds and images that this produces are loud and shrill; quite the opposite of John Cage's or the sober austerity and aggressive complexity of Karlheinz Stockhausen's early pieces that Paik finds so fascinating. In *Gesang der Jünglinge* (song of the youths) from the mid 1950s Stockhausen transposes, combines, and modifies the recording of a single boy soprano's voice into a fascinating electronic choir. At its debut performance on 30 May 1956, at a concert titled "Unerhörte Musik" (literally unheard-of, incredible music) in the large auditorium of West German Radio (WDR) in Cologne, there are no musicians on the stage, it is only "dehumanized music"[108] that issues from huge banks of loudspeakers and a spherical construction with twelve loudspeakers on the ceiling. And *Kontakte* (1958) sounds (today) like an anticipation of Jimi Hendrix's live performances.

---

108 Hans H. Stuckenschmidt, in *Die Reihe* [1955], quoted in *Wege elektronischer Musik* (1991), p. 22.

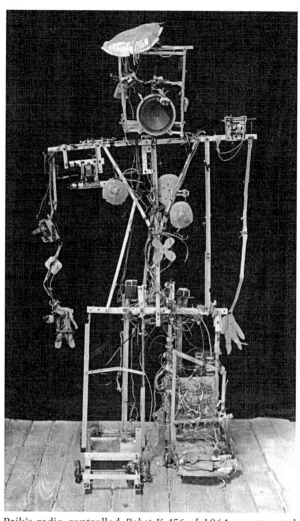

Paik's radio-controlled *Robot K-456* of 1964, constructed together with Shuya Abe. (Paik, Kölnischer Kunstverein 1977, p. 94)

Wellenübertragung: Karlheinz Stockhausen 1962 in the Studio for Electronic Music of the WDR in Cologne (photo: © WDR Köln, *Wege elektronischer Musik, Sechs Konzerte,* 1991, p. 42).

Paik's crude cannibalization of old pianos and their opulent draping with barbed wire, plants, baby's rattles, alarm clocks, and other material (*Klavier intégral*, 1958–1963) treads a fine line between critique and outright kitsch, as do many of his early objects, like *Schallplattenschaschlik* (*Record Shishkebab*) of 1963. Here lower middle class daily life and the will to avant-garde combine into an integrated whole. Whereas young electronics engineers tend to avoid appearing on stage in the flesh, the Korean artist brashly inserts the body as an attraction into the ephemeral action onstage. Deeply impressed by Paik's anarchic imagination, the master and shaman of art as sacralization of the profane, Joseph Beuys, wrecks one of the piano exhibits at the opening evening of Paik's first solo show, organized in 1963 by Rolf Jährling in Wuppertal-Elberfeld.

The bloody ox's head, which Paik had hung at the door to the exhibition, results in the Galerie Parnass being reported to the police for infringement of the Cadavers Act. For the exhibition, however, this turns out to be a highly effective PR stunt. It is due to the success of this spectacle that the exhibition's twelve electromagnetically manipulated televisions are still celebrated today as the genuine beginning of media art practice. In spite of the fact that Vostell had worked at least four years before Paik's exhibition on technically intervening in typical images from the cathode ray tube.[109]

---

109 Cf. the *TV-Dé-Collage* set from the 1970s Hahn Collection in *Video End* (1976), p. 7.

Nam June Paik (right) at the hanging of the freshly slaughtered ox's head at the entrance to Galerie Parnass for the exhibition *Exposition of Music — Electronic Television*, March 1963. Photo: Rolf Jährling, © Dr. Anneliese Jährling; The Museum of Modern Art, New York. The Gilbert and Lila Silverman Fluxus Collection Gift, 2008; Zentralarchiv des internationalen Kunsthandels e.V. (ZADIK), Cologne.

"From the first it has been the theatre's business to entertain people, as it also has of all the other arts. It is this business which always gives it its particular dignity; it needs no other passport than fun, but this it has got to have," writes Brecht in *A Short Organum* in 1948. In the age of staged capitalism, in which the arts are integrated, the objective cannot be to play in a venue that is located outside of it; this would come at the price of not being heard or seen. Even the Foucauldian heterotopias are part of the system of established locations, even though they fulfil decadent functions there. Yet the minimum demand of an artist is at least to codetermine the rules of the game, and to repeatedly risk an attempt to confront the business with its own impossibilities. When Brecht declares entertainment to be an obligation, he formulates an idea that is similar to the *unconditionality* that we find in Derrida's famous lecture in Frankfurt (1989) with regard to the university. Unconditional pleasure, which also exposes itself to ridicule, becomes Paik's speciality. In the context of aesthetic processes, which have to do with advanced technologies, it is highly fragile, very rare, and extremely beautiful.

To work unconditionally is an attitude that incurs the danger of being declared useless. The only economy that art can accept for itself is that of uncompromising luxury. "The theatre must in fact remain something entirely superfluous, though this indeed means that it is the superfluous for which we live. Nothing needs less justification than pleasure."[110]

After World War II, in light of the historic failure of both concepts of productivity — capitalism as well as socialism — the category of excess not only plays a large role in the work of Georges Bataille. Understanding artistic activity as a special practice of expenditure distinguishes Paik (who comes from a Buddhist-influenced culture) as though he held an aristocratic title. He carried this distinction with great dignity throughout his life.

Time

"There is no rewind button on the Betamax of life."[111] This saying of Paik's is an instant formula and puts the essence of all theories of time-based media in a nutshell. The time we live through cannot be repeated. Only when life is recorded by technical means and fed into a storage machine is it reversible. Time that is objectivized in a machine can be run forwards and backwards; it can

---

110   Brecht (1964), quotations p. 180 and 181.
111   Paik quoted by René Block in the Preface of Paik (1984), n.p.

be paused, slowed down, and sped up. For these operations it has buttons for the past and the future which one can press. A film or a video shows movements driven by algorithmic commands: the principal and most significant attraction of these media is the fact that they can manipulate the flow of time. Exotechnical existence, by contrast, is mercilessly irreversible.

Paik is fully aware of the special temporality of technical existences. In Tokyo, Stuttgart, and Cologne he studied music and Schönberg in particular, the subject of his thesis, with whom Cage had studied. The time-based art genre par excellence, music, is the most important artistic frame of reference in Paik's oeuvre. This is something shared by many protagonists of the new art scene. "My computer programme is like a piano," said the pioneer of *expanded cinema*, John Whitney. A time image is not painted but composed.[112]

In the shaping of objectivized time, Paik achieves the greatest poetic density when he combines modernism's thinking as intervention with the myths of his own Korean cultural traditions and those of Japan. *Zen for TV* (1963) is the result of a serendipitous accident. During transportation of the objects for the Galerie Parnass exhibition, the tube of one of the black and white TV sets is damaged. When it is plugged in, it only shows a white horizontal line. Paik turns the set by ninety degrees and celebrates the electronic message as a vertical signal. A few months later he makes *Zen for Film*. The work exists in several forms. As an object it is a plastic box containing a reel of 16 mm unexposed film that runs for approximately twenty minutes. Uncoated and thus unexposed film is not normally projected. For certain aesthetic intentions it can be painted, scratched, or processed in some other way and then projected. Paik left it unexposed for the *Zen for Film* performance. When

---

112   Cf. Youngblood (1970), p. 207.

projected with a film projector, the film stock shows an almost empty image on the screen. Its temporality is articulated only by the dust particles that dance in the light and as tiny shadows on the screen. On its packaging, Paik glued a scene from the shooting of a Hollywood film. The contents of his film canister empties the scenery.

When the work is created, around 1964, the visual idea is not entirely original. Guy Debord's *Hurlements en faveur de Sade* (*Howlings in favor of Sade*) consists exclusively of empty white and black film frames that create an abstract projected space. But whereas the young adult Debord at the premiere on June 30, 1952 at the Ciné-Club d'Avant-Gardes at the Musée de l'Homme in Paris uses a soundtrack consisting of readings of prepared dialogue fragments and protests — the howlings — of the audience, Paik forgoes any additional acoustic mise-en-scene. Only the sound of the projector structures the silence. The temporal dimension of the machine articulates itself unfiltered, in its own rhythm, its own time.

A similar maximal density with minimal effort is only achieved by another film in which Paik acts *in front of* the camera. Wolfgang Ramsbott, a filmmaker in Höllerer's Berlin Literary Colloquium and later the first professor of experimental film at the University of the Arts Berlin, shot the film in 1961 without establishing any distance and in a very intimate setting. The film was completed in 1962. *Performance im Hause Ramsbott* begins with a close-up of Paik's lower leg which is relaxed to start with but then begins to describe strangely mechanical movements, swinging to and fro. From a fade to black a detail opens showing Paik's mouth which is articulating words that are not heard. Paik is seen close-up playing a fascinating game with fingers spread in front of his face. He appears to be imitating a flicker machine; a device that projects light intermittently and rhythmically through an aperture, like the slits of a projector's shutter.

As far as the invention of technical images is concerned, which significantly differ from those of established apparatuses, the most attractive medium to experiment with in these years is film. In 1963, Andy Warhol makes his best films about simple, everyday sensations in the Factory: *Kiss*, *Eat*, *Blow Job*, and *Haircut*. These are followed in 1964 by *Empire*, a silent, black-and-white film of over eight hours of continuous slow motion footage on 16 mm film which shows a single stationary shot of the Empire State Building in New York. Jonas Mekas shot the pictures with an Auricon camera from the 44th floor of the Time-Life building. And in the second half of the 1960s Warhol begins to make exquisite audiovisual hybrids consisting of photomechanics and electronics. From 1966 Paik is working with Yud Yalkut on such symbioses. Paik's "electro-madness" combined with Yalkut's "delicate kinetic consciousness" develops into a third media reality that balances between film and video.[113]

Paik's *TV Buddha* (1974) is as iconic for the time-based arts as Warhol's famous colored prints of a photo of Marilyn Monroe, which Gene Korman took in 1962 shortly before the star's suicide, are for the graphic arts. Simplicity and complexity are ingeniously related to each other in Paik's installation. A heavy Buddha statue sits before a video monitor. Over the monitor a camera is installed, which records the cult object electronically. Its electronic image is seen on the screen of the black-and-white video monitor. This videographic close-up view is in contradistinction to classical tele-vision. The Buddha sees himself looking at himself — a closed loop that is formed like the figure of magical time, elliptical, nonlinear, but infinitely repeatable because a technical medium is interposed between the object and the image: aeon is the time dimension in Greek mythology that extends beyond the lifespan of mortals into eternity. Aeon is the

---

113   Ibid., p. 330.

time of machines, a time that in principle is empty. The Dutch composer, Fluxus and media artist Dick Raaymakers devoted one of his early compositions to this time period in 1964.[114]

Since 1974, Paik has realized the Buddha installation in numerous aesthetic variants; in one the monitor is embedded in a heap of coal that appears to supply it with the energy needed to power its rays (1982); another has the Buddha buried in soil (1997), and as the self-contained sculpture of the artist it gets a nail in its mouth for a cigarette and a clothes peg attached to its head; there is also the variant where in a performative act Paik himself sits before the camera and monitor as he did in 1976 in the Kölnische Kunstverein art association. With regard to the radical nature of the time concept, some of the later variants created in the 1990s are especially impressive. The video monitor is divested of all its technical inner life and reduced to its casing. Within this frame, where a tube once flickered, a simple candle now burns. The Buddhas who sit in front of these objects watch something akin to a primeval film; a flickering candle as a symbol of one of the first time-based artifacts that humans created: a fire. In these late variants of the Buddha work Paik returns to his early installations. In the early 1960s, he had already worked on emptying the television image and substituting candles for the flickering electronic image.

The archaic expressive power that informs the time theme in *TV Buddha* is rivaled by another installation of Paik's that he also realized in several variants from 1965 onwards. For millennia, people of all cultures have observed the night sky and taken the moon as the projection screen for their longings and utopias. Looking at the moon is the natural *dispositif* of tele-vision. Four years before the first astronaut sets foot on our satellite,

---

114   Cf. *Dick Raaymakers – A Monograph* (2008), p. 408.

without shame but with a claim to ownership thus rendering a sacred place profane, Paik deconsecrates the moon which is sacred for the sense of time on Earth. *Moon Is the Oldest TV* is the name of the installation in which Paik sets up twelve monitors on tall black pedestals in an open semicircle in a darkened room. At the center of each screen a white sphere shines, from very weak new moon to luminescent full moon.

"Zen consists of two negations," says Paik in an experimental essay written immediately after his exhibition at Galerie Parnass in 1963, "the first negation: The absolute IS the relative; the second negation: The relative IS the absolute."[115]

"Heideggar" as Chelsea Girl

In 1964 Paik is invited to the New School of Social Research, the famous progressive split-off from Columbia University which offered a haven to exiled scholars such as Claude Lévi-Strauss and Hannah Arendt or Hanns Eisler, and where John Cage later taught musical composition until 1960. During these years Paik's techno-philosophical deliberations and experiments become more intense and radical. The program for his initial exhibition at the New School lists the artistic ramifications of Paik's microuniverse that will be decisive for the next decades. We first see the manipulations of black-and-white and color televisions, followed by demonstrations of the robots which Paik increasingly declares to be part of his family, the performance of Pop sonatas, some Minimalist Zen pieces, and early performances with Moorman and other Fluxus activists.

---

115 The text was published in the June 1964 edition of the New York Fluxus newspaper *FLuxus cc fiVe ThReE*. Paik kindly gave me the broadsheet to include in my *Reader* (Zielinski 1992a), pp. 123–124.

NEW SCHOOL OF SOCIAL RESEARCH NEW YORK BRECHT (GEORGE) LENNON/ONO NOORMAN ELLUL

MACIUNAS THE BEATLES THOMPSON TWINS

DUCHAMP CAGE KUBOTA YALKUT WARHOL MONTANO

VOSTELL ABE BRAKHAGE

SCHOENBERG BEUYS GINSBERG NEKAS CUNNINGHAM

BRECHT PAIK BLOCK KATROW GABRIEL BELLMER

JÄHRLING BIOLEK PLESSI

KAGEL STOCKHAUSEN PIENE FLUSSER ANDERSON KEANE

GLASS RAAYMAKERS HERZOGENRATH EISENSTEIN LÜPERTZ

HEIDEGGER RAMSBOTT GALERIE PARNASS RITTER

JASPERS MCLUHAN WIENER DALI WEIBEL

THE MONTHLY REVIEW OF THE UNIVERSITY OF AVANTGARDE - HINDUISM

An uncommented circuit diagram of an electronic television set is printed on the back of the invitation to this exhibition in January 1965. Paik attempts to unite the attitudes of a Benjaminian magician and operator in a single person, himself. Around the time of the exhibition in the Galerie Parnass, George Macunias, the father figure of the Fluxus artists at that time, noted approvingly that Paik had secretly studied electronics for one or two years in order to be able to carry out the various modifications to the electromagnetic fields of the television sets.[116] It is clear that the crazy electrician has acquired a vast knowledge about the fast electronic tubes and increasingly he collaborates with technicians and engineers, particularly with Shuya Abe. From the beginning this genius instrument builder and electronics engineer appears in connection with Paik's work when it is a question of intervening in the structures and processes of the electronic image. A few years later their collaboration leads to the joint invention of the audiovisual time machine of the video synthesizer.

---

116 Maciunas in a letter to Robert Watts, in Hendricks (1988), p. 438.

On October 4, 1965 Paik is riding in a taxi through Manhattan, New York. He is accompanied in the back seat by one of the first portable video recording units from Sony, probably a VC 2010.[117] From out of the moving vehicle Paik takes pictures of the Pope's visit to St. Patrick's Cathedral. He is not taking the pictures for some TV station and its anonymous audience. A short time later he presents the unedited recording at the hip night club Café au Go Go on Bleecker Street in Greenwich Village. The audience consists entirely of friends, artists, writers, musicians, and acquaintances. This quality of public was entirely appropriate to the new medium, both from an artistic and a political perspective. With this action Paik inaugurated that part of the history of video art which concerns its own images.

Paik writes a lot at this time. He calls the texts essays, yet their genres are more the pamphlet, the manifesto, or the manual. Incisive, argumentative, polemical, anarchic in form or with a deliberately exaggerated formal structure, in these writings Paik is far in advance of his time and anticipates both terminology and themes to come. "We are in open circuits," he concludes a short reflection on the dialectic of "cybernated art" and "art for cybernated people," the ideal representative of which he sees as the Minimalist George Brecht ("Maybe George Brecht's simplissimo is the most adequate"), who continues to work as a chemist and engineer until the

---

117   It was definitely not one of the later legendary Portapaks, which did not exist in 1965. I asked Paik many years ago to solve the riddle and he wrote: "The first SONY half inch 2010 series (i think it is VC 2010) was also often so called from the same reason. compared to the ampex studio geraete... also this sony was sometimes called micky maus, because it was so small, like a toy, and often broke down. needless to say, for the first day shooting (indeed on october 4) i had to borrow a zerhacker (dc-ac converter)." Paik, personal correspondence with the author, 1984.

mid 1960s.[118] Cybernetics interests Paik as a science of pure relations, indeed as *the* scientific relation per se.

In a provocative short-circuit, Paik connects in a 1967 text, *Norbert Wiener and Marshall McLuhan*,[119] the mathematics professor from MIT who has enthusiastically read the *Encyclopaedia Britannica*, and the Joycean hippie, as he calls the Canadian cultural critic. The core idea of this coupling is the fetishization of signals which is common to both authors. Wiener and McLuhan disregard the semantic context where processes of technical communication are concerned. McLuhan's famous phrase, "The medium is the message," has existed implicitly in cybernetics since the 1940s. This corresponds to Wiener's assumption that the signal with which a message is sent plays an equally important role as the signal with which no message is sent. In Shannon's famous formula they are one and the same.

During the first months of his tenure on a Rockefeller grant at The State University of New York at Stony Brook, Paik writes his first report titled *Expanded Education for the Paper-less Society* wherein he develops audacious perspectives for future academic work in the sector of art and media. In a manner similar to how twenty years later Kittler introduces his *Gramophone, Film, Typewriter* as the last publication that can just about be written in book form, Paik reproaches McLuhan for the fact that although he talks about electronic media, his words are still published in classic form, that is, on paper and bound between the covers of a book. With existing video technology and the ease of mailing videotapes Paik

---

118 In *Something Else Press* (New York 1966); cited here from Paik (2004), n.p. The connection between pharmaceutical experiments, pharmacist and inventor toolboxes with regard to the early Fluxus artists would be worth investigating as well as their relationship to music. The performing arts in the tradition of Fluxus did not develop primarily from the visual arts, but from various experimental praxis.
119 Published in the Bulletin of the ICA London; used here from Paik (2004).

suggests setting up a university network which he calls "mailable television." A lecture recorded in New York could be exchanged with a course module from the collaboration program between the universities of Tulane and Nairobi, or from Tel Aviv, in an economy of academic friendship. In this way university education could be *"mondialisé"* for the students at low cost. Continuing a famous paradigm of the Russian Revolution from the 1920s, Paik enthuses in the 1960s over the electronification of connections, from brain to brain, from planet to planet. With an ironic Maoist gesture he projects a technoculture of thousands of small transmitters and for the 1st of March 1996, that is, for a day thirty years hence, he plans a program that gives us an insight of Paik's tele-universe: Duchamp begins at 7 o'clock in the morning with a lesson about chess; in the afternoon Maciunas explains "how one can lose money fast" with a report on the stock exchange; Diter Rot fills up the prime time slot with a baby-sitter program; a midnight discourse about art and politics with Vostell follows; then films by Brakhage, Mekas, and Vandenbeek are screened; finally, in the early morning there is an alcoholic beverage drinking contest between all participants.

A highlight of Paik's *Expanded Education* text is the discussion of future forms of teaching philosophy classes. The act of "philosophieren"[120] is supreme and requires the total involvement of the teacher's whole personality. It is high time that great philosophers are recorded, and their thoughts made available for the study of philosophy worldwide. Here Paik has in mind a decidedly low-key, easy method of production comparable to what Warhol is practicing in his Factory for film at this time. Thus it comes about that two completely different circles of people meet within a single sentence:

---

120   Paik uses the German word for philosophizing; see *Expanded Education for the Paper-Less Society* (1968).

155

"The interviewer should be a qualified philosopher himself and the camera crew as minimal as possible, so that Jaspars or Heideggar can talk as naturally as 'Chelsea Girls.'"[121]

Associates

In 1961/1962, Paik develops an idea for a most unusual concert. In San Francisco one pianist plays the left hand part of Johann Sebastian Bach's Prelude and Fugue in C Major from the "Well Tempered Clavier" and another plays the right hand part in Shanghai. At midday, 12.00 hrs Greenwich mean time, both parts are then broadcast on the radio exactly in time using a metronome set at 80 beats per minute. Telecommunications would enable the two separate performances on different sides of the Pacific Ocean to be put together in a techno-imaginary way. This plan of Paik's is now half a century old.

Paik's thinking is also Brechtian in this regard. His notion of education expanded by means of complex technology reads like a didactic play in which courses of action under future conditions of communications can be tried out. In the imaginary center stands the idea of an infinite number of transmitters which even enable extremely elitist interests of a small minority to be catered for or some individuals' need of luxuries. What Brecht had demanded in his radio theory fragments and realized aesthetically in his didactic play *Flight across the Ocean* (1929/30), Paik develops in a continuous performative act. The art adept on the receiving side — either as an expert or an amateur — is integrated in the transmission praxis. As Paik, like Beuys, Cage, or Vostell, assumes that there is no difference between art and life, this means

---

121   Paik's strange spelling of the philosophers' names is retained here as in the original; Paik (1968)

that potentially anyone who wants to be appreciated artistically can become an actor within the expanded sets of interactive events. An audience that merely ratiocinates or contemplates is just not viable with Fluxus.

In his work on cooperative and collaborative projects Paik is an exceptionally gifted communicator, seducer, and agitator. In this he races far ahead of the existing conditions of technical communication. He constantly acts within real and imaginary nexuses, and operates as a pivot and generator of many events that establish the tradition of Fluxus in contemporary art. He creates a network of philosophical and aesthetic associates, a community whose members are bonded by art and experiment.

The climax and endpoint of this development appears to be the gigantic project *Good Morning, Mr. Orwell!* that Paik realized on January 1, 1984 to greet the new year. At 18.00 hrs Central European Time viewers could be televisual participants in a colossal Happening staged in the new Centre Pompidou in Paris and broadcast via satellite in four variants from four countries and seven cities. Over twenty million people watch the event. Its success is principally due to Paik astutely organizing an extremely heterogeneous mix of performances that has the character of an electronic variety show. International pop music stars like the Thompson Twins, Sapho, Peter Gabriel, and Laurie Anderson are included, as well as Yves Montand for the cinematographic business and art icons like Salvador Dalí; there are fashion shows and international comedy interludes ("Big Brother"), as well as the event's core of super stars from various contemporary art and music scenes: Beuys, Cage, Merce Cunningham, Allen Ginsberg, Phillip Glass, Charlotte Moorman, and many others.

Paik, the operator and magician, succeeds in bringing art and commerce together in a wild and radical mixture such that the individual ingredients of the dish remain clearly recognizable. At the same time this "montage of attractions," as Eisenstein called such exhibition fights in the ring on the public stage, is the prerequisite for the fact that TV broadcasters in Paris, New York, Seoul, and the four largest cities in Germany engaged with the project and financed it.

At the highest level of development of the telecommunicative *dispositif*, Paik succeeds with this difficult balancing act in the age of the outright spectacle. The juggler uses the laws of gravity and at the same time finesses them illusionistically. Vostell, Paik's friend from the Fluxus movement who is also trained in Zen Buddhism, aptly sums this up when he says "in art as in the happening it is not important that you cross the river but how you cross it."[122]

Paik worked for a year on the electronic happening. Once it is over he seems exhausted. He has achieved everything. His art has been distributed in real-time all over the globe and has met with great resonance. He is a star. Already in the early 1970s he did not pale in comparison with John Lennon and Yoko Ono. Even before the New Year Happening he had been invited by Alfred Biolek to appear in a major entertainment show on German television (Bios Bahnhof) where he was at liberty to furnish the entire studio with his artworks. He is given jester's license and offered work opportunities all over the world. When he occasionally visits his class at the Düsseldorf Art Academy, where he has been teaching since 1982, he falls asleep when the students show him their new work. The twenty years leading up to securing his livelihood through his art practice have been very strenuous and exhausting.

In retrospect *Good Morning, Mr. Orwell!* seems like the fulfillment of the needs and wants that Paik had projected onto the once new technologies. Afterwards, things

---

122 Vostell: Leben=Kunst=Leben (1993), p. 150.

do not go forward; everything just gets bigger, more confused, and more duplicated. In 1989, in New York's Whitney Museum, he proclaims the *Fin de Siècle II*. 201 TV sets in the entrance hallway greet the visitor with an overwhelming barrage of flickering electronic images and sound, which are sourced from laser discs and controlled by computers. The title of the exhibition is a clear sign that the electronics-based arts have come of age and arrived at the center of Western economies: *Image World: Art and Media Culture* is its postindustrial, pragmatic title. (And hundreds more with a similar thematic attitude will follow in the years after). In the very same venue in 1982, Paik used 40 scrapped TV sets for the sculpture *V-yramid*; now, in 1989, the TVs used are current standard models. He builds *Beuys/Voice* (1987) for the Documenta 10 like an altar which consists of 44 stacked monitors showing computer-controlled images from three videotapes. The middle section of the triptych shows a recording of Paik and Beuys' last concert together, in the Coyote series, in Japan. Beuys had died the year before.

Paik is far too passionate and involved to develop any distance to the media euphoria that is gaining momentum. Paik goes along with it; the name of the game is that the media are becoming strategic. South Korea discovers their distinguished native son and finances his gargantuan installations. At the Seoul Olympic Games he installs a tower of images and sounds on 1003 monitors; a gigantic audiovisual techno-Babel for which TV broadcasters from 12 countries deliver programs. The attitude of the title, *The More the Better*, is an ironic commentary given the presence of the *dispositif* in such sheer masses.

The precious temporality of the fleeting actions, the fragility of the technical microuniverse that Paik had developed in the preceding thirty years, is transformed into a space, and makes its presence felt there. The activity of the artist is monumentalized in the way that Ritter says is characteristic of the second stage of his operational anthropology, which is distinguished by three-dimensional objects. The video sculpture is the contemporary emerging art of recollection, interspersed with aperçus of nervous temporality.

"thus in the next few years there will likely be a development away from the production of videotapes and toward spatial, architectonic, three-dimensional, sculptural video solutions, because at the moment this is where people suspect the secret of video, its art, lies."[123] In 1977 Peter Weibel already anticipates the development toward decorating the transition to the information society. In Venice Fabrizio Plessi constructs huge water wheels with monitors, the Studio Azzurro group constructs pyramids with them, and even the British feminist Tina Keane scales the monumental heights with twenty stacked televisions in her *Escalator* (1988).

These are all grand analogies before the onset of the digital, the arrival of an imaginary spatial experience that is interconnected by telematic technology. The generation that begins to engage artistically and actionistically with the new menetekel of the Internet at the beginning of the 1990s only laughs at the old masters. Paik is feted at one retrospective after another, while for the younger artists the future becomes attractive as a Web-based context of acting and thinking, which Paik had sounded out in the past in myriad ways without actually having access to Internet technology.

The self-possessed Paik is, however, still capable of producing liberating laughter. He still delights in intervening with poetic stimulators, as Bellmer called his toys, in the fine minimalistic mise-en-scène, and in fooling about surface time and again. In 1989 he creates *Eine Kerze* [*One Candle*] for Frankfurt's gallery of contemporary art Portikus. A video loop of oscillating electronic

---

123   Weibel (1992), p. 151.

images of a real candle point to its ancient origins and vice versa. Three years after Documenta 10, he arranges nine old color televisions into a weird figure, feeds them with identical pictures of the Tokyo concert, and puts a felt hat on the (TV set) head of his anthropomorphic techno-creature: he calls the work *Beuys Voice 1990*. His family of improvised-looking TV robots seems to grow exponentially, spawning ever more variants; one of them he even lets ride a scooter (*Video Scooter*, 1994). *Auf Wiedersehen meine Geliebte* (*Goodbye my beloved*) is the title of a minimal installation consisting of two small bird cages and a pair of monitors with pictures that hold an imaginary lover captive.

Cultura experimentalis

In Paik's oeuvre one can study how excellently artistic and analytical work mesh, how the philosophical and world-staging practices intertwine that were characteristic for the techno-avant-garde after World War II. He brilliantly embodies the self-confident artist who commutes between the cultures of the Far East and the Near West, and how a radical culture of experimentation can become established and develop over a longer period in a market culture that is equally radical. The sublimity that Paik achieves has nothing to do with any naive idolization of machines.

Slowly and with difficulty we have learned that we are creatures full of defects, full of inadequacies, not at all effective and fast, but instead rather lethargic. The Modern age is distinguished by the circumstance that it developed texts, calculations, images, sounds, and machines that were supposed to help compensate for these defects or even overcome them. With the aid of propaganda and communication technology, what is unwieldy

161

or does not fit into the system can be integrated, as Ellul writes. The impossible is rendered a little more possible. In this respect technological advancement is successful. Machines learn to compute and combine, to write, to make music, to draw, to play, to associate — usually far faster than we are capable of doing. The intelligent machines make us happy with their degree of perfection and durability that it is not our lot to achieve. In the past we responded to their obligatory nature in that we began to believe in the machines. Many people even develop affection for the world of synthetic constructs, and trust the individual artifact in the same way as they trust more complex systems of connected units. They love their cars, their audio systems, their BlackBerrys, their jet airliners, their nuclear power plants. This is above all the success of cybernetics, which originated from the fear of noncontrollable inaccuracies, of states that, according to Rössler, everyone knows machines simply do not have.

In the situation that has come about there are at least two diametrically opposed options for thinking and acting. We can see to it that in the future the functional circuits are closed even more flawlessly. Or we can try to confront what has become possible and may become possible with its own impossibilities. A project and thinking of this kind I call *cultura experimentalis*.

Here I programmatically formulate a position that runs through my entire text like a thread. When I refer to art I am addressing a theory and praxis that is affected by science and technology and that is at least to a certain degree interested in them. When I write about science and its particular capability of experimenting, I have in mind a concept that is porous and curious about the theories and praxes of art. When we engage with the focal point of art, we do not need just any science, but a science that is able to think poetry and poetically.

162

In such a system of coordinates, research could possibly take on the status of a third entity in the true sense of the word: it could be a medium; that is, the processual element that operates between the arts and the sciences. Nils Röller formulates a concept of media from this perspective like the one Ernst Cassirer developed in the 1920s in his *Philosophie der symbolischen Formen* (*The Philosophy of Symbolic Forms*);[124] a concept, namely, that "while maintaining the differences, is able to portray heterogeneous forms of mental articulation."[125] The experiment would be the practical expression of this kind of research. A culture of experiments and experimental art are conditional upon each other. However, in a society that understands itself as a test department this reciprocal action cannot develop.

In the decades when media-as-strategy was becoming established, Paik was not the only one to take up such a position. His friends and allies from music, literature, dance, and the visual arts with whom he had worked and made appearances, each in their own way represented a microuniverse of functioning deviances and successful irritations: Beuys and (George) Brecht, Cage and Cunningham, Allen Ginsberg and Allan Kaprow, Joe Jones, Mauricio Kagel and George Maciunas. The arts that are realized with and through media, the culture of experiment, had found a whole range of outstanding activists. Marina Abramovicz, VALIE EXPORT, Richard Kriesche, Thierry Kuentzel, Muntadas, Marcel Odenbach, Ulrike Rosenbach, Tommaso Tozzi, Vostell, and Weibel are active for decades to ensure that the sector of artistic practice with advanced technologies, which is a highly sensitive area through its proximity to power, continues to be challenged by the unpredictable. But it is precisely

---

124 English translation: Ernst Cassirer, *The Philosophy of Symbolic Forms*, vols. 1–4. New Haven, CT: Yale University Press, 1965–1996.

125 Röller (2002), p. 12.

because, time and again, Paik has sought extreme confrontations with laughter and tears that he is so valuable for us as a protagonist of a *cultura experimentalis*.

Meatphysics

After World War II the avant-garde understood its activities with the then new technical instruments as an extension of the reality that they themselves experienced. Expanded Reality describes the concept of intervening with machines in nontechnical reality to expand it to its advantage.[126]

At the beginning of the twenty-first century, two tendencies in the conceptual arts are vying with each other for attention. Various practices are assembled under the term physical computing in which algorithms are developed to control physical material that lies outside the computer. The commands do not primarily serve to organize the computer hardware and user programs in order to generate texts, images, or sounds. Instead, they are used to animate three-dimensional moveable objects, such as constructions made of wood, synthetics, or metal, or fluids, magnetic fields, and many other things. Therefore, a more apt name for these experimental activities would be "computing the physical."

The second trend, which has existed for quite some time now, carries out manipulative interventions in biological material — plants, animals, and humans — or its simulations. So-called evolutionary algorithms are implemented in artificial organisms, and interventions organize short-term or long-term changes in real biological structures, or they create an entirely different, living world that only exists in the computer. For example, for the past

126   In 1992, I commented on this in a text titled: "Expanded Reality," in: *Cyberspace*, eds. Florian Rötzer and Peter Weibel (Munich: Boer 1992).

thirty years the Japanese artist and scuba diver Yoichiro Kawaguchi has "grown" stunning structures through the complex generic algorithms that he invented.

All these variants are experimental and, in part, testing practices that I would assign to the twentieth century. They have in common, through and via technical media, that intentional effects are organized with hard physical, fluid chemical, or soft biological material, or an internal digital world is generated that consists entirely of effects. The attraction is the sensational physical reality.

It has been said that we live in an age of augmented realities. Sensorially perceived realities are being enhanced by information technology. The semantics that resonate in "augmentation," however, are rather tricky. *Augmentation,* the action or process of making or becoming greater in size or amount, is closely related etymologically to "auction," which also designates an increase in amount, in value, and in the price paid. Augmented reality may be a form of enhanced experience of reality but it is also an auctioned reality, and that is the opposite of an enriched experience; it is, namely, impoverished sensuality. An auction deducts the sensational from a real attraction. Augmented reality is a prime example of something belonging to the process that Giorgio Agamben characterizes as de-subjectivization.

Let us look out for artistic practices that are located qualitatively *after the media*; then we will seek works, processes, and experiments that have wholly abandoned the will to create or use effects. In the twenty-first century it is no longer necessary to prove that media technologies can be effective and possess wondrous powers. Both in the limelight of the art market and the twilight of the laboratory, valuable approaches to art after the effects are developing.

For some years now the Berlin artist Jana Linke has been building machines which accomplish work that did not exist before the advent of machines. In this way Linke turns our familiar logic of rationalization on its head, and at the same time creates her own unique and fantastic world of an impossible human–machine relationship. The Swiss artist Yanick Fournier has produced a series of works that thematize his dramatizations of the augmentation of reality. Out of simple timber roofing laths, screws, and hinges he builds constructions that we know from the simulations in computer games, and stages them in performances as real spaces of action. With his own body he becomes an actor in the built spaces, suspended on ropes that can be pulled from outside the realization space of the simulation. Those who have only recently been ennobled as competent *users* vis à vis machines are shown here to actually have the status of functioning marionettes. Exploring the imaginary in the real has been practiced for years by the Italian artist Armin Linke who lives in Berlin. His works revolve around the terrific success that the augmentation of reality through artificiality has already achieved, but without intervening using digital technology. *Mapping the Imaginary* (2009) is a series of works with technical images that at first glance look like highly staged, textbook examples of digital postproduction. Yet the images are in fact carefully selected excerpts of reality outside of machines in which the effects of artificial gazes are firmly imprinted, as a three or four-dimensional lived reality. This reality behaves as though it is a manufactured technical reality, it lives in "as if."

For ten years now, under the bright spotlight of the international art market, the British brothers Dinos and Jake Chapman have been making their art at an advanced level. It is bizarre, loud, acidly humorous, in the worst possible taste, and not located anywhere near the razzle-dazzle effects of technology. The Chapman brothers not only seem to be able to imagine the people who will look at their works very accurately, they can also program their emotions superbly. The reception of their work, and the possible reactions of critics, are already built into it, particularly in the catalogs and books which they often take a hand in.

They are highly amenable to discourse, stylistically elegant and eloquent, and at the same time just as at home in the nonverbal, in the greatest horrors and in grotesque laughter, which in the last century Bataille opened up philosophically to all who do not see squandering and transgression as disastrous categories but as opportunities for poetry. The insignia of German Fascism, Hitler and the Holocaust, the ghastly wars, the industrialization of the erotic by pornography and automata, instant sex, instant food, instant politics, Stephen Hawking as Superman in a wheelchair floating toward the abyss: everything monstrous that the last century brought forth the Chapmans seem to have gulped down and now regurgitate it at its end. The eye that Simone had ripped out of the priest and inserted in her vagina the Chapmans have long since removed from the rotting corpse. In the meantime vile worms have eaten their way into the flesh around the sight organ (*New Art Up Close 3*, 2003). We are living a good eighty years after God ejaculated into the *Histoire de l'oeil* (1928) and after the cut that Buñuel and Dalí in *Un Chien Andalou* (1928) made through the eye of an ox, in honor of their lover Federico García Lorca, in his own words "the dog from Andalusia."

A specialty of the Chapman brothers is longer narrative texts that are cut up, defamiliarized, and put back together again with the result that they teeter on the brink of being unreadable; this is also an aesthetic practice that Bataille used many times, although in a much more restrained fashion. In *Enjoy More* (2002) they take another author's text — Keith Ansell Pearson's agitational essay on "Viroid Life" — and dissolve its graphic layout into everyday symbols of the twentieth century.

Meatphysics (2003) was written by Jake Chapman on his own. Whole lines and entire pages of Mac symbol fonts intervene in Jake's dense semantic orgies which ignore grammar, structure, punctuation, and pagination. "[...] scooped out of flesh, meat strand strung to bone, hip disjointedÖ≈ÖÄ□□□ÚÚÚÚÚÚ [...] □□□'Ö-Öx the whole wide world in his www.hands.cum.on.ucnt [...]." The book ends with a metaphor that is hard to take: "_____a ho-locaust of words has no end." Then the text disappears into a blank, blood-red sheet of paper that is inserted before the book's endpaper.

The Marriage of Reason and Squalor (2008) by contrast dispenses entirely with typographic and syntactic irri-tants. On 308 pages of closely set type Jake Chapman parodies the standard romance novel à la Mills & Boon. His tale develops its subversion entirely through lan-guage, through the meaning of individual words and sentences in this scurrilous story, which linguistically spirals out of control, about a heroine named Chlamydia Love who is caught up in a matrix of power, vanity, love, treachery, and death. Will Self, author of *The Quantity Theory Of Insanity*, said in his review that "my eyes bled."

Two pages from Jake Chapman, *Meatphysics* (London 2007), n.p.

Edmond Jabès, too, in his *Little Book of Unsuspected Subversion* (1996)[127] favors the tactic of subtle literary infiltration. Chopping up, scratching, demolishing — this is not difficult, as the first twentieth-century avant-garde abundantly demonstrated with the experimental film. To vary things that exist, to alter them qualitatively in sublation and in this way to produce new things is much more of a challenge.

This idea also plays an important role in the homage paid to love and death machines in the dissident theater of objects of the Polish artist and director Tadeusz Kantor; the Chapmans call them *Little Death Machines* (2008). On the surface the idea of variants appears to play a significant role in the Chapmans' "rectification" of a set of rare prints of Francisco de Goya's *Disasters of War* and *Los Caprichos series*. "El sueño de la razón

127 Published by Stanford University Press.

produce monstruos" — "The Sleep of Reason Brings Forth Monsters." From out of the mouths of maltreated heads genitals protrude; eyeballs pop out of sockets and multiply in the imaginary space like blowflies; volcanoes erupt like nuclear explosions; and images of the deepest abyss that Bataille described recur time and again: the black sun, microcosmically applied to the human body — *L'anus solaire* (The solar anus). The highest regard that one can accord to historical works is, from this point of view, to transform them into the present. It is not only the theater that has lived off this for centuries.

Definitely their masterpiece to date is *Hell* from 1999. The immense tabletop installation was destroyed in 2004 in a fire at a fine art handling company's London warehouse; one can almost imagine this as part of the Chapmans' staging of their art. Their works are blasphemous in all senses of the word. However, with numerous helpers they meticulously reconstruct several new versions of the *Hell* installation. The real thing is to be preferred to the recollection of an object, for otherwise it becomes a myth. Especially this work they do not want to see become just a glorified recollection. In 2008 the Chapmans present the new work to the public — *Fucking Hell*. Nine landscapes in glass cabinets arranged in a broken swastika contain tableaux depicting creation as a horrifically gruesome nightmare of the real. Over 30,000 tin soldier-sized figures populate the apocalyptic scenarios in the cabinets. Somewhere among them, on a small hill, the system of annihilation is personified, thus exonerating the many henchmen and fellow-travelers, which corresponds to German postwar ideology: Hitler hangs on the cross like Jesus Christ. *(Fucking) Hell* plumbs the depths artistically of what is unendurable, but which in the meantime art and media have designed in due form down to the last detail.

170

Everything in this installation is hard, physical material. And yet it has not only taken the route through memories and history books. It appears to three-dimensionally freeze all the cinematographic and electronic imaginings with which these events have been and will be abundantly exploited. In this area reality far outsrips the imagination, particularly in England. In the 1980s, tour operators offered holidays in facilities that bore a marked outward resemblance to the extermination camps of the Nazis, but with modified rituals that were bearable: "Thirty pounds for three days of torture with full board." The porn industry invented subgenres in which panties with swastikas, SS militaria, steel helmets, and other insignia of Nazi terror are employed to stimulate seriously warped sexual appetites.[128] The Chapmans' artificial figures populate *Fucking Hell* like marionettes, like media through which we can contemplate history and stories like these.

Heterotopias, as Foucault understands them, are not idyllic places. Rather, they should be understood as "counter-sites," sites of resistance which insinuate themselves into a culture and at the same time represent, challenge, and change it. *Fucking Hell* was bought by one of the wealthiest art collectors in Europe. François Pinault purchased it for his second Venetian museum, worth many millions. In a lavishly converted former bonded warehouse at the tip of the Fondamente Zattere, located between the mouth of the Canale Grande and the Canale della Giudecca, the Chapmans' huge installation has been given a place that resembles a macabre viewing platform.

The contrast could not be greater nor the mis-en-scène more ideal. In a city of moribund beauty that is doomed to disappear, the historically unique, murderous terror of the Nazis is laid out for viewing in *Fucking Hell*'s

---

128   See Knilli and Zielinski (1982), p. 411 and 109.

glass vitrines as though it is going to be used to make an animation film. Completely shielded from all outside noise by soundproof windows, the visitor's gaze wanders from the kitschy gondolas packed with overweight tourists, the expensive hotels, the facades fringing San Marco, to the killing fields of history, staged by the Chapmans as screaming praise of the most horrible surfaces. It's crazy that this extreme balancing act does not tip over in one's perception in favor of the dolled up, undersold, and rouged cadaver, as Agamben has referred to twenty-first century Venice.[129] In spite of all the media spectacles that have found entry into the Chapmans' installation, the terrible resistance of the *ontological event* of Auschwitz remains untouchable.

---

129   Agamben (2010), p. 67ff.

3. Thinking Media Explicitly and Implicitly — and the Intimation of a Perspective: For an Exact Philology of Precise Things.

Looking back at the past half-century of work on theory, one sees that with respect to media phenomena there has been a split into two main strands. That these two contrary meta-methodological modes occasionally come into contact with each other and can overlap, I take as a given when comparing them. Juxtaposing such ideas only makes sense when they are used with the intention of clarifying, which in the meantime has become a necessity. As soon as clarity is achieved, rigorous comparison as a method becomes unnecessary.

In connection with Foucault and Derrida, I have elaborated the relevant qualities above. I suggest a simple distinction between media-*explicit* and media-*implicit* discourses. In the first case, individual media or a random collection of media or the media in the strategic generalization *expressis verbis* are the subject of my exposition — media as the attractive focus on which a given text's curiosity centers. As a rule this mode coincides with a declared aspiration on the part of the author(s) to make a conspicuous contribution to media theory.

In the second case, media phenomena are integrated as subjects of research in wider discourses or epistemes. They are thematically incorporated into other foci or overarching contexts, such as history, sexuality, subjectivity, or the arts. Here the media phenomena are not the sensational center of the investigation. The authors of this variety of text come from fields of discourse other than media theory and it is not their intention to make a career in it.

On the mondial theory-markets of the sixties and seventies of the last century, the studies which explicitly center on *dispositif* systems such as radio, television,

173

cinema, photography, or the media as a generalized concept, experience a boom. They are the new thing and artists, scientists, and engineers alike feel equally challenged. McLuhan is the scene's international star. He formulates media theory explicitly in the form of catchy, instant formulas. Postulates like the medium is the message or massage, we live in a global village, electronic media tribalize us, or every new medium includes the old ones, promote and accompany the media in their implementation in society.

Similarly, the aesthetic realizations of the media, such as radio plays, TV series, films, or comics, set a precedent. To see through their structure, their organization, their grammar, their inscribed programs; to develop a language to critique them as well as a means of treating them; to provide an open framework for their artistic development, is a big theoretical challenge. The challenge is initially taken up for individual media by literary studies and linguistics before more empirical and applied disciplines, such as sociology, economics, political science, and psychology, try their approaches to the phenomena of the technologically new. Media theory consists in thinking about the conditions of the production, distribution, consumption, and perception of explicit things, which have had the label of "media" forced upon them by communication technology. This is also the time of writings that weigh opportunities and risks. One praises what is new, and at the same time condemns with some harsh aperçus that it ousts valuable old things.

In the late 1970s and 1980s, the specialized analyses are replaced by extensive discourses. Embedded in the metatheories of post-World War II, French master-thinkers such as Lévi-Strauss for ethnology, Lacan for psychoanalysis, Foucault for history, Barthes for the diffusely aesthetic, and Derrida for text and grammar, the new *gay sciences* of the poststructuralists articulate themselves entirely in the spirit of relief that Nietzsche formulated in 1882: "No, life has not disappointed me. Rather, I find it truer, more desirable, and mysterious every year — ever since the day the great liberator overcame me: the thought that life could be an experiment for the knowledge-seeker — not a duty, not a disaster, not a deception!"[130] Nietzsche probably wrote these lines in Genoa, where European ships had once set out for the open oceans and as yet unknown lands.

Undogmatically, energetically, and undisciplined in the immediate sense of the word, in Germany the media analyses by Kittler unfold transversely to the established disciplines as applied discourse analyses. Informatics and aesthetics, philosophy and psychoanalysis, are woven into dense fabrics of reflection — especially about texts. Flusser activates a wayward, intellectual association and storytelling machine, which he feeds with knowledge cultures, such as magical thought and alchemy, with encyclopedic manuals of the natural sciences, Buber's philosophy of dialog, and the phenomenologies of Husserl and Heidegger. The latter two especially link him with the French master-thinkers, to whom Flusser otherwise hardly ever explicitly refers.

In the late 1980s in certain German states, the significant restructuring of the traditional capitalist economies into economic systems working principally on the basis of flexible, high-end technological services and financial businesses begins. Baden-Wuerttemberg and North-Rhine Westphalia assume pioneering roles; they generously fund new academies and institutions of higher education to accompany and support, with art and culture, the dawn of the information society. From the outset conservative Swabia puts great emphasis on proudly displaying what is new, on exhibiting progress, whereas the state of miners and comrades favors the concept of the laboratory, the advanced workshop.

---

130   Nietzsche [1882] (2001), Aphorism §324, p. 181.

What Becomes Explicit?

The action-oriented theory discourses ready themselves. The Internet is celebrated as a new lead medium. Without such a construction, it seems rather difficult to think about systems with any reliability. For some time now television has ceased to be a vanishing point toward which everything gravitates and which usurps everything. The mass realization of communications that link texts, images, and sounds also leads to a new impetus toward the explicit, albeit with an important break with the past. Criticism appears to have become anachronistic due to the loss of any orientation that could furnish critique with a perspective, but also because of the realization of a technology-based utopia or, to put it better: a utopia that is technology, a utopia one has the opportunity of witnessing. The new telematic media context as a cultural technique that is interwoven with everyday life, is made explicit as the attractive center of curiosity and inquiry: this means that the act of implementation has already taken place. The Internet becomes the object of theoretical and design praxis, from which other questions that are occasionally posed derive. Boris Groys will later reflect on such gestures in his *Introduction to Antiphilosophy* as the changeover from criticism to command, from contemplation to instructions.[131]

Pierre Lévy, who teaches at the University of Québec in Montreal, Canada, and is the author of a condensed technological history of the computer (1989) for a project of Michel Serres', is one of the first theoreticians to systemically follow the introduction of the Internet as a mass medium. The ground for his concept is prepared by his earlier books *La machine univers* (1987) and *Les technologies de l'intelligence* (1990), in which he adapts Turing's ideas and nomenclature for the technological and

---

131   Groys, *Introduction to Antiphilosophy* (New York, 2012).

cultural upheavals at the twentieth *fin de siècle*. His universal machine, however, is not of a locally active variety like that of the British mathematician, but a planet-spanning mega-machine. In 1994, Lévy propagates the possibility of developing a "collective intelligence" in his book *L'intelligence collective*, which is provided for by the new technological parameters. He ramps up the cybernetic space anthropologically with the advanced human intellect. For Lévy, *"cyberespace"* consists of an infinite number of universes existing in parallel, as in the many-worlds interpretation of quantum physics. Lévy understands these as individual spaces of knowledge. They must be connected in a smart, nonhierarchical way, through discrete, mechanical knowledge-generators and the intelligent activities of their free users. In this way, it is possible to realize "the universal without totality," as Lévy writes in the lead article for the inaugural issue of German Internet magazine *Telepolis* in 1996.[132] Derrick de Kerckhove, also from Canada and the heir to McLuhan's difficult intellectual legacy, later assigns the term *connected intelligence* to the paradoxical desired outcome. As Kerckhove understands it, in connectivity the lightning flashes of thoughts skim around at the speed of light. Hypertext — as Ted Nelson invented it in 1960 and formulated in his Project Xanadu— becomes the paradigm of how each field of intelligence is organized. The person who writes while reading and reads while writing emerges as the ideal figure of the new literality.

The architects of the information societies appear to have been waiting for such promising constructs. Shortly after publication of Lévy's at once tractable and pragmatic Internet utopia, the Czech Prime Minister Václav Havel invites members of the European artist and intellectual elite to Prague Castle, with its Golden Lane and

132   Also in Pierre Lévy (2001), *Cyberculture*, trans. Robert Bononno, Minneapolis, University of Minnesota Press, p. 92.

alchemists' quarters, to debate the cultural future of the continent at round table discussions. Lévy is one of the leaders of the conference. An incident at the event graphically illustrates the political and cultural reality that stands in opposition to his ideas. After the first discussants have made their contributions, a Russian-speaking scientist intervenes forcefully because the conference languages, into which the proceedings are being translated, are only English and French, despite the fact that two-thirds of the people present speak Russian as a second language, or are at least conversant in it. One of the moderators from the Brussels administration answers flippantly that this had been taken into account but it was decided to translate only into the most important official languages of the European Union. Slight turbulence ensues in the dignified hall of Prague Castle (which even rouses the mathematician Benoît Mandelbrot from his deep slumbers). When it's the turn of Antoni Muntadas (from Barcelona) to speak, the artist immediately addresses the forum in Catalan; the translators in their cabins remain silent. Everyone in the hall listens attentively to his statement, although no-one understands what Muntadas is saying. The dilemma cannot be demonstrated better. Muntadas' spontaneous performance is a marvelous satire on the allegedly power-free, horizontally organized cultural space that can purportedly be produced by means of technology and energy.

In the 1990s, with the spread of private and public databases, telecommunication reaches the stage of mass use; up to then it had only been accessible to an elite. In the beginning, thousands of research assistants, professors, and students trade their quite reliably functioning stationary home computers for PCs and MACs with ISDN-compatible modems and get connected for several hours on a daily basis to deal with their correspondence *online*, which is how they signal they are a part of these developments. Billions of sentences are sent and received, but in the beginning no images. Publications are quickly finalized over long distances, conferences are organized, the first theoretical magazines such as *CTheory* by the Canadians Arthur and Marie-Louise Kroker appear, and there are opportunities to try out the political resistance potential of the new Internet communication. For example, in 1994, when the Baden-Wuerttemberg Prime Minister Erwin Teufel tries to force the biochemist and theoretical physicist Otto E. Rössler to undergo psychological tests after disputes with his employer, the University of Tübingen, before he can get clearance for a guest professorship at the Santa Fe Institute. Speedily, institutions and scientists in the field all over the world are informed about the outrageous incident. Within a few days, hundreds of letters of protest arrive at the Institute for New Media in Frankfurt and the Academy of Media Arts Cologne, among them letters from Nobel laureates. They are handed over to the Baden-Wuerttemberg administration, and the deeply provincial Swabian politicians stop what they are trying to do.

Normal everyday life in large institutions adapts to other ramifications of the networking that is just beginning. In important work areas, offices lose their function because the rooms of academics and researchers transform into administrative bridgeheads. Academics and researchers do not stop writing, quite the opposite. Their quantitative output of texts is immense, although in large part it is bureaucratic and statistical. With the arrival of computers the size of a large book which are connected to the grid and the Integrated Services of the Digital Network, the new workplaces become mobile. By this point in time, they are long since image- and audio-enabled. The techno-social basis of the mainly immaterial work of a band of many individuals is the installation of electronic nodes usable everywhere for international data traffic.

Sociologists, who seek to work at the cutting edge of the times, will call this social phenomenon the "new creative class" at the end of the decade.

The digital becomes an analog for the alchemical formula for gold. The new explicitness is quickly joined by affirmation. One no longer gets tangled up in nets, but allows oneself to get caught by them and carried off as a bought commodity. One works with nets and inside them; structures that are permanently available and dependence on the communicative centers are reinterpreted positively. Technical connectedness becomes obligatory, and Get Connected! is a social order.

Through its Anglicization, the German concept of *der kybernetische Raum* is enhanced in an odd way. This is largely due to how the fancy label *cyberspace* is used in the context of aesthetics and human sciences. Because of this, it loses its not-quite-respectable character, and appears less bureaucratic and militaristic. In becoming the term *cyberspace*, even art historians write about the cybernetic space by simply extending the concept of immersion into the distant past. Thus painted ceiling frescos from the sixteenth century become a case of *virtual reality*, a second magic term, which — like the first — also has only a short half-life on the theory-market. Today no artist or theorist dares to talk seriously about this obscene kind of reality any more.

From 2005 to 2010, Miao Xiaochun stages a sky-high, jubilant farewell to the short-term exaltation of cybernetic space from the art academy in Beijing. His grand-scale computer animations using three quintessential paintings of the European Renaissance, *The Last Judgement of Cyberspace, H_2O,* and *Microcosm,* boldly and impertinently hold up the mirror of the Macintosh computer as the new Creator to European iconography from Michelangelo to Cranach and Bosch. The apple that glows on each one of these computers that are found

180

particularly in myriads of ateliers, seminar rooms, and offices, is the fruit with a bite out of it that we find in the Old Testament. In every moment, by day and night, it points out that paradise is irretrievably lost forever. It must be reinvented.

In the discourse surrounding the now shining golden calf of media phenomena, entrepreneurs appear on the scene whose attitude previously was either condescending or indifferent. These include protagonists of art history and art theory. Horst Bredekamp, once an assistant at the Marburg Institute for the art historian and later founding director of the ZKM Center for Art and Media in Karlsruhe Heinrich Klotz, practices a certain resistance to the new theoreticians of the image in Hamburg until the early 1990s, which only gradually transmutes into an intellectual openness toward the new phenomena. In close institutional proximity to Hartmut Böhme, Christina von Braun, Wolfgang Coy, Thomas Macho, and Friedrich Kittler at the Humboldt University Berlin, in the second half of the 1990s Bredekamp becomes the leading image scientist, who is more and more aware of the apparatus-conditionality of visual production and perception. In the previous years the seminal work of Hans Ulrich Reck and Florian Rötzer had laid the foundations for an understanding of art that is connected to the energies of change, for example, via the journal *Kunstforum* and publications such as *Kanalarbeit* (Reck 1988) and *Digitaler Schein* (Rötzer 1991). Without any connection to the technological conditions of producing, distributing, and perceiving images, the academic disciplines which only accept as art what fits into a slide as a photographic reproduction and satisfies the criteria of the classic canon of art history risk sinking into insignificance.

Surprisingly enough, an "iconic turn" is proclaimed. Such a paradigm shift, however, can be found to have taken place in the nineteenth century, when the machines began to work at top speed on the technical (re)producibility of images. Henceforth the technical image, which is how Flusser summarizes the phenomena that arise in the course of the process leading to abstraction, began to intervene massively in all sectors of cultural expression — from mass print media, literature, criminology, and art, to medicine, psychiatry, and the experimental natural sciences.

After this fundamental technical innovation further thrusts of technical visualization follow, especially with cinema and other diverse time-based forms of images. In a superb essay Gilbert Cohen-Séat ushers them in with the assertion that from now on the image will "decisively influence" the whole of civilization.[133] The 1960s see a further boost in the intensity and extensive reach of images, because of the massive spread of electronic television as the leading mass medium. And with its endless stream of instantaneous image (re)production, television radicalizes the conditions of visual perception again, which contemporary art historians had failed to notice at the time. They also struggled for a long time with the art of Fluxus and with Performance. And computer-generated images were completely alien to them.

With the arrival of the Internet on the world market of the academe, *image sciences* increasingly turn up in the early 1990s in the USA. Barbara Stafford, among others, tours Europe on an intellectual sales campaign. Whereby Stafford processes in particular iconographic material from Europe that has been purchased and collected by wealthy North American educational institutions and their libraries. Now we can marvel at these works in opulent reproduction in the printed *wunderkammers* of Zone Books and other prestigious book publishers, albeit from a strangely displaced perspective. Here the strata of deep time traditions in Europe are reinterpreted from

---

133   Cohen-Séat (1963), p. 137.

the flat temporal perspective of the modern construction of the United States of America. The motto on the Great Seal of the USA formulates the universal claim that will distinguish the global market: *e pluribus unum* – Out of Many, One.

As if one turn were not more than enough, a *pictorial turn* is also proclaimed, which revolves around the same thing as the *iconic turn*. At least this makes it perfectly clear what this is all about: the staking of claims to interpretive authority by the various academic disciplines and their hegemonial aspirations. With the *iconic turn*, certain sections of art history who have an icono-logically substantiated monopoly at their disposal, attempted to assert their exclusive competence for every last kind of visual form of expression suspected of being aesthetic in some way or another. The *iconic turn* would provide a justification for founding a new academic faculty in German-speaking countries, that of "Bildwissenschaft," which is merely a translation of *image sciences*. At the same time, scholars engaged more in pragmatic and scientific applications of images attempt to use the *pictorial turn* to establish that they possess credentials compatible with and relevant to visual culture and the fine arts. Otherwise one could easily mistake *image sciences* for a type of marketing strategy, which begins to be introduced in business management around this time.

The media-explicit literature of the 1990s develops like a guidebook for solving topical problems of the most diverse areas — smart advertising and communication agencies, design and architecture firms, as well as the digital activists and electronic agitprop groups who understand themselves as revolutionaries. Technology-based praxis is fetishized. Writing theory is confused with writing recipes and manuals. And the never-ending round of first destroying the Internet's security measures and then systematically building them up again begins, for the Internet can only exist as a vulnerability. The protagonists lose themselves — in some cases in severe pain — in the endless labyrinths of the subcultures of the Internet, which they fondly call *webs*. The seductive Circe, however, is wooed without her destructive quality. A root system without a main stem, which is not organized hierarchically, is in Deleuze and Guattari's interpretation a rhizome: this becomes the aesthetic and political paradigm for action. A function like this cannot really be sustained by such a mellow and poetic category; nevertheless, it is brazenly applied to processes that are in principle mechanical and thus run vertically.

Lev Manovich, a Russian émigré to the USA, writes a book at the end of the 1990s summarizing the decade of Internet parties, which in the hangover that follows the short high of the so-called New Economy becomes the Bible for newcomers to the information society, in colleges and academies as well as the many private institutions of higher education that spring up around the putatively still golden calf. The work promises to at last bring some clarity to the intoxicatedly happy experiences with the new media. What had been developed in the previous decades in the way of communicologies and mediologies is declared by Manovich to be useless for a theory of the so-called New Media while at the same time he shamelessly makes use of them as a quarry for building his own disputatious house.

Eclectically and far removed from the theoretical capabilities of the Russian formalists and structuralists, the Prague School, or the protagonists of the linguistic turn after World War II, Manovich repeats that the New Media possess their own language that we must learn if we want to understand them and use them to our advantage.[134] But first and foremost we must assume that the new world Manovich writes about obeys informational commands. The original starting point of the new algorithmic era is declared by Manovich to be the symbiosis of computer and cinematic technology, which Konrad Zuse created with his Z1 in 1936. This is in fact not correct because Zuse used 35mm film merely as the physical storage medium for his programs. His computer did not function as a media synthesis consisting of cinematic and computing machine.

---

134 In the meantime this message has even reached the Pope. "We must be attentive listeners of the languages of the people of our time, to be attentive to God's work in the world," said Benedict XVI. on 2/28/2011 in a speech titled "Listen to the language of new media" to the Pontifical Council for Social Communication (gloria.tv – "the more catholic the better": accessible on Pope Tube at www.http://en.gloria.tv/?media=133972, 3/28/11).

Telecomputing und die digitale Kultur

Art Com Front End, 1989, Menu für interaktive Computerkunst-Installation, für Macintosh Computer. Konzept von CARL LOEFFLER, Programm von FRED TRUCK

"Keiner weiß, ob das das Beste oder das Schlechteste sein wird, was die Menschheit sich selbst angetan hat, weil das Ergebnis zu weiten Teilen von unsrer Reaktion darauf abhängen wird und von dem, was wir damit machen. Das menschliche Gehirn wird sicherlich nicht von der Maschine ersetzt werden, zumindest nicht in der näheren Zukunft. Aber es besteht kein Zweifel, daß das weltweite Vorhandensein von Phantasie-Verstärkern, von intellektuellen Werkzeugkästen, von interaktiven elektronischen Gemeinschaften die Art verändern wird, in der die Menschen denken, lernen und kommunizieren."

Aus: Howard Rheingold, "New Tools for Thought: Mind-Extending Technologies and Virtual Communities", 1989

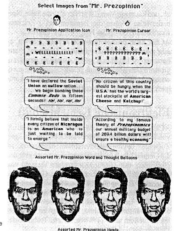

JOE ROSEM, Mr. Prezopinion und Vibrabones, 1987, interaktive Computerkunst, für Macintosh Computer

In the autumn of 1989 *Kunstforum* magazine published "Im Netz der Systeme" (In the net/network of the systems) edited by Gerhard Johann Lischka and Peter Weibel. The Art Com Electronic Network (ACEN) had been set up in the spring of 1986 in San Francisco. The illustration is a montage of elements of the first two pages of the essay.

All the ostensibly specific qualities that Manovich cites in *The Language of New Media* are not new but the result of previous decades of experimental and theoretical work: the logical-mathematical-informational basis of the immaterialities, the modularity of the structure of information, the variability of the language, the translatability of the codes between different communication processes, aka *transcoding*. In the New Media world there is also a screen between us and the experienceable things, and this screen has the function of an interface between the computer users and the world, which was an inside-joke as soon as Manovich's book appeared. Manovich runs through what Shannon, McLuhan, Flusser, Kittler, Lévy, the Krokers, de Kerckhove, and many others have defined as concrete phenomena contradistinguished from traditional media; he rarely uses terminology other than that which has already been written down many times and is in circulation, but he structures it clearly and formulates it in a way that is easy to understand. This is theory with the categorical will to be relevant to practice, which naturally is successful on the market.

Ten years later Manovich rather presumptuously modifies the title of Giedion's famous work *Mechanization Takes Command* of 1948 for his follow-up book in which he proclaims the advent of a phenomenon that at this point in time has already been established as a cultural technique for a long time, namely *software*; "immaterial machines," as Matteo Pasquinelli likes to call this phenomenon.[135] The unstoppable proliferation of social networks has made it clear to him that knowledge of programming is urgent, topical, and cannot be put off any longer, as Manovich says in a lecture in Venice in October 2010 to explain his change of perspective and the

---

135   On Matteo Pasquinelli see, for example, www.republicart.net/disc/empire/ pasquinelli01_de.htm.

187

necessity of achieving proficiency in the grammars of the programs and making them productive for art.

Over half a century after the beginning of experimental computer-generated poetry in various countries, including Southern and Eastern Europe, after Max Bense had formulated basics of a *generative aesthetics*, after the famous commencement of visual research with the aid of the computer and the countless cinematographic experiments with it in the 1960s, and forty years after Jack Burnham's famous exhibition at The Jewish Museum that put "Software" and "Its New Meaning for Art" on the daily agenda of the creative scene in art and design, after the legendary chess game concert between Duchamp and Cage in which each move was also a command selecting a fragment of musical composition, after Gene Youngblood's seminal *Expanded Cinema* (1970), and two decades after the spectacular interventionary projects with a type of software which we provocatively termed "collaborative,"[136] Manovich's insight seems rather antiquated. The artistic processes he is demanding have been around for a long time and exist in many formulations and formations. Their protagonists, however, are only wary of using highly ideological terms like *social networks* or *social webs* or of using these to lubricate their theory and practice. One of the most powerful artistic critiques of the concept of network was created offline after in-depth analysis and research using untold numbers of handwritten index cards: Mark Lombardi's *Global Networks*, published and exhibited posthumously in 2003, is a painstakingly hand-drawn visual narrative of real-world connections of economic, political, and criminal power. Giedion's book had already been a swan song of the age of mechanics in 1948.

---

136 See, for example, various works by the group *Knowbotic Research* from 1992–1998, who now teach at Zurich University of the Arts; on Max Bense, see Bense (1965), pp. 11–13.

2600

The Hacker Quarterly $4   *VOLUME SEVEN, NUMBER TWO*
SUMMER, 1990

Just as open source software has long been an important option for business and marketing strategists, the idea of a "collective intelligence" powered by free access has also proved suitable as an incubator for young managers and stock exchange speculators. These are by no means grounds for abandoning the ideas completely, only for why they should not be naively sold as a techno-utopia for the twenty-first century.

Geert Lovink from the Netherlands belongs to a group of activists who, during the 1995 Venice Biennale, meet in the back room of a crumbling theater to inaugurate techno-enabled subversion in the minimal form of an Internet mailing list. Over the next three years this communicative underground circle works in the spotlight of telematic curiosity. Berlin's most ambitious curator after German reunification, Klaus Biesenbach, secures international recognition for the Nettime project in the art world at Catherine David's Documenta X (1998).[137] A short time later the revolutionary élan has already dissipated.

The digital activists of Nettime initially primarily operate in the newly accessible countries of Eastern Europe. They travel to Ljubljana or Tirana, to people plagued by poverty and armed conflict, where they suggest getting connected to the global networks as a possibility of improving their existential situation through effective communication. The objection that an invitation

---

137 Historiographies change quickly, in this scene as well. Pit Schultz, who in recent years has devoted his energies to an independent cultural radio station, is cited in the as-if-encyclopedic reality of Wikipedia as cofounder of Nettime. The initially strong presence of the young media philosopher Nils Röller is mentioned by Lovink in his published texts, as well as that of Paul Garrin, who at this time is a brilliant video engineer of Paik's; Garrin brought with him the flair of a militant street fighter along with the ubiquitous electronic camera attached to him in the scene since "Free Society" (1988) and "Man with a Video Camera (Fuck Vertov)" of 1989. Heath Bunting, British graffiti star with the nimbus of artistic anarchy and street credibility, wore a shiny CD round his neck like a techno-totem, an amulet signaling his close libidinous affinity with the juvenile culture of the digital.

190

to dinner would be of more value to the people there than a few hours surfing data networks that belong to the West anyway, is laughed off by the activists as hopelessly old-fashioned. After all, it is a great historical moment: effective and fast access to the progressive world of telematics and thus to information as the most important resource of any future economy as well as the resistance to it. With laptops and power packs under their arms or in their backpacks, many of the young activists are like a highly intelligent, mobile *lumpenproletariat*; they dress in a demonstratively casual way in dark T-shirts printed with strange text messages and mysterious pictographs, wear sneakers, baggy pants with large pockets and woollen beanies even in summer, as though they are protecting their most important asset, a well-functioning brain, from sudden cold snaps. Intensive work on algorithms is mental acrobatics. The activists are the equivalent to young athletes who seek recognition in the world of competitive sport. For the activists, however, all physical and external things don't seem to be worth the hassle. They have an innate aversion to all institutions, which they simultaneously allow to fund their projects, albeit begrudgingly. Unless of course the speculator George Soros deems it appropriate to finance the projects in the east at least initially, and sometimes for a longer period.

A few years later there is ample access to the Internet, including in Eastern Europe. The new international service economies need this as an unconditional prerequisite for their existence. Prostitution in front of webcams is the only source of income for hundreds of thousands of poor young women and men in Romania, Bulgaria, and Hungary. Discovering possible ways out of the established infrastructures is rather difficult. What is still seriously lacking are the most important resources for a life with sensational qualities like clean water, nonpolluted food, healthy air to breathe, gender equality access to all levels of education, and peace at least for the foreseeable future.

In the meantime the next generation of individual activists on the Internet, particularly in the Arab-Islamic world, already use the widespread commercial networks and their applications linked to propaganda to send out their concerns into the world of the associated to get their messages multiplied by the millions. But without the living conditions in Libya, Egypt, or Syria effectively improving.

In Western Europe, Lovink develops into the relentlessly forward thinker of a heterogeneous movement which constantly invents new publics and subcultural constellations in and around the Internet; nurtures them for a time and then abandons them when they have exceeded their short half-life of subversive attractiveness. Against the clock and parallel to the advancing telematic complex as a *dispositif* structure, Lovink's writing follows each successive stage of the progress of Internet culture and its everyday techniques in a timely fashion using current jargon to at least extract a grain of revolutionary action from it. Bob Dylan's *Forever Young* is the aspiration of the contemporary *zeitgeist* and it's tough going to keep up with it. To stay forever young, also in the slang one uses, is as important in this aeonically loaded scene as it is in Pop music.

"By and large, German media theory has been, and still is, offline — old-fashioned Gutenberg knowledge stored in books. [...] The history-driven speculative approach bounces back, having little to contribute in the economic and political debates over the network parameters"[138] says Lovink in his *Dark Fiber* of 2002; a German translation is commissioned by the German Federal Agency for Civic Education (Bundeszentrale für politische Bildung), a public authority of the German Federal government,

---

138   Lovink (2002), pp. 29–30.

and appears in 2003. Does this contention mean that shrewd theories about prisons can only be developed on the basis of inmate experience?

Lovink's reproach contains a rhetorical device that had already been worn thin by the first Russian avant-garde as well as the radical Left of the late 1960s. Only those who had worked on the production line were in a position to develop a useful critique of the ruling political economy. With regard to areas of theory pertaining to the media, the reproach is as old as the strategic establishment of the media itself. Fifty years ago McLuhan wrote about the dying culture of the scholarly mandarin classes,[139] to which as a Catholic bibliomaniac he naturally considered himself as belonging.

One can only make vague guesses about what theory might be like from those who are characterized by the development of their identity online. Perhaps it is distinguished by the instantaneous concurrence of writing, reading, thinking, and publicizing? Since Nietzsche, we know that profound contemporaneity can only be produced at the price of untimeliness. To conform at all costs to the needs and expectations of the present creates dependency of thought. Only when there is no compulsion to be up to date is it possible to identify differences in the here and now. Flusser typed his interventionary theorems for dialog-oriented telecommunication on a mechanical typewriter.

In 1995/1996, the Rotterdam media collective V2 launches a project for collaborative development of interface theory. Five writers are selected to develop their positions in intensive dialog on the Internet. After only two rounds of deafening discussion there is a call for an editor who will supervise the texts and moderate the communication. The five authors go back to their computers and write their contributions for the publication

---

139   Cf. Röller (2000), p. 193.

offline, and in doing so return the computer to the role of a local writing instrument. The resulting book is actually an adaptation of Raymond Queneau's *Cent mille milliards de poèmes*, which in 1961 was still a rather courageous experiment. His book, bound in white cloth, contains the separate lines of ten sonnets printed individually on cards so that readers can combine them into different verses, like a children's book about heads, bodies, and legs. In V2's book the arguments of the different authors can be separated horizontally along perforated lines and combined vertically with the arguments of the others.[140]

In keeping with the generally oral character of Internet communications, the texts by the Internet activists seem to derive more from the spoken word than from focused writing. With regard to their main subject, the telematic networks, they are often put together in self-referential loops; one engages in debate and gladly confirms one's own praxis. The texts vary the core message that the connectedness of the worldwide networks is an inescapable fact from the perspective of advancing techno-liberal mass democracies and discreet dictatorships. We are familiar with this hypothesis from Lasswell and Ellul's propaganda research in the 1920s and 1960s. The insistence on market nonconformity is very important to the Internet underground that has developed from Nettime and other initiatives. Over and above its power functions for the technologically associated, the Internet realizes indispensable utility values which were previously unknown to our civilization, in science, the arts, design, architecture, and politics. That it is a motor for progress is no longer up for discussion. From this perspective communication always means a good society, and the expansion of communication necessarily a better society. This is why we have to get involved with the expanded facticity of communicative action. We have to

---

140   *Interfacing Realities*, published by V2 (Rotterdam 1997).

learn the skills and tricks of the new mental and manual crafts so that we are prepared to implement possible subversive applications. The essence of communication as an extremely ambivalent event, as a "risky adventure without guarantees,"[141] in which, according to Kafka, the breeding ground for the activities of avaricious minds are always created, remains alien to such a way of thinking.

The published texts complain that there is no useful theory of the Internet, but they are not offering one either. This is due, on the one side, to the fact that it is not possible for them to really engage with the techno-political operating and protocol structures. For this purpose there are other gangs in which qualified programmers are active, like the Chaos Computer Club. And it is also because such texts remain vague about the ethical, political, and aesthetic viewpoints upon which their arguments are based. This includes the decisive question as to what kind of community and what kind of subject identities should be created, supported, and served by the telematic networks. Grand gestures toward Michael Hardt's and Antonio Negri's as well as Maurizio Lazzarato's enlightened new sub-proletarian International, which will apparently arise on the basis of networked, immaterial labor, do not provide clarity. Their dichotomy of *Empire* and *Multitude* suffers from the fact that the first concept, in spite of all endeavors to effect some conceptual shifts, still exudes Trotskyist-Leninist charm, whereas the second concept is so vague that it does not seem to be of any use for interventionary thinking and action. This also applies to other prominent Italian theorists like Paolo Virno or Matteo Pasquinelli. There is no convincing argument in favor of a communist Internet.

Manuel De Landa, born in Mexico City and a resident of New York, who has also written a strong plea for a multilinear historiography, knows what he is talking

---

141   Peters (1999), p. 267.

about when in the early years of the telematic boom he explicitly engages with networks (*Meshworks*), the Internet, and digital interfaces. Before De Landa begins to write about computers and their connections, he acquires a profound knowledge of programming and studies the hybrid materialities of electronically based communications. Already in the mid 1990s De Landa calls attention to the fact that the Internet is "a hybrid of meshwork and hierarchy components." For this incisive thinker heterogeneity is not the same thing as multifariousness at all, and an increase in heterogeneity by no means necessarily results in an improvement of social and cultural conditions. "But even if we managed to promote not only heterogeneity, but diversity articulated into a meshwork, that still would not be a perfect solution. After all, meshworks grow by drift and they may drift to places where we do not want to go. The goal-directedness of hierarchies is the kind of property that we may desire to keep at least for certain institutions. Hence, demonizing centralization and glorifying decentralization as the solution to all our problems would be wrong. An open and experimental attitude toward the question of different hybrids and mixtures is what the complexity of reality itself seems to call for."[142]

Associated with New York University in Washington Square, which was once the hub and the most expensive address in the market economy-functioning world, a pair of restless thinkers appear who engage in a specific manner explicitly with the *dispositif* features of the Internet — Alexander R. Galloway and Eugene Thacker. They are versed in European philosophy since Nietzsche as well as trained through extensive practice with and in

---

142   De Landa (1997), available online at: http://www.t0.or.at/delanda/meshwork.htm.

196

the new media systems of the USA. *The Exploit*[143] is the title of their monster construct for which they want to develop a theoretical base. "Exploit" means a daring feat and it is also the hacker term for manipulating the flaws and vulnerabilities in a network system. Hackers exploit weak points and for those on the other side of the fence this shows where security can be breached and action is necessary.

In essence *The Exploit* is about the extreme ambivalence of the Internet as a paradigm for cultural globality. For Galloway and Thacker, networks have evolved to become the dominant technical form of the nature of control and are thus a contemporary equivalent of the panoramic view that is representative of the Enlightenment. Particularly important here is Foucault's emphasis that the *dispositif*, which is so difficult to grasp, is itself the network in which the various discourse practices are linked and regulated.

Galloway and Thacker also consider it possible to organize resistance through network-like structures. The network is at the same time the plan and the failure of the plan.[144] The conservatism articulates itself in the transfer protocols of the network systems, the analysis of which is Galloway's area of expertise. They are concealed, for example, behind the abbreviation *http* and organize the communication from the one to the other. By contrast, the inflammatory potential resides in the swarm, or swarming behavior, which is Thacker's focus. He is particularly interested in biological questions and their connection with philosophy.

---

143 An exploit means a bold or daring feat, a notable or heroic act, and is the hacker term for a program that takes advantage of a flaw in a network system. To exploit, also exploitation, means to make full use of and derive benefit from (a resource), as well as make use of (a situation) in a way considered unfair or underhanded, or to benefit unfairly from the work of (someone), typically by overworking or underpaying them (Oxford English Dictionary).

144 Galloway and Thacker (2007), p. 4 and 155. On the *dispositif* as a network see the Introduction in Agamben (2008).

To write advanced theory today means above all to embark on the adventure of writing advanced codes. This is the solution of those writing in the first tradition, including Galloway, who has also reactivated Debord's "Game of War" of 1977 and adapted it so that it can be played on the Internet. By contrast, the swarm stands for an anti-Web, which does not have a center. Resistance is always asymmetrical. Unlike the Internet with its innumerable individual connections, in swarms it is a question of connections of the many with many others and the attendant complexity. These connections are not of a human nature, and therefore theoretical constructs associated with them are not anthropocentric.

The theoreticians from the USA's East Coast differ markedly from the one-time computer hippies of the West Coast who with their metaphysics of telecommunication, their strange theologies of absence of the body while at the same time propagating hedonism and drug use, dominated the 1960s and 1970s and to a large extent also made Silicon Valley possible.

Galloway and Thacker are also searching for at least partial answers to the question of what subjectivity and sovereignty could still mean in the age of the Internet; whether and how they can still be effective as concepts. "Connectivity is a threat."[145] Proceeding from this courageous statement that connectivity now has a principally menacing character, it becomes possible to develop opportunities for action that are more free, which must not necessarily renounce all purposive associations.

There are only ten years between Lévy's concept of intelligence augmented by connections into infinity and this harsh criticism of the essence of connectivity. It is also reflected in the work of the Canadian researcher Anne Galloway on the rediscovery of local forms of

---

145   Galloway and Thacker (2007), p. 16.

communication as "locative media."[146] They are dependent on developed technologies of control like the Global Positioning System (GPS), the contemporary realization of the panoramic view into the microstructures of spatio-temporal conditions.

Entirely superfluous ideas are once again making the rounds — unfortunately also in the sphere of art — concerning flat analogies between social, technical, and biological structures. Once again, allegories and metaphors of living organisms have to serve as technological products. Organismic analogies surface at regular intervals in theoretical discourse at junctures where things threaten to get seriously unclear. Life serves as a concept for harmonization — is not nature the model realm which is full of differences and at once identical with itself in its heterogeneity? As Karl Popper pointed out in 1967, the difference between *clockwork* and *cloud-work*, the friction between the perfectly predictable and the always somewhat indeterminate, is rendered null and void by using the image of a cloud for specific services of the Internet and other networks. The techno-imaginary clouds, as linked offerings of computer hardware and software resources, do not foster cloudiness but instead its opposite: the transparency of the actions that take place in its environment. In the same way birdsong (Twitter) is a singularly inappropriate comparison for an activity and a service in which online activists consent to the compilation of statistics about what they like to talk about the most, their political and cultural interests, what they spend their money on, and so on. In a popular variant this concept of a collective culture of databases, generated by swarmlike superorganisms, disastrously draws from a model of society which was believed to exist among ants.[147] Unintentionally, a genealogical

146   Galloway (2008).
147 A naive example of this is Kuai Auson's installation *Oh!M1gas*, which even received an award at the Turin Festival "Smart Mistakes" in 2010. A complex society of organisms is kept under surveillance, visually and auditively, in order

pitfall of the concept is articulated here. *Der Ameisenstaat* (*The ant colony*) was one of the early radio plays written by Wulf Bley in 1934 eulogizing Hitler's state and its "command and obey" structures.

After the turn of the new millennium and the collapse of the New Economy, the manuals are particularly excruciating, "aids," and guide-type publications which are churned out in their masses for the new social class and the administrators of progress. With disquisitions on digital change and digital revolutions, on computer literacy and automatized knowledge, on users that will at last now all become artists or disappear inside emotional interface design, unlimited memory, unlimited penetration of communications, and once again even more collective intelligence, their authors cozy up to the movers and shakers of the information society, offering themselves up as effective escorts. They possess neither the means of production nor the infrastructures that they write about, nor as service providers do they occupy positions of power within the networked structures that they cling to — in the main as temporary employees. On these grounds we can refer to them, then as now, as petit bourgeois. Hans Magnus Enzensberger erected a fine textual monument to this type of sociality in the mid 1970s when the course was set for today's communications situation in terms of policy, economics, and technology:

> "Today this social class is teeming with progressive men, and nobody jumps at the opportunity more avidly than they to latch onto the latest trend. They are always *au courant*, up to speed. Nobody changes ideologies, clothes, form of intercourse, and habits faster than the petit bourgeois. He is the new Proteus, adaptive to the point of loss of identity. Perpetually fleeing from what is outmoded, he rushes along in pursuit of himself."[148]

---

to translate its communicative behavior into the realm of human perception.
148   Enzensberger (1976), p. 5.

Operationally, one can summarize the last sixty years of theoretical media thought as consisting of three stages:

1. After the great disaster of everything ontological, in the beginning structure is discovered by the humanities as a sensation. On the basis of de Saussure's linguistic theory intellectuals from various disciplines reactivate thinking about and in differences. The second avant-garde draws on the first from the 1920s. Structure determines the various positions, from semiology to political economy, from psychoanalysis to cultural studies. An exhibition titled "World Made of Language" at the West Berlin Academy of Arts in 1972 points out the hegemony of the linguistic paradigm, and brings closure for the time being.[149] Everything is code, but code is by no means everything.

2. This rigorous thinking in differences is irritated somewhat by the merry postmodern transgression of boundaries and its main rhetorical figures, which softens up the transitions between disciplines with the result that theory can become more fluid and smooth. As an orientation, organic multiplicity replaces the mechanical, majestically vertical structures. The processual, the becoming-in-the-horizontal supersedes the rigidly structured in the vertical. Rhizomic branching complexities are not fought against, but euphorically celebrated, preferably on plateau-like formations.

3. This is the transition to thinking in associations and connectivities, which no longer appears to need any hard and fast differentiation as an intellectual and artistic act. Everything can be interconnected with everything

---

149   The essay that gave the exhibition its title was written by Walter Höllerer; its subtitle was "Auseinandersetzungen mit Zeichen und Zeichensystemen der Gegenwart" (Interrogating contemporary signs and sign systems) (Berlin 1972).

else horizontally. With the paradigm of the equality of connections created by technology, the techno-based mass democracies have passed their cybernetic litmus test. Beyond this there is only dictatorship, fundamentalism, post-colonial corruption, or phenomena which those at the communicative center ignore entirely. Every instance of those who were previously excluded joining in is now celebrated as a resounding victory by the billions who are already connected. And the number of such new members joining continues increasing rapidly, because the model of a *societas* which is bent on free and uninhibited consumerism and promises a share of the already largely divided up whole effectively functions telematically.

The New Implicitness

The inflationary henchmen and underling literature of a media-strategic, tactical, and practical nature is contrasted in the last decade by a band — in the sense intended by Deleuze — of thinkers who appear to be indifferent to the interdiscursive field of the techno-imaginary third party. On the contemporary theory market they represent a strange phenomenon that is influenced by the writing and thought of the Romance countries. For decades Alain Badiou, Jean-Luc Nancy, Jacques Rancière in France and Giorgio Agamben in Italy have worked in the broader sphere around Althusser, Foucault, Derrida, Deleuze and Guattari, and other intellectuals who do not argue systemically, but without being accorded much attention.

In 1996 Turia + Kant in Vienna publish a volume of texts by Badiou and Rancière *Politik der Wahrheit* (*The Politics of Truth*), two series of lectures given by the authors in 1992/1993 in Ljubljana, which unleashes a veritable discourse machine at the margins of established society. Two major concepts, which postmodern discourse seems to have abandoned long ago with its pointed trashing of rationalism, are put back on the agenda of current debate. The printers of the German language publishing houses Diaphanes, Merve, Passagen, and Turia + Kant work faster than the protagonists (newly proclaimed as master-thinkers) can develop or sharpen their arguments, or revise their older texts for an international readership.

Various and diverse members of the critical intellectual scene rub their eyes in disbelief. Hardly anything at all in the texts that are published in quick succession — mostly short, fragmentary texts — is original, including the way they are written. Yet at the same time it is obvious that the band from Paris is responding to an intellectual and emotional crisis. After the wars in the middle of Europe, which accompanied the reconfiguration of the continent and its Eastern countries in the wake of the entropic decay of the Soviet Union, utmost importance is again attached to the political which is explicitly an object of curiosity. As body or gender politics, as biopolitics or micropolitics, it has also been constantly present in Western Europe in the decades before, not to mention the committed authors writing on postcolonialism in India, Africa, or South America. A quarter of a century after the events of May 1968, like a menetekel, people start to speak of the return of politics, which is rhetorically only possible if one assumes that it had previously disappeared. The endeavor is to bring philosophical thinking and politics in the broad sense into a relationship of meaningful tension with each other. In this, media phenomena only play a marginal role at best. In the following interpretation I shall be brief and inexcusably guilty of overstatement.

What might a *communitas* that does not follow a bu-reaucratized, socialist productivity paradigm, and its regimes of surveillance and prison, look like? Is the only alternative the creation of a community built on the powerful identification that results from the capitalist imperative of accumulation and consumption? Is it (still) possible to name socialities that have the ability to resist?

Society has successfully abolished itself. Accompanied by massive processes of individualization and privatization in which telematic networks are already actively involved, in the course of the 1990s, however, questions as to the validity and quality of community increasingly gain in importance, as well as questions as to the relation between lies and truth. Bataille, Leiris, Blanchot, Caillois, and many others had worked since the 1930s on concepts which could potentially transcend what actually exists. In poetic self-expenditure they discovered and propagated an effective and fascinating alternative to increasing universalization under the aegis of the market and technology. But the waning twentieth century is not suitable for either poetry or resacralization. For the great challenge that remains is the obligation to ensure that multifariousness continues, that pluralities are preserved and their long-term development supported if it is not possible to expand them continually as positions within areas of certain discourses. Thus the heterologies, heterotopias, and other options for plurality will have to be worked on again; the Marxist *multitudes* of Hardt and Negri are clearly an insufficient proposition.

The main issue is to establish a different aura in the arenas and forums of intellectual discourse, which one does not want to abandon to Slavoj Žižek and the former militant left-wing radicals in Italy. Concepts and terms which had not been the subjects of careful consideration for a long while are again tabled proactively and in opaque wording. At the margins, murmurs and rumbling begin to be heard much like at the end of the 1970s and the beginning of the 1980s when it appeared that Structuralist and Marxist positions day was done as meta-orientations. In Germany, journals like *Tumult, Freibeuter,* or *Konkursbuch* published texts critiquing Western hegemonial rationality which one frequently did not understand, also because they were deliberately formulated in an obscure way. At the same time they reinforced critical intellectuals in their conviction that things could not carry on much longer with what was currently offered in the way of politics and truth.

"There are Indians in town," Urs Jaeggi told the Governing Mayor of Berlin in an open letter of 1980, "redskins, expelled students, drop-outs, the disgraced. Relentlessly culture is changing back into nature. In full swing is the terrorism of the eco-friendly brigade, of cyclists and pedestrians; the struggle of the old, the lovers, and the ineducable in solidarity alone with the counter-terror of [police] batons and legal paragraphs."[150]

The idea that all truths are events, which is deemed a characteristic of Badiou's thought and to which proposition he has devoted an entire book, is one of the categorical universalisms of nonuniversalist thought of the last hundred years. In the twentieth-century history of science the work of Alfred North Whitehead, particularly his essay *Process and Reality* (1929), establishes this idea. Virtually all of his contemporaries who think in the logic of multifariousness operate with it intellectually. Žižek embodies the irruptive event. Agamben has devoted an early etymological case study to Heidegger's concept from *Being and Time,* which to my knowledge is not available in English translation. The Italian title is "*Se. L'Assoluto e l''Ereignis'*" and the text seeks to link the consciousness of the self with the idea of what has no restriction, exception, or qualification and the event.

---

150   *Konkursbuch. Zeitschrift für Vernunftkritik,* no. 5 (1980), p. 9.

This idea is deeply entwined with Bataille's philosophy of *inner experience* and his concept of *erotic rebellion*. "God is what does not happen, if you will, but is well determined as if what does not happen had happened," writes Bataille in his text on friendship in.[151] We also find the idea of an event in Blanchot's writings as well as the philosophical and poetic texts of Klossowski. Derrida ties the event to his concept of *deconstruction*. The event, in which the non-falsehood between the discourses is expressed, is the most important category with which Foucault undermines the claim of traditional historiography to truth, and on this basis — following Nietzsche — he develops his concept of genealogy. An essential component of Gianni Vattimo's concept of "weak thought" is the event-nature of history. If truth is understood, not as an absolute proposition but as a specific practice of intellectuals that has to be thought through and expressed time and again, then apart from the event there is nothing that can really interest us. Consistency exists, says chaos theorist Rössler, but in each moment anew. It is expressed in the particular instant. This was also the creed of the artistic movement Fluxus and of Action art. "Events are weapons for politicizing art," wrote Vostell in *Happening und Leben* (*Happening and Life*) with his hand on the bastard title of the catalog — in 1970. His manifesto for architects and urban planners titled *Ereignis* (event/happening) was written in 1968. And the series of performances that Vostell stages in the late 1960s, including at the Berlin Wall, he also called "Ereignisse."

151   Bataille (2002), p. 44; Bataille's erotic rebellion was used as the title of an excellent essay by Giorgio Cesarano, that was published as part of his *Manuale di Sopravivenza* (*Handbuch des Überlebens* 1983) [survival manual] in 1974 in Bari.

51 77 83

A U T O M A T I S C H E R T E L E F O N B E A N T W O R T E R

KOMBINAT 1 / KÖLN

VOM 1.10.1969 – 31.10.1969 /TÄGLICH 12–15 UHR,und 21–24 UHR

V I D E O K O M B I N A T 1 – I D E E N

Vostell: Action art with telephone network and Anrufbeantworter/ answering machine 1966. The number was Vostell's telephone number; the machine pictured is a 1/2-inch reel to reel video recorder for taping black-and-white television images; *Wolf Vostell elektronisch*, Neue Galerie im Alten Kurhaus (Aachen 1970).

EIN 3 KONTINENT HAPPENING

(11 MINUTEN + 48 STUNDEN)
VON
ALLAN KAPROW NEW YORK
MARTA MINUJIN BUENOS AIRES
WOLF VOSTELL BERLIN

AM 24.OKTOBER 1966
VON 0 UHR BIS 0.11 UHR SIMULTAN
IN DEN 3 STAEDTEN NEW YORK BUENOS AIRES UND BERLIN AUFGEFUEHRT
DIE AKTIONEN KOENNEN
VON BELIEBIG VIEL MENSCHEN DIE MOEGEN
ZUR GLEICHEN ZEIT AN JEDEM ORT
SELBST INTERPRETIERT WERDEN

ZEIT	ORT	AUSFUEHRENDE	AUTOREN	AKTIONEN
0 UHR -0.04	BERLIN	VOSTELL	VOSTELL:	"NEHMEN SIE EINE FLASCHE
0 UHR -0.04	NEW YORK	KAPROW		MILCH SCHREIBEN SIE
0 UHR -0.04	BUENOS AIRES	MINUJIN		FALL-EX DARAUF UND STELLEN
0 UHR -0.04	UEBERALL	JEDER DER WILL		SIE DIESE AN DIE NAECHSTE
				STRASSENECKE UND FUELLEN
				SIE EIN TELEGRAMM AUS AUF
				DEM MILCH STEHT UND DIE
				NAMEN DER STRASSENECKE
				SCHICKEN SIE AM SELBEN TAG
				DAS TELEGRAMM ANS WEISSE
				HAUS IN WASHINGTON USA."
0.04 UHR -0.07	BERLIN	VOSTELL	KAPROW:	"BESTREICHEN SIE IHREN
0.04 UHR -0.07	NEW YORK	KAPROW		WAGEN GANZ MIT MARMELADE
0.04 UHR -0.07	BUENOS AIRES	MINUJIN		LECKEN SIE DIESE DANN AB
0.04 UHR -0.07	UEBERALL	JEDER DER WILL		UND OEFFNEN SIE DANACH DIE
				WAGENTUEREN UND LASSEN SIE
				LEUTE HERAUSFALLEN DIE MIT
				METALLFOLIE ODER SILBERPA
				PIER UMWICKELT SIND."
0.07 UHR -0.10	BERLIN	VOSTELL	MINUJIN:	"
0.07 UHR -0.10	NEW YORK	KAPROW		
0.07 UHR -0.10	BUENOS AIRES	MINUJIN		
0.07 UHR -0.10	UEBERALL	JEDER DER WILL		
0.10 UHR -0.11	BERLIN	VOSTELL	POLAROID	VON JEDEM EREIGNIS GENOMME
0.10 UHR -0.11	NEW YORK	KAPROW		NE POLAROID FOTOS WERDEN
0.10 UHR -0.11	BUENOS AIRES	MINUJIN		DURCH TELE-FOTOGRAFIE
0.10 UHR -0.11	UEBERALL	JEDER DER WILL		(FUNKBILD) NACH DEN 3
				STAEDTEN GESCHICKT UND DORT
				NACH ANKUNFT 48 STUNDEN
				PROJEZIERT FUER PUBLIKUM
				IN BERLIN IN DER GALERIE
				BLOCK FROBENSTRASSE 18

"Events are weapons for politicizing art": Vostell, Kaprow, Minujin, jeder der will [and anyone who wants to], 1966 (Vostell 1970), p. 143.

Obviously, one can think all that through over and over again. However, we should also remember the power of the event to bring out differences has long since been discovered as an aesthetic and actionistic category by marketing strategists, advertising agencies, finance sector tacticians, and the mediaocracy and has thus been rendered functional for the system. Just like the edgy, irritating film techniques of the Nouvelle Vague have long since been absorbed into the arsenal of hegemonial aesthetics. The production of discontinuities, events that seemingly erupt but are in fact artificially engineered, serve today to make effective propaganda for services and commodities. Here communicative networks, whose gateways are wide open for eventualities and contingencies, play a significant role. With *The Black Swan: The Impact of the Highly Improbable* (2007) the Lebanese-American scholar and finance industry specialist Nassim Nicholas Taleb has produced a highly successful literary landmark for the extreme impact of certain kinds of rare and unpredictable events.

Badiou's contrast of event and institution finds its reflection in Rancière's dichotomy of politics and police, and also, slightly shifted, in Agamben's state and non-state dualism.[152] That which is commonly referred to as politics is for Rancière the realm of expert administrators, managers, and government technicians who all speak the language of power peculiar to this realm. He summarizes hegemonial phenomena under the term "police." Against this, there is growing unrest among the other, those who are excluded, the struggle of those who do not have a share articulates itself in opposition to the symbolic order of the governing community, in opposition to the established *communitas* and its promises.

---

152 Working together at the European Graduate School in Saas Fee, Switzerland, has also contributed to the fact that the themes of this discourse's protagonists increasingly overlap and secretly correspond with each other.

This articulation is actually politics in the proper sense, which must be strengthened and must never cease to be developed in practice. It is entirely beyond me why this identity of the political, which over the last decades has been so fundamentally repudiated, should still be significant and meaningful.

Peter Weibel, *Polizei lügt* [the police lie], from the series *Anschläge* [means both attacks and posters], 1970/1971 © Peter Weibel.

In this context I would also like to mention someone now virtually forgotten who developed an intellectual energy in Germany comparable to that of Cesarano in Italy. In a tour de force, Erik Grawert-May has sifted through concepts of power from Machiavelli and Casanova up to Bataille and Foucault and thirty years ago was farther ahead than Rancière is today with his book *Zur Entstehung von Polizei- und Liebeskunst* [the origin of the arts of policing and love] (1980). Grawert-May writes that in its remit to prevent social entropy, "police logic" has taken on important functions in observing errors and catastrophes and even integrates Adornian positions on its way to becoming a disciplinary power. He draws particular attention to the interplay of the different modes in which power is generated and developed. There cannot be a power-free sphere in what is termed society. After Bataille and Foucault, the much more important question is, what is disciplined sovereignty produced for and what will it be used for. "Power and discipline are not evil per se; when they don't instill fear, they can be fine."[153]

This venturesome idea against convenient dualisms, as formulated by Grawert-May, resonates in the practical consequences of how the Deleuzian Manuel De Landa characterizes the relationship between centralization and decentralization in network-like structures in the 1990s. To condemn out of hand what is centralized, with its stabilizing factors, simply on the grounds that it was frequently misused in the past, is a big mistake. Different hybrids and mixtures of the structures make sense as technological and communicative realities. Not all processes of centralization inevitably lead to dictatorship. "Hence, demonizing centralization and glorifying decentralization as the solution to all our problems would be wrong."[154]

By contrast, Rancière is drawn to praising the power-free space in which those who are excluded from the language of the steersmen, whom he refers to as "anonymous people," are located. Yet the blueprints, which stand in opposition to a bourgeois existence and are radical to a greater or lesser degree, have to be rendered concrete time and again. It is clearly not enough that artists like Pasolini or Boris Mikhailov stage them as grandiose and desperate heroes or that rock music celebrates them time and again in ever new identities to the point of self-destruction. Philosophical thinkers feel obliged to

153 Grawert-May (1980), p. 134.
154 De Landa (1997), p. 42.

211

rename them over and over again in spite of the reservations that artists in particular have concerning this mania for naming. In his commentary on "The Althusser Case," Heiner Müller writes "as soon as young people are in a position to say what they hope to achieve, paralysis has already set in.... As long as a force is blind, it remains a force. As soon as it has a program, a perspective, it can be integrated, it belongs."[155]

Similar to Badiou, Rancière introduces a string of nonwords which correspond to his invention of *mésentente*[156]: the not-own, the unsayable, the unshowable, the unrepresentable, the aesthetically unconscious, the unbelievable, the unpredictable. Depending on discursive context, Rancière uses them to denote phenomena and properties, which are virulent on the side lying opposite to that of power; on the side where the share-less people are, who naturally — like the Situationists — are not sedentary but on the move, roaming.

"Antiphilosophy" knows what's what. After making a differentiation in principle it is in this strange non-difference that Rancière ultimately locates art. Art's task is to aid the reshaping of the world in which we live (he uses Husserl's term Lebenswelt — lifeworld — which Flusser was also very fond of) into a more just world of equality. The eventual and obvious accusation that he — for example, in *The Future of the Image* or *The Politics of Aesthetics: The Distribution of the Sensible* — assigns tasks to art within the framework of "what is really political," and thus instrumentalizes art. Rancière attempts to preempt this accusation by including it at the end an emphatic plea against the normative. Now, who wants to be labeled normative because they resist standardization?

155   *Konkursbuch*, no. 7 (1980), p. 205.

156   Jacques Rancière (1999), *Disagreement: Politics and Philosophy* [*La Mésentente. Politique et philosophie*], trans. J. Rose, Minneapolis: University of Minnesota Press.

The lacuna that arises because of Rancière's unwilling-ness to draw conclusions is again filled with one of his quirky words which underline the obscurantism of what are at bottom rather conventional deliberations: the "un-decidability," which articulates itself between the two opposing poles of politics, between which art operates at its undefinable heart.[157]

Jean-Luc Nancy's idea of *Being* [in] *Singular Plural* can be regarded, from the perspective of science, as project-ing aspects of chaos theory onto the subject matter of ethics and aesthetics. To see the greatest resonate in the smallest and the smallest in the greatest is a basic per-spective of thinking about fractals and a rhetorical fig-ure which we find archaically formulated in the Pre-So-cratic natural philosopher Anaxagoras, a lesser known contemporary of Empedocles, and finely elaborated in Johann Wilhelm Ritter's plan of an electrical universe ca. 1800.

Most notably, Nancy's text-universe contains a reac-tivation of the dialogic philosophical reflections of ex-clusively twentieth-century Jewish thinkers, first and foremost of Edmond Jabès (whom Nancy has published on), Emmanuel Levinas, and some aspects of the politi-cal ethics of communitarianism as developed by Martin Buber. "Being-with" becomes an open impossibility as an alternative to the hermetic "self for-itself." For Nancy this idea of communality is not — from a Marxist per-spective — primarily bound with the world of labor, but with the realm of aesthetics. The world of artists is the special place where fractures, discontinuities, detours, and fragmentation are particularly at home; this feeds into his idea of community as coexistence of the singular with the plural. The Subjection of art to a good cause is not an option for Nancy.

---

157   See the end of Rancière (2006), p. 99.

Many decades after Molinier declared his ecstatic travesties to be holy artistic acts, after Beuys let the coyotes howl in the spaces of art, after VALIE EXPORT's *Touch and Tap Cinema* invited random passersby on the street to grope her breasts and she also crawled across the stage through electrified barbed wire that sent electric shocks through her naked body, after FM Einheit from *Einstürzende Neubauten* demolished the back wall of the stage in Berlin-Kreuzberg's club SO 36 with a percussion drill opening a hole onto the Oranienstrasse and thus used a rock concert to spontaneously rearrange the block … but also in view of the mondial multifariousness of highly contemporary artistic expression, for example, Thai director Apichatpong Weerasethakul from Bangkok, Shirin Neshat from Iran, Mahmat-Saleh Harroun from Tchad, 01.org from Bologna, the Mesopotamian dramaturge Kutlug Atamans from Istanbul, or Ali Kazma's encyclopedic *Obstruktions* about circular consistencies in the contemporary world of labor, the ideas of these authors from France seem curiously lackluster. Of course this may be an effect of the fact that, under the enormous pressure from the super-rich from all over the world who live in Paris and the predominance of fashion, design, and the demonstratively prestigious culture of the metropolis on the Seine, a young and rebellious generation of French artists has not surfaced for the last fifteen or twenty years. But it is also due to a deficiency in the argument. It has become a matter of some urgency to get rid of the classic dichotomy between an ostensibly hermetic bloc that is the market, and the purportedly "open" events at the noncommercial margins. This pairing, too, does not work anymore — also because of the withdrawal of public institutions from the cultural and subcultural scene — at least for those who work there. Social and cultural daily life is now replete with fractures, fragmentation, and discontinuities. It is high time to consider different figures of therapy.

And to accuse Benjamin, sixty-five years after he wrote his legendary *Work of Art* essay with courage and in great isolation, that he was too much the advocate of Modernity's technological optimism,[158] is a tawdry critical position in view of today's interventionary media theory. Adorno formulated this criticism while Benjamin was still alive, more incisively and precisely, and Benjamin himself had begun to revise his opinion. His angel of history took flight in panic with its back turned to progress.

Artistic processes or media works do not really interest the aforementioned French authors in contrast to Derrida or Deleuze. In his profound study of the painter Francis Bacon, *The Logic of Sensation* (1995), and in his treatment of individual photographs or philosophical thoughts on time and cinema, Deleuze has written an exquisite and implicit theory of art and media. The only explanation that occurs to me as to why aesthetics, as a vague field of activity, has become so en vogue for certain thinkers is that, above all, art is again being celebrated as a refuge in which insurrection can still take place and unfold. Nancy's concept of *vestigium*, of "residue," in which possibly Rancière's "undecidability" finds itself, corroborates this assumption.[159]

If one does not accept any term that cannot be deconstructed, if one doesn't want anything to do with the divine it must be very difficult to write about art in a way that is profound and goes beyond what one immediately sees and hears. This distinguishes Badiou, Nancy, and Rancière from the French master-thinkers after World War II. Their categories are not uniquely their own and they are not strong enough to fill the empty space effectively left behind by the death of God proclaimed by Nietzsche. Bataille's heterology, Lacan's imaginary, Derrida's *différance*, Deleuze and Guattari's *becoming* all offered

---

158   Rancière (2006), p. 50ff.
159   Nancy (1999), p. 139ff.

such qualities; in Germany it was Heidegger's *being*, and the community of communicative activists as devised by Habermas. Foucault was possibly the first member of this band to dispense with formulating a substitute for God. For now one is certain with a curious determination of one thing; namely, the breakup of all dependabilities, gravitas, consistencies — especially with regard to the subject. Although it has lost "its last bastion, namely, to be the fundament of knowing" at the latest with "the objectification of German idealism."[160] Self-disempowerment and self-flagellation.

Different: Giorgio Agamben

"Never should anyone have to endure what a human being is capable of enduring, and never should anyone have to witness how this suffering of the greatest potency has nothing human about it at all."[161] Agamben is still teaching in Venice when, his thoughts circling around this unprecedented sentence by Grete Salus, he makes the attempt to write about the impossible that has become reality. Auschwitz was not about dying but about "something far more appalling. In Auschwitz people did not die; rather, corpses were produced." Criticism of the technical rationality that pervades the entire catastrophe could not be more incisive. Productivity changes abruptly into the greatest perversion imaginable. In their philosophical fragments, *Dialectic of Enlightenment*, Adorno and Horkheimer practice critique that is similarly mordant,

---

160 Hübener (1986). My thanks to Eckhard Fürlus.
161 Agamben uses part of the Salus quotation as the title of an excerpt from *Quel che resta di Auschwitz* (1998) (*Remnants of Auschwitz* [1999b]), which is translated into German in 1999 on behalf of the Heiner Müller Society for the first edition of *Drucksache N.F.* [Neue Folge] before the first volume in the *Homo sacer* series is published by Suhrkamp Verlag. For the following quotation, see Agamben (1999b), p. 71f.

as does Günther Anders in his later aggressive criticism of civilization.

Isn't it absurd to interrogate the writings of an essentialist and fine practitioner of hermeticism about the traces that technology and media leave behind in thought? At first sight the intellectual world of the Italian philosopher seems utterly devoid of media; however, this is absolutely not the case — on the contrary. Agamben hails from a country where in every kitchen, every living room, as well as the cafés audiovisual spectacles of rare and incomparable stupidity are celebrated. Berlusconi's power resides not least in the fact that it occupies these stagings and employs them imperially. Technical media are by no means foreign to Agamben's anthropological and civilization-philosophical reflections. Their presence is strong but rarely explicit.

Like Benjamin, whose writings Agamben has translated into Italian, the realm of media is also roughly divided into two parts. The locally operating techniques of reproduction that were industrialized in the nineteenth century, photography and film, command positive interest. Electronic communication media, which operate over distances, are potentially threatening and — insofar as they are an issue for him at all — are an expression of the power of a *dispositif*.[162] And there is a third facet: everything that exhibits propagandistic, bureaucratic, and journalistic tendencies arouses Agamben's contempt. "Journalists and mediacrats are the new priests of this alienation from human linguistic nature," he writes in *The Coming Community*.[163]

The collection of short texts titled *Profanazioni* (*Profanations*), published in 2005, is not as extensive as Barthes' *Mythologies* or the text fragments of McLuhan's

---

162   In relation to Benjamin I have discussed the distinction elsewhere (Zielinski, 2005).
163   Agamben (1993), p. 81.

217

Mechanical Bride. However, it has a similar argumentative function. In ten miniatures Agamben discusses media content and rhetoric, but without explicitly naming the particular medium in the title. What attracts his interest are the modes of operation and not the technical objectifications of the *dispositif*'s system.

"Judgment Day" is a minimal treatise on photography as "a prophecy of the glorious body" that "represents the world as it appears on the last day, the Day of Wrath." "The Assistants" is about translators and "intermediate creatures," about "angels, messengers who do not know the content of the messages they must deliver, but whose smile, whose look, whose very posture, 'seems like a message.'" "Parody" is a short discourse on theater, literature, and the cinema (of Pasolini). "Desiring" treats the imaginary of images, as does "Special Being" which focuses on the mirror as an artifact that generates images; an artifact that also had fascinating importance for Foucault in his text on Velázquez's *Las Meninas*. "Magic and Happiness" considers play as more than likely a squandering activity. Before the book closes with an aperçu on fantasy in the cinema, on Sancho Panza and Don Quixote — Orson Welles' grand project on this perfect embodiment of dignified failure was never finished — Agamben inserts "In Praise of Profanation" to sum up the collection of essays. Starting from Benjamin's famous *Capitalism as Religion*, Agamben reexamines a central category of WB's "Work of Art" essay, the "exhibition value," which has assumed an independent existence in "the system of the spectacular religion." His formulation "pure means," as the "inviolate place of expression," we could substitute with the notion of pure media — without causing any epistemic break — which determine the "new condition of objects." This is a religious idea familiar from Christian painting. In Agamben's text it is the models and porn stars who are the extreme protagonists

218

of a gesture that dominates and pervades everything, the gesture that shows nothing more than engaging in an act of showing. "The profanation of the unprofanable" makes it possible to move the sacral into the sphere of the largely secularized world; a nice Bataillean notion.

At the end Agamben becomes a missionizer when he characterizes this act as "the political task of the coming generation."[164] And to tear what is unmediatized away again from the media is certainly one of the options for future subjects to act in order to avoid their own virtualization. At the end of his essay on the *Dispositif* he returns to this theme when he describes as an urgent task "the profanation of *dispositifs* — that is to say, the restitution to common use of what has been captured and separated in them." Viewed as an aesthetic tactic — epic, anti-Aristotelian — it reads almost like Brecht. And Agamben does indeed refer to future subjects intervening, "in their own processes of subjectification and in the *dispositifs* [...] in order to then bring to light the Ungovernable, which is the beginning and, at the same time, the vanishing point of every politics."[165]

The fragmentary miniatures that Agamben publishes in 1990 as *Communità che viene* (*The Coming Community*, 1993) read like extensive prefatory remarks to *Profanations*. Once again he sets out to tackle the problem that Foucault left behind for today's intellectuals; namely to outline, or even help develop subject identities that differ from traditional concepts of individuality. The task is far from being finished. Again, his thoughts circle around the big picture and its systems that are so difficult to pin down after the collapse of the last great political identifications; he attempts to develop alternatives to the community generated by advanced capitalism, the mediaocracy, and the factual constraints of cybernetics,

164   Agamben (2007), p. 27, 23, 29, 73–90.
165   Agamben (2009), p. 24.

which result in a short reflection on the demonstration in Beijing's Tiananmen Square that Chinese students organized to commemorate the passing of Hú Yàobāng and to demand his official rehabilitation. The subsequent unrest culminated in huge protests and an embodiment of the revolt: the young man who on June 5, 1989 stood in the path of four approaching tanks.

The focus of *The Coming Community* is the provocative and ambivalent "whatever singularities." They are not to be confused with *qualunquemente* (whichever-ly) that is a defining feature of Berlusconi's corruption-based republic as highlighted in a 2011 film by director Giulio Manfredonia of the same name. Agamben understands "whatever singularities" as those who "cannot form a *societas* because they do not possess any identity to vindicate nor any bond of belonging for which to seek recognition."[166] Whatever singularities form a community simply on the strength of the fact that because they are singularities they are different and belong together. The identity of whatever singularities is a notion of community that the state simply cannot deal with because it does not fit in with the being-in-language that is specific to the state. "Wherever these singularities peacefully demonstrate their being in common there will be a Tiananmen, and, sooner or later, the tanks will appear."[167]

Agamben does not use the adjective *arbitraria* to characterize his special notion of *singularità*. "Arbitrary" means above all random choice or personal whim, rather than reason or system; unrestrained or autocratic; in Latin *servum arbitrium* is the ever-subservient, enslaved will as opposed to free will which is able to do good and which Descartes exalted as a human being's greatest possession in a letter to Queen Christina of Sweden. Agamben attaches great importance to *quod libet*, which

---

166   Agamben (1993), p. 81.
167   Agamben (1993), p. 86.

220

is related to the adjective *qualiscumque* (Italian: *qualun-que*). Its translation is reminiscent of the Shakespearean titles *As You Like It* and *Twelfth Night* or *What You Will* which celebrate the opposite of arbitrarily subjective, and thus subservient actions, and invite the audience to decide whether the play matters and what it means. In old scholastic treatises, *quodlibet* stands for "what you please." The lovable, including in the sense of what is desired, is the oscillating center of this specific form of identity that Agamben proposes.

A fragment of an implicit theory of the mediatized imaginary is included toward the end of *The Coming Society*, the miniature on the "Shekinah." Agamben writes it as a reaction to the "immense accumulation of spectacles in which all that was directly lived is distanced in a representation." In principle this is familiar to critiques of the hegemony of the (techno-) imaginary in the Lacanian tradition. However, here Agamben explores surprising territory; namely, the difficult area to penetrate between Kabbalah and media theory, which was once before important, in the early Modern age.

The theological thought system of the Sephiroth, which generally consists of ten axioms that can be combined in perpetually new combinations, describes in the Kabbalah the (self) expression of the divinity and at the same time its manifestation in the universe and to human beings. Agamben conceives the structure of the Sephiroth as vertical — this is not mandatory for there are many circular constructions — and on this basis he determines that the Shekinah is the last of the forms in which God or the infinite reveals itself to humankind. Shekinah, which is also called Malkuth, concerns in particular "God's abiding in the world." Through a cloud or firesmoke, veiled, not really visible, God appeared to Moses and both revealed and hid his glory. He speaks to Moses, his abode is on

Earth — as Agamben summarizes — the "word." In representations where the combinatory system of the Sephiroth is projected onto the microcosm of an individual organism, the Shekinah also functions as an ideal mediator. It stands for certain sense organs, particularly skin,[168] which I have discussed elsewhere as an ideal interface with reference to Empedocles' theory of pores. Together with Hod (associated with the biological, organizing communication systems) and Netzach (actively cyclical, repetitive principle) Shekinah forms the great trinity of the vegetative foundation of an organism.

The system of the Sephiroth is open to many interpretations; according to context, the individual dispositions can differ considerably. The activity of a Kabbalist essentially consists in constantly interpreting and reinterpreting the divine revelations and their relations to each other. This is something the three monotheistic religions have in common; they all have one God, one master text — Bible, Koran, and Talmud. Amador Vega, the Catalan aesthetician, Ramon Llull expert, and respected scholar of mysticism has engaged profoundly with this and published extensively on the subject.

With explicit reference to "Marxian analysis of the fetishistic character of commodities" and Debord's *Society of the Spectacle*, Agamben uses the Shekinah to state the aggravated situation that we have got into with the advanced technologies of mediation: "The spectacle does not simply coincide, however, with the sphere of images or with what we call today the *media*: it is 'a social relation among people, mediated by images,' the expropriation and the alienation of human sociality itself." With the escalation of the spectacle to the most extreme

---

168 Flusser attempted to develop a media theory with the skin as its focus. The pertinent texts (*Von der Dermatologie und von Hiob; Hiobs Dermatologie; Haut*) can be studied at the Vilém-Flusser-Archiv in Berlin. See also Silvia Wagnermaier's introduction to Flusser's "Von den Möglichkeiten einer Leibkarte" in: *Lab. Jahrbuch 2000 für Künste und Apparate* (Cologne 2000), p. 114.

degree, the mediating authority, the word, has begun to separate from what it reveals. In my words: the media have assumed a completely independent existence. Debord says that telecommunication can only connect what has already been separated. For Agamben, individuals are de facto separated by what appears to connect them; namely, the media. "What hampers communication is communicability itself."[169] Agamben refers to the ongoing work of separation of artificial connections in his later text on the *dispositif* as a process of "desubjectification." This is now so far advanced that the problem with *dispositifs* cannot be "reduced to the question of their correct use."[170] Those who argue that it can merely reveal they are the products of the media *dispositif* in which they are captured.

An Exact Philology of Precise Things

There is a fine line between feeling trapped and feeling at home. The question of correct or incorrect use of technology arises for media theory when even in the age of the technical producibility of art and other media things it must be assumed that in principle the relationship between technology and cultural expressions is an instrumental one. If this is the case, the latter are brought forth by the former. However, if on the other hand I assume as an operative precondition that there is a relationship of interdependency in the form of "nontrivial interaction"[171] between the two fields of discourse, then the problem does not arise. For then we find ourselves in the midst of a *cultura experimentalis*, whose components are technological media.

---

169 Agamben (1993), pp. 79–84.
170 Agamben (2009), p. 21f.
171 Here I use a term of Hans-Jörg Rheinberger's; see: Rheinberger (2001), p. 26.

The generation of media theorists who engaged with Baudry's, Pleynet's, and Flusser's apparatus heuristic, with Kittler's technical media *a priori* of all aesthetic expressions, as well as various materialist concepts of media archaeology and media anthropology, direct their epistemological interest to exact knowledge of the things which negotiate between the one and the other. In the friction-laden entity consisting in technical and ideal identities, which relate to each other in a feedback loop, what is important is to recognize the interactions as realms of possibility and to let them evolve.

This presupposes thoroughgoing knowledge of both: of aesthetics, its formal laws and particularities, and of the technical artifacts, their structures and mode of operation in wider contexts, their scientific fundamentals. Furthermore, this implies using a special approach that we are familiar with in art. By attaching the same value to technical objects and ideas, we treat them with the same respect. We encounter them on equal footing; not from a worm's-eye view that elevates the observed objects, nor from a bird's-eye view that scales them down and renders them indifferent. And at the same time we consider them from an oblique standpoint; Nils Röller speaks, in his dissertation from 2000, of the possibility of elucidating the otherness — in his case, of mathematical thought — using the tools of philology.[172]

The *philològos* has a great affection for the spoken word. With a view toward a potential media-theoretical perspective that is already developing, let us sketch the figure of a researcher who is fond of speaking and writing about things that have been thought up and invented as technological means of communication to inspire and extend our thought horizons. As our good philologist is also conversant with hermeneutics, she/he is acutely aware that these things are all embedded in history. This

172   Röller (2000), p. 194.

means that in this regard, too, our philologist's interpretation must be exact, while being fully cognizant of the fact that it can only ever be an approximation.

We are thus sketching the concept of a philology of precise things that is as exact as possible. To the extent in which it already exists as a practice in the concrete form, our philology did not come out of nowhere. Our philology maintains certain indispensable links to the tradition of individual elements in this edifice of ideas, which I have outlined above for approximately the last fifty years. A very basic idea is the notion that language can also be understood as an artifact and that artifacts themselves are eloquent. Things thing, as Heidegger says, including technical things. Depending on their degree of complexity, technical devices of communication can speak volumes.[173] That was one of the basic ideas that was always floating around in the Berlin Institute for Language in the Technological Age. A Steenbeck was not just a film editing suite for 16mm and 35mm film, but also an aggregate for complex narratives. In the course of discovering Structuralism, the idea that technical things can be "read" arose; not as an ideology but as a source of ideas for a basic method of working. The intense interplay between the act of taking apart and putting back together again is not merely a possibility to make linguistic systems transparent and transformable. If we master this technique it can help us to understand "the game of generating new knowledge" upon which "experimental systems" [the systems in which experiments are conducted][174] are based, which in a variety of disciplines are referred to as research. Naturally, the arts that take up the challenge of experimenting are included here.

---

173   A quarter of a century ago [1985] I devoted an entire monograph to one media-historically attractive artifact; see Zielinski (2010).
174   Rheinberger (2001), p. 27.

Technology, understood in the material sense as a sensational artifact, is produced by a variety of activities in which parts of nature are initially taken apart according to a specific plan, in certain cases right down to the smallest particles; then we arrive at conditions which are only accessible through nanotechnology or are electronic, dynamic. The components are then assembled in an order which is not the same as their previous one. In such transformation processes the imperfections of natural things are carried over into the artificiality of the new order; these are the most exciting moments of an experiment.

Perfection does not exist in nature and it does not exist in technology. We know only of attempts to approach the highest possible precision. Henry Petroski, who with *The Pencil* has produced an admirable case study of a seemingly humble artifact, cites David Pye: "Everything we design and make is an improvisation, a lash-up, something inept and provisional." This "ubiquitous imperfection" of technical things and systems induces us to modify our concept. I advocate a philology as exact as possible of nonperfect precise things, which will be devised and developed to support communications with others, to facilitate them, to make them a sensational, even perhaps scandalous happening. This philology is not interested in the systemic function of things.

Like Benjamin, Giedion also carried around a major unfinished work with him in which he wanted to describe the shifts that the nineteenth century had brought about in the mental states of the subjects. *Die Entstehung des heutigen Menschen* (*The Origin of Present-day People*) was conceived as an attempt to understand a pivotal period in the history of civilization through the objects constructed by humans.[175] This means that Giedion ascribes media functions to technical artifacts. What the people who

175   Cf. Georgiadis (1989), p. 18f.

designed and built them knew and wanted is passed on through these things. Because scientific, technical, as well as design thinking and reasoning is objectified, they can be understood as *Denkdinge* (thought things).[176] They provide food for thought. They are thought-provoking and are capable of changing our way of thinking and our aesthetic sensibilities. To listen to the tales they tell, to read these narratives in the artifacts themselves, is something that connects our kind of philologist with the alchemists.

In the indissoluble unity of theory and practice an identity of alchemy was prominent where work on the particular did not need any strategic generalization. The "immense variety of things 'that are not, and cannot be; but that have been imagined and believed'"[177] went through amazing developments by virtue of the wildly proliferating sphere of imagination and experiments with nature; probably its last flowering before the civilization of European Modernity commenced its relentless work of standardization and universalization. The production of concrete results, despite boundless imagination and factoring in the possibility of failure, was a necessary part of this culture of experiment. Punishments for misperformance by the royal rulers who invited the adepts and sorcerer's apprentices to their courts and financed them were drastic and could even be lethal.

The theory and practice of alchemy in early Modern times served the (self-) understanding of a subject who was still unsure, indeterminate and rather provisional, and who sought a relation to the other — that which was not yet understood, including nature — which was both rational and frictional. The cosmos crackled with atmospheric noise and to listen to it was exhilarating. Acoustically, it projected itself via natural phenomena and the

---

176   Here I use a different term to Rheinberger, because his "epistemic things" have a specific meaning: the new knowledge generated by an experiment.
177   Charles Mackay (1995), p. 100.

227

auditory system into the souls of the adepts. They had decided in favor of participating in the world and not just observing it. A new model for experiencing and working on the world: when alchemy was understood in this way it did not only point back to a magical past but also forward to a possible future. Our exact (as possible) philology of (nonperfect) precise things feels comfortable in this tradition. Artifacts and their connections are not only read as evidence of a distant past, that is, examined archaeologically, but also investigated in order to understand the "game of generating new knowledge," as Rheinberger calls today's scientific experiment,[178] that is, prospective, forward-looking.

Alchemy was "a dream one could only listen to, and in recounting it one could only stammer. When people were no longer able to dream at their firesides and listen to themselves in material things, the dream of alchemy retreated back into the night."[179] It is worthwhile to undertake the experiment of reactivating the dream at the current state of our knowledge of the world. This would correspond to the *cultura experimentalis* that I described above in connection with the arts. The cosmic, or however we wish to call the general, which is indispensable for establishing an individual's identity, is articulated in various ways in things; in the manner in which they are put together, mixed, and formed. It is up to us to verbalize what the things themselves are not aware of, to make it sing, hum, or stammer.

In artistic experiments, this is being and has been done with impressive success. "The rushing sound that we had heard earlier in the air was familiar; it was not in the air now, it was with us. In the depths of the forest it continued without respite, swelling up as branches and twigs crashed to the ground. What made it more terrible was

---

178   Rheinberger (2001), p. 27.
179   Fierz-David (1952), p. 132.

that everything else did not move at all. Nothing of the shiny glitter moved, not a twig, not a pine needle.... We stood still and looked; I don't know whether it was admiration or dread to drive into the thing." These strange sentences are from Adalbert Stifter's icy story, published in *Die Mappe meines Urgrossvaters* (*My great-grandfather's notebook*). The composer and director Heiner Goebbels used them as the springboard for his production *Stifters Dinge* (*Stifter's things*) of 2007. In a dense fabric of associations, from the "thing-becoming" of landscapes, various vocal artifacts of William Burroughs, Malcolm X, or Claude Lévi-Strauss, to fantastic projections of image artifacts and a spectacular mechanical theater, an artform unfolds and develops for which there is still no name. What the label Media art once denoted this piece has left far behind. The venue where it is performed is not a classic theater, nor a museum or gallery. In a laboratory of hearing and seeing which is open to the public, *Stifters Dinge* confronts us with the shifts that have taken place at the borderline between media-people and media-machines. In the space where the performance takes place there are no staff; only two people who set it up at the beginning. On a huge platform at the back of the space, overturned upright and grand pianos play music automatically, controlled by computers. During the performance the platform moves slowly, at first imperceptibly, toward where the audience is sitting. Exactly at the end of the piece the platform with its mechanical ensemble stops right in front of the visitors. One can almost see it taking a bow; but in any case it gets an enthusiastic ovation for its grandiose performance.

In *Coro Spezzato: The Future Lasts One Day* (2009) the Sicilian artist Rosa Barba, who lives in Berlin, connects five optomechanical film projectors which perform a complex choreography. They speed up and slow down in a prescribed aesthetic order whereby they generate very different individual noises. The projectors project text fragments on the wall which are taken in part from a Venetian choral work of the late Renaissance. The artist has dissected and reworked them into poetic polyphony. The running projectors fulfill their technical function (almost) perfectly. They act like a choir which draws lyrical attention to itself in the rhythmic, changing text fragments.

The South Korean artist Yunchul Kim works in a completely different way, but also with poetic energy and precision. In recent years he has made a series of complex artifacts that combine heterogeneous materials, liquids, colors, chemicals, and different metals that through computer-aided interventions of the artist, (which are also acts of interpreting the material) transform into kinetic artifacts that produce sounds. *Epiphora* (2009/2010), which translates as unstoppable tears, has crossed the boundary between natural and technical things. Although they are in separate containers within the exhibition space, magnetic-sensitive fluids appear to communicate with each other over distances in a mysterious way. Inside the main attraction of this work, seemingly uncontrolled overflowing reactions constantly take place within a branching glass pipe that I recognize as similar to forms shown in early Modern treatises on alchemy. This hybrid of hard mechanical and supple vital parts, located somewhere between principle and accident, appears prone to recurrent states of hysteria.

The artifact *oK* (2009) is also situated in this precarious terrain and Kim calls it a symptom generator. According to the artist, it is a pataphysical machine. Kim has invented a technical object constructed from computer scrap metal that looks like the structure of DNA transformed into a sculpture. The thing vibrates, sings, hisses and crackles; it behaves like an electrical organ. The viewer can examine this techno-aesthetic sensation installed under a glass dome like a patient being asked about their health. Under observation, the lively artifact constantly changes from one state to another.

As a scientist, Arianna Borrelli, a quantum physicist and doctor of philosophy from Rome, dances the difficult movements that the practice of thing-philology most elegantly requires. Her masterpiece to date is a study of the astrolabe of the Latin High Middle Ages with its connections also to the traditions of Arab-Islamic science. With reference to modern scientific method, she first makes a rigorous distinction between the mathematical, the technical and practical, and the philosophical aspects of this fascinating device that has been called an ancient analog computer. After further study of the texts, however, Borrelli finds that these strict divisions are not helpful. The three aspects are merely different hermeneutic tools used to describe a single complex instrument, and they clearly overlap in its genesis. Thus in many respects the astrolabe turns out to be an instrument for communication that does not necessarily have to be spoken or written down. In philosophical terms it can be read as a world machine (*machina mundi*) in the sense employed by Vitruvius, which makes it possible to apprehend the laws of the universe. It is also conceivable as a device to calculate movements taking place in time, of time cycles that can be experienced on Earth which are influenced or caused by celestial constellations, as a geometrical measuring instrument, as an algorithmic artifact, or as a mechanical device for measuring time.[180]

The three aspects can only be developed in Borrelli's study as equal, reciprocal, hermeneutic tools. This is because Borrelli is able to think and deal confidently and competently with the scientific, technical, and practical aspects, including those of an aesthetic and philosophical nature. This is a distinguishing feature of other deep time

---

180   See Borrelli (2008).

231

studies by the physicist-philosopher. She has investigated the thermometer, the connections between pneumatics and the alchemy of weather, why wind exists and why it blows, as well as especially challenging themes involving mathematics and geometry, such as crystallography, and mathematical notations as the specific philosophical tools of preeminent scientists like Isaac Newton and René Descartes.[181]

Borrelli's research "workshop" in recent years has been mainly the Berlin Max Planck Institute for the History of Science. It is above all Rheinberger's achievement that an expanded conception of what science understands by an experiment has been developed at this institute. The research projects that the biologist and translator of Derrida's *Grammatology* into German has initiated and implemented revolve around an idea that makes all the difference. Here the experiment is like a "search engine" that facilitates what could be described as a fortuitous finding. Starting from the premise that at the beginning of a project "one doesn't know exactly what one doesn't know" (otherwise one wouldn't need to do the research anyway), Rheinberger sets up the laboratory as an open and adventurous space of possibilities where provision is made "for producing unpredictable events." By following a specific plan, differences or variable aspects, are produced.[182]

The porosity of the boundaries between artistic, cultural, scientific, technological, and philosophical questions is inherent in this concept. A concept of an experimental culture arises that some authors, like Bruno Latour, take to such extremes that all of social reality becomes a laboratory, a view I do not subscribe to or find useful. That which is still referred to as "society" has

---

181 Arianna Borrelli's work has been published, for example, in our *Variantology* book series on deep time relations of arts, sciences, and technologies; see Zielinski (2005–2011).
182 Rheinberger (2007), p. 87.

degenerated into a test department wherein practicing for an emergency constantly takes place. The emergency case is to avoid differences and not to produce them, the achievement of uniformity for what threatens to drift apart and not the generation of diversities. The test department has nothing to do with the respect for thought things and natural things which both underpin and drive the *culture of experiment*, as a 2004 anthology in German co-edited by Henning Schmidgen is titled.[183] The idea of a space of possibilities where both the inputs and outcomes are not unequivocally defined is as far as possible from a policy of cybernetic short-circuiting that distinguishes the cultural technique of testing.

Schmidgen, whose doctoral dissertation investigates the concepts of a machine in Deleuze, Guattari, and Lacan, addresses in his exact case studies technical setups and artifacts in which the measurement of time plays an important role. His main interest is directed at the minimal, sometimes dramatic, events that can suddenly prevent the execution of a plan, the unpredictable. "It is precisely in the inconsistencies, the resistances, and frictions, which arise while handling experimental systems and repeatedly force the experimenter to make interventions, that the epistemic potentials of the structure lie," as the anonymous author of the introduction of *Kultur im Experiment* states (probably Schmidgen himself). The conditions under which an experiment is conducted, its location, architecture and acoustics, the individual properties of the instruments used, and many other factors not only greatly influence the objects under study, but at the same time those who are conducting the experiment.

These are considerations that we have encountered before in connection with cinema and the apparatus heuristics of the early 1970s; the period in which Deleuze and

---

183 The title is *Kultur im Experiment*, eds. H. Schmidgen, P. Geimer, and S. Dierig.

Guattari wrote their first work on the relationship between capitalism and schizophrenia, *Anti-Oedipus*. No apparatus is neutral. Technology does not determine aesthetic and ideological perception, but it is an active component of a process in which interactions between technological and nontechnological aspects constantly take place.

A history of science and technology that is open, via the culture of experiment, for issues of communication and aesthetics, is one of the possibilities in the immediate future to advance theories of the media. Perhaps the proponents of such implicit media theories will not be accredited historians of science, but is that important? For whom would it be important? Today media technology pervades nearly all scientific processes on a massive scale, particularly experiments, as well as other prerequisites for producing, evaluating, and disseminating scientific findings. To know one's way around at the interface with media conditionality is no more scandalous today than it was to engage seriously, as a philologist-to-be, with Spaghetti Westerns, comics, or audiovisual magazines in the 1960s and 1970s.

Such an envisaged expansion can also have effects in the opposite direction. Media theory that is not only open to the history of science and technology but also deploys its philological expertise within these fields will likely be in a better position to understand communicative processes and much more. For centuries, science and technology have played a pivotal role in these processes. Media theory can also provide communicative processes with thought-provoking input and particularities that are valuable additions in an age of undecided identities, of horizontal vagueness, of over-colorful and blatant spectacles. With regard to technical things of communication they could also be understood from the perspective that the best way to critique a book that has been written is always to write a better one.

Henri Chopin, object from the series *Graphpoemachines*, May 2006
(Archivio F. Conz, Verona, 2006), n. p.

Kittler's philological studies that extend into technology and its mathematical foundations may sometimes be inexact and effusively metaphorical with regard to technical details of the actual artifacts and systems that he deals with. But his interdiscursive analyses still hold a great power of fascination, particularly with regard to their intimation of possible connections with philosophical, historical, psychoanalytical, and aesthetic dimensions. For the generation of academics that came immediately after Kittler, his writings possess a very strong suggestive potential.

Some of Kittler's former aides and collaborators are systematically advancing the concept of the technical and media *a priori* in media theory. The archive specialist and media theorist Wolfgang Ernst's engagement with material devices is so dedicated that he has even installed a laboratorial museum and workshop for time machines at the Berlin Humboldt University. With *Kulturtechnik* (cultural technique) Bernhard Siegert adapts a concept that emerged in the 1980s in the course of engaging with Birmingham Cultural Studies.[184] Peter Berz and Claus Pias are pursuing their own individual paths through the labyrinth of interactions between literature, science, and technology. After receiving his PhD for a dissertation on the standardization of machine technology around 1900, and researching the early years of high speed projectile photography, Berz focuses on possible creative interdependencies among biology, history, and philosophy (morphogenesis, mimicry). Pias is developing into a respected humanities expert on cybernetics and epistemological issues of the digital. As a former programmer and trained electrotechnician Pias is one of the few contemporary theorists with a thoroughgoing knowledge

---

184   In the final chapter of my book *Zur Geschichte des Videorecorders* (History of Videorecording) of 1985 I discuss in depth the utilization of this audiovisual time machine as a *Kulturtechnik*.

of machine languages and their command structures. In this still relatively new tradition, Bernhard Dotzler from the Center for Literary and Cultural Research Berlin already published an unconventional media-philological study in 1996. In taking as his starting point that what was written and published in the seventeenth and eighteenth centuries consisted mainly of mathematics transformed into text, Dotzler makes a thorough investigation of the reciprocal connections between communication and control in the development of paper machines for computing.

Dotzler's starting point (adapted from Turing) that everything for which an algorithm exists can also be constituted as a machine, is used again ten years later by David Link for a very special purpose. Link is also a philologist and philosopher who, in addition to the art of interpretation, has taught himself computer languages. His particular archaeology of algorithmic artifacts seeks to identify the mathematical and informatics command structures in technical things which to laypersons do not appear as being algorithmically constructed devices. The high point of his study on artifacts that attempt to generate ultimate truths using rotating letters or characters is a meticulous analysis of a thought-thing called a Zâ'irajah, which was described in 1377 by Abd ar-Rahmān Ibn Khaldūn in his *Muqaddimah*, a universal history of the world in seven volumes, but which in fact has far older origins. The Zâ'irajah, which at first sight looks a bit like a mysterious astrological mandala, is revealed by Link to be a *machina mundi* of a special kind. With its help it is possible to ask simple questions about the world and to get answers in rhyme. The artifact proves to be not only a poetry machine, but something more: a kind of master model of cryptological, knowledge-generating machines — from Ramon Llull and Alberti to the Enigma of the twentieth century.[185]

---

185   See Link (2010), p. 215ff.

Link's particular philology of precise things, however, goes a considerable step further in its methodology. I am not aware of any comparable studies which have the same practical consequences for art. His analytical case studies can become prolegomena for installations that are at the same time experimental systems. In an earlier project, his in-depth study of poetological grammars leads to the construction of a *poetry machine* that is able to generate poems and lyrics for rock songs on the basis of semantic affinities between different kinds of texts. And in his *Loveletters* project, Link succeeds in doing something that would have made the Bletchley Park computer buffs look over his shoulder with curiosity and admiration. While searching for early examples of texts that had been mainly generated by computers, Link came across the fact that with "the first industrially produced computer," the Ferranti Mark 1 (its forerunner was the Manchester Mark 1 developed at Manchester University), texts were generated "that are intended to express and arouse emotions." In the course of his investigation Link discovered the program for *Loveletters* among the papers of its author Christopher Strachey, but found only scant documentation on how the Ferranti Mark 1 functioned. It seemed it would be impossible to study the program for loveletters in operation. Link then constructed an emulator which duplicated the functions of the Ferranti Mark 1, built a replica of the console and user interface, and made it possible to run the *Loveletters* program again, here and today.[186]

This is how far media theory as a variant of an exact philology of precise things can go when it is capable of explicitly intervening in technological practice. The part of a complex machine of 1952 that was expressly designed to communicate feelings has been saved from

---

186   The process is described in detail in Link (2006), pp. 15–42; the emulator can be found on David Link's website: http://alpha60.de/research/muc/.

oblivion in a maximal form. In its new environment the program again runs within the framework of the special aesthetic and apparatus accentuations of the philologist, philosopher, and artist Link. The history of science and technology from this perspective is not just a collection of what has been. It is an aggregate of possible states in the past, of the installation of what also could have been, and what definitely is in the present.

In one of their most recent series, Dinos and Jake Chapman carefully overpaint parts of watercolors purportedly painted by Adolf Hitler adding colorful artistic elements. With their intervention they make these originally amateurish artifacts, allegedly painted by an art academy reject, into sought-after attractions on the contemporary art market. If Hitler had applied to art school with these paintings, from today's perspective he would probably have been accepted and the history of the twentieth century might have taken a different course, perhaps a less horrific one than that which millions had to suffer. The British siblings think this idea is ridiculous because it propagates the ludicrously overrated value ascribed to the opinion of artists or juries as to what is good or bad art. Yet with *If Hitler Had Been a Hippy How Happy Would We Be,* Dinos and Jake Chapman allow us to think about the subjunctive tense for the past — in a grotesque manner but at the same time unafraid. With the aid of a prospective archaeology it is possible to carry aspects of this forward into the future.

4. Be *Offline* and Exist *Online*

No More Secondhand God
Buckminster Fuller, 1963

On the Way Things Go

If one casually says the words that the abbreviation "PC" stands for, they sound remarkably antiquated. Although computers in Europe only came into service in mass twenty-five years ago, the concept of a personal computer gives the overwhelming impression that it is a concept from the past.

On the one hand, devices driven by algorithms and microelectronics have gotten very close to the bodies of their users, certainly comparable with the functions of Oswald Wiener's *Bio-Adapter*. In the 1980s the mouse that nestles in the hand and glides over the table or the mouse pad began to gradually render the alphanumeric keyboard obsolete, at least for GUI users. The ever-ready users, always on standby, carry the latest interface for the mobile terminals close to their bodies before it disappears inside the body in the next step. The smooth, rounded artifacts of communication snuggle into the hand. Their flat, translucent displays are caressed with the fingertips, as though they are the porous skin that covers another's body. One wakes up to them in the morning, and for many people they are the last things they touch before going to sleep at night, for example, when they want their constant electronic companion to wake them up. The small, dynamic data packages with techno-sensual access organize people's private lives as well as work, study, and school.

The office, and therefore management, is ubiquitous. Life is managed administratively. The artifacts have

241

become intimate appendages of biological life forms: they help them to cope with techno-logical reality and facilitate their orientation within it. These artifacts are an integral part of the paradise aggregates that we require to live harmoniously with the world and in order that the world can tolerate us to some degree. The "pleasure suit" (Wiener — *Glücksanzug*) is today called an interface, although I prefer the more dramatic German word: *Schnittstelle* (point of intersection; cutting point).

On the other hand, there is nothing personal about computers any longer. They have ceased to be autonomous stations for work and for amusement like the Atari ST (Sixteen/Thirty-two) or the C (Commodore) 64 on which we cut our computing teeth and the PCs that came afterwards. The algorithmic prostheses of today are no longer independent units. No matter where the users of contemporary digital notebooks and workstations happen to be, they are connected to telematic hubs for giving and receiving instructions, ordering, distributing, informing, and for propaganda. As a rule, much of the data that inhabits the devices is personally encoded, and only means something to the device's owner. But the individual machines are no longer terminals; they function as interfaces of a telecommunication and informatics system to which many others are connected at the same time and who engage to a greater or lesser extent in dialog with or against each other or are just casual users. They are fast-flowing conduits for information and communication processes. Here the individual laptop, PowerBook, or their smaller, more mobile variants without their own hard disks, are individual connections within *dispositifs* effusively dubbed "social networks." The word "social" stems from the Latin "socius," which in the adjectival form is reduced to its original meaning; namely, being a participant, consorting with others, being in a relationship of reciprocal exchange — no more, no less.

The users are operating updating machines. The individual devices function as convenient and temporary receptacles for a myriad of other artifacts of a programmed kind, the applications. Apps are only used when needed. Their particularity consists in instantaneous realization. Just as the first hundred years of cinema established a particular variant that involved paying a certain sum of money to rent designed and shaped time, players in the telematic networks pay for software updates to their application programs. The applications have left the various hardware devices and are imported as needed. Programs are now service providers on loan; they are treated like guest workers or leased laborers. The hardware devices are increasingly designed and configured as casings for using the so-called social networks, which are developing into the contemporary marketplaces.

Does this updating really signify an activation of the present? There has never been so much remembering and so much biography as in the age of the technologies of oblivion. At present, the future is planned with great immediacy as that which one will remember or should remember: it is becoming binding. One phenomenon is particularly strange which, by modifying the name of an appliance of 1967 manufactured by Ampex called "Instant Replay" and continuing Vilém Flusser's idea concerning electronic recording technology, we could call it "instant archaeology."[187]

This cultural technique, which was developed at the end of the 1960s for professional elites, sporting activities, and for work processes involving fine motor skills, is now a mass phenomenon. It is particularly conspicuous in digital photography. Because the time between

---

187 "Instant philosophy" is the heading we assigned to a section in Flusser's *Bochumer Vorlesungen* (Flusser 2008, p. 179f.), which engages with the speculative qualities of video. Annika Kuhlmann recently completed a thesis at the Berlin University of the Arts entitled *Instant Nostalgies*. My thanks to her for our discussions.

recording the image and playback is so short, anyone can get to see what they looked like just a few seconds ago, and with this knowledge they make a face so as to be forearmed for the next picture. Young people practice this real-time archaeology to an extreme degree. Platforms such as YouTube or MySpace are the playgrounds for the excesses of this cultural technique.

Is this really a form of remembering at all or merely a slight stretching of the present moment into the past? Is this not a kind of pro-spective archaeology or even an advanced form of "de-membering?"[188] Instant archaeology is not concerned with looking back, but looking through what has just transpired while looking forward. Yet to already be the subject of a past event in the instant that something happens is tantamount to abolishing the present. The present becomes merely an extremely short effect for the future; a miniscule, no longer quantifiable amount of time; simply a moment of updating. The extreme shortening of storage times coupled with simultaneous expansion to near-infinite storage capacity have not led to the past being forgotten; rather, the facility of enjoying the present is the victim. There's no time for that anymore. Future and past are joined together directly and effectively.

Essentially, this means the implementation of cybernetic ideas in a psycho-social context. The increasing ability to perform an "instantaneous calculation of highly complex interactions" was already identified by Zbigniew Brzezinski in 1970 as a principal characteristic of a "technetronic society." Now that the willingness and the necessity to engage in social interaction have become required qualifications in job descriptions, immediacy as an ability is the next "greatest good" in the indirect handling of technical communication.

---

188 German: *entinnern*; for more on this neologism, see Bartels (2000), pp. 7–16.

Nevertheless: The *YouTube therefore you are* of the contemporary modern era, which many theorists continue to call "postmodern" for lack of a better term (which means that modernity is still in crisis), is progress compared to the conceitedness of *cogito ergo sum* (I think therefore I am) of the classical modern era. Lacan's reservations about the logical consistency of the relation between the thinking and the being "I" are spectacularly confirmed by the technologically based everyday rituals of the late twentieth century. It can also be the starting point for action that has long since been fully aware of the impossibility of sovereign subjectivity. All the more so as the fragmented subjectivities are confronted by material worlds that are just as fragmented. The notion of a closed bloc of the hegemonial was always a chimera, just like the idea of a powerful subject as the center of the universe. The notion of a fragile subject, however, could be useful, the concept of a floating and oscillating identity, as proposed by Gianni Vattimo. By this the Italian philosopher understands a weak subject; in my view, such a subject can only derive its vital force from its relationship to the Other, and in this way can also become a strong subject through the Other. Many good ideas are paradoxical.

The "you" advances to become the center of attention, be it only as an electrified "you." Vilém Flusser, intellectually trained in Martin Buber's philosophy of dialog, in the last years of his life defined this as a possibility for the individual to get closer to God again after He had so completely hidden His face in Auschwitz. In this variant of Jewish religious philosophy, the encounter with "you" (or "thou") is the only possibility of beholding the countenance of God. In terms of a telematic network this would mean for Flusser from monitor to monitor, from one terminal to another, if there is mutual affection:

245

"Only by loving my neighbor I can love God. Then the only admissible image is the face of the Other. But the synthetic image is the other person; [...] through the computer image, I can talk to the other person: he sends me his image, I work on it and send it back to him — so this is the Jewish image. This is not an idol. This is not paganism. It is a way I love my neighbor, and by loving my neighbor, to love God. I am not a good Talmudist, but I would say that from a Talmudic point of view, the synthetic computer image is perfectly Jewish."[189]

This is how Vilém Flusser conceived telematic dialog before it became a mass phenomenon in reality. The concrete quality of the synthetic images that Flusser has in mind remains obscure. He did not go into more detail in any of his other texts. But these cannot be representational images either from the perspective of his theological argument or from the point of view of media theory. From the narrative experiment *Vampyrotheutis infernalis*, which is also — even without the illustrations by Louis Bec — a tale told in images, we can only deduce that it concerns visual artifacts that produce a different reality than the one outside of images that we know; science fictions, for example.

In his last film, the British filmmaker Chris Petit masterfully staged the mood of those people who, twenty years after the establishment of the Internet, seek dialog with a fictitious counterpart on a daily basis. At first sight *Content* (2009) is still driven by the notion that camera and automobile are two devices that originate from the same *dispositif* context. On the other hand the film remains entirely inside a private and intimate living space, actually even inside the apparatus of telematic communication. In this sense *Content* is at once a road movie and a home movie.

---

189   Vilém Flusser interviewed by László Beke and Miklós Peternák (1990); the interview is in (Flusser 2010).

"Just once, for one day in my life, I would like to feel that I and everyone speaking to me, were talking full sense."

"I would like to fall in love before it's too late, don't care who with."

"I would like a feeling of assignation to life, not sitting here calculating how many fucks I have got left. The middle-ground is hardly there anymore."

The middle-ground — in a temporal perspective that is the present. Petit's young characters move in front of the camera, which in the passage from *Content* quoted above is a simulated webcam, as though they are in a strange hall of mirrors where they perpetually encounter different people who all want to snatch their image. They style themselves for total visibility while at the same time trying to hide inside it; under the brims of hats, behind cascades of hair falling over their eyes, behind oversize sunglasses, by turning their heads to present their faces in semi-profile. Such games of hide-and-seek are familiar to us — under completely different historic circumstances — from the existentialist shadow figures in John Cassavetes' early films *Shadows* (1958) and *Faces* (1968). "Technologies of the self"[190] is what Michel Foucault calls such regimented exercises in identity. Andy Warhol's Factory in New York was the ideal laboratory for developing attitudes and poses of this kind.

"I'll be your mirror" is the soundtrack to this quest for another identity, composed by Lou Reed in 1966 for Velvet Underground and sung inspirationally by Nico, the icon of Andy Warhol's factory: "I'll be your mirror / Reflect what you are, in case you don't know / I'll be the wind, the rain and the sunset / The light on your door to show that you're home [...] Let me stand to show that you are blind / Please put down your hands / 'cos I see you." The imaginary overcoming of

---

190   Discussed in the context of the Internet in Campanelli (2010), p. 173.

Lacanian separations, the cause of so much pain, through the romantic reunion of the gazes of the one and the Other, the Other and the one, at least in an ecstatic moment of rock poetry.

At the height of the Vietnam War, William Burroughs formulated the reason why the Romantic ideal had to be broken in post-Romanticism via the *dispositif* of the technological. The hot-wiring of the cybernetic loop of human and technology-based systems is the focus of his polemic *Electronic Revolution*, the cover of which features a stray dog shitting electrical cables. "Consider the *IS* of identity. When I say to be me, to be you, to be myself, to be others — whatever I may be called upon to be or to say that I am — I am not the verbal label "myself." The word *be* in the English language contains, as a virus contains, its precoded message of damage, the categorical imperative of permanent condition. To be a body, to be nothing else, to stay a body. [...] If you see the relation of the I to the body as the relation of a pilot to his ship, you see the full crippling force of the reactive mind command to be a body. Telling the pilot to be the plane, then who will pilot the plane?"[191]

A conclusion that be could reached after superficially and cynically observing the lives of young contemporaries in European and North American technology-based societies is that while having a great familiarity with others they are simultaneously at pains to be alien to each other. A militant and radical extension of a rhetorical figure of Agamben's the French theory group *Tiqqun* enthusiastically celebrates such singularity that is arbitrary. Formulated as critique of the effects of cybernetics-based power, such a notion of singularity carries the danger of changing into fascistic actions. Radical arbitrariness does

---

191   William S. Burroughs, Electronic Revolution, also available online: http://archive.groovy.net/dl/elerev2.html accessed10/22/2012.

248

not admit any responsibility toward the other person. It is prepared to jeopardize the inviolacy of the individual.

To be sure, those who spend their work hours and spare time in social networks do not form a *societas* in any traditional sense of a binding communication community. All communication has its roots in the experience of blockages, breaks, separations, and deficits. The connected individuals, however, cannot possibly be completely random singularities, because with all its attractive user interfaces and endorsements the telematic *dispositif* has long since had an identity-generating function for them. Through their techno-communicative activity with each other they constitute a community to which they have a positive relationship; just how they want it. However, it can degenerate into attitudes of arbitrariness in the sense of subservient caprice when the telematic aspect is the only thing that lends the community temporary stability in its perpetual updating.

Every generation creates its own paradises, and every generation needs its own access to the non-locations of aspiration and promise once called utopias; they have every right to this. The common inhabitants of the so-called social networks are effective product endorsers, disseminators, and products. But they are also solitary individuals who are seeking meaningful occupations for themselves and above all respectful attachments which go far beyond the statistical expectations of friendship and moments of happiness that they experience every day. They do not want to be merely associates within a functional mechanical network where the best possible sensation they can have is to be permanently wired. Their communicative activities are driven by the hope that the friendships in the technical beyond can perhaps be extended into the here and now of an experience. That there is perhaps someone on the other side who is capable of listening and who speaks a language that is not the same as that of the hard-nosed integrators and minute takers.

The individuals who are interwoven with and lost in the techno-social networks may also be looking for reflections of the innumerable splinters of their largely unspectacular egos. (For spectacles the tiny displays are hardly suitable). The central attraction of their activities, on the other hand, is the longing for a counterpart to their own existence and actions, is the "you," to be acknowledged by "your" gaze even when the concrete formulation of this gaze is only a projection.

One does not necessarily have to call this a search for a single deity, or the one God. Yet if one understands the world of the Other in such a way that God is manifest "in every smile, in every caress, and naturally in every special act of peace or every special act of tenderness" as the Fluxus artist Wolf Vostell once said in a conversation,[192] then one can use that big word here. The postwar avant-garde self-evidently equated life with art, and many people still find this admirable. Why do we react, then, with incomprehension to those who have grown up in digital culture when they declare communication and life to be identical?

Hegel's *Elements of the Philosophy of Right* is one of the most fruitful texts for the rigorous definition of philosophical concepts that Germany has produced. In a supplement to the chapter on the state (§ 270) Hegel makes a differentiation that I have adapted for the following Manifesto. The differentiation is between "existing" and "being." Not only in Heidegger's philosophy does this play an important role, as the differentiation between *existentia* and *essentia*, between merely extant and unconditional being. This pairing, straddling the different notions of what is essential, runs through the history of Western thought.

---

192   In Vostell, *Leben=Kunst=Leben* (1993), p. 145.

In Hegel's *Philosophy of Right*, the difference concerns the question as to if and how the individual is connected to the whole, whether this connectedness to the whole is perceived and reflected as a necessity, or whether its particularity is seen as sufficient; that is, simply to exist: "Actuality is always the unity of universality and particularity, the resolution of universality into particularity; the latter then appears to be self-sufficient, although it is sustained and supported only by the whole. If this unity is not present, nothing can be *actual*, even if it may be assumed to have *existence*."[193]

Looking at the so-called social networks of the Internet, which play a similar role for young people today as the state did for Hegel, I distinguish on the one hand between living a life that amounts to little more than engaging in technology-based communication and at the same time through this act seeks to constitute itself with reference to the obscure "net community," and on the other hand, the type of being that is aware of the interwovenness of its communicative activities and in a broad sense can realize itself relatively independently from them without adhering to any disastrous notions of essential unities. I distinguish between a subject that, by and large, merely functions (and is therefore subjected), and an individual who has the courage to be self-possessed at times and and other times has the ability to escape the self, which from the perspective of dialogic philosophy presupposes intentional communication with the Other, including in (technical) experiments.

If one understands the two modes as gradations on a scale, existence relates more to the universal in the particular, whereas for being it is a priority to perceive the

---

193 Hegel, Grundlinien der Philosophie des Rechts, Dritter Teil: Die Sittlichkeit, Dritter Abschnitt: Der Staat. Zusatz zu § 270, in: G.W. Hegel (Frankfurt 1986), vol. 7, p. 428f; English edition: Georg Wilhelm Friedrich Hegel, Elements of the Philosophy of Right, ed. Allen W. Wood, trans. H.B. Nisbet, Cambridge University Press, 1991, § 270, p. 302.

particular in the universal. God can exist, but not be. Humans are, but they cannot merely exist. This is also a question of the awareness of time, which is closely tied to the machines for communication. To exist on the Internet means first and foremost to act and perceive in the *actualitas* mode, to participate techno-psychologically in updating. Deep time experience of being contains updates, but is not absorbed by them.

In my Manifesto, I discuss some fundamental prerequisites for this differentiation to remain effective for individuals, or to become effective again. At the calendrical onset of the new millennium, *The Cluetrain Manifesto* (2000) proclaimed that under the conditions of the digital networks all business markets are conversations. By contrast I maintain that not all conversations must inevitably be markets.

In formulating my thoughts, several texts that seek to formulate theory in an appellative form were a great help. In May 1983, Giorgio Cesarano published his tribute to Georges Bataille. In 98 items, his pamphlet revolves around the changes in the subject's mental state in a situation subject to the hegemony of productivity mania/delusions. "The object par excellence is the fictitious subject, the sublimated commodity, which coheres only in a form of emptiness. A body, it is a stand, an empty one, the brand of the self. That which one speaks is the sound, the soundtrack of emptiness. With or without a guitar, every song is the feature that fosters absence, that celebrates the omnipotence of the past and the have-not-been, inseparable from the apology of future credit. Thus being is established exclusively in remembrance."[194]

The title of my Manifesto is a *hommage* to two works from the heyday of the age of industrialisation: Baron Richard von Krafft-Ebing's *Psychopathia sexualis*

---

194 Cesarano (1983), § 61, p. 72f.

[Sexual Psychopathy] (1886) and Oskar Panizza's *Psichopatia criminalis* (1898). In his meticulously detailed study of sexual deviance, the psychiatrist and forensic scientist Krafft-Ebing succeeds admirably in maintaining a balance between the multifarious phenomena of deviancy and the scientist's idea to achieve integration. Panizza's pamphlet, modeled on Krafft-Ebing's book, on the surface purports to be a guide to identifying the energies and manifestations of criminality, but actually emerges as an unconscionable manual about melancholy, agony, lachrymosity, and paranoia as the inevitable consequences of being subordinated to authority. "Only when they have communication with the infected, with no-hopers, [...], with left-wing liberals, with the previous crop of the lunatic asylum, does the seed begin to grow in the hearts of these young people, some of whom probably once belonged to the Young Men's Christian Association where they sipped the tea of innocence [...] and takes the form of spine-tingling passion for evil," as Panizza writes in the first paragraph about *paralisis cerebri,* the softening of the brain.

Vademecum for the Prevention of *psychopathia medialis* [Manifesto]

1. Arts and theories that possess an affinity to advanced thinking and advanced technologies demand maximum movability. This movability is not the same as the mobility that is demanded of us day in, day out, and proclaimed as an inherent necessity. Movability does not offer itself for exploitation and, in turn, it does not exploit. Our movability gets by with a minimum of possessions — albeit carefully selected ones. It cultivates a life of wandering and attempts to orient itself in the world without prescribed disciplines. It is in the best sense undisciplined. It cannot be disciplined. This is a plea for theory and practice situated in the in-between of disciplines, between staked-out territories, between the *dispositifs* of power, which Michel Foucault identified above all as sexuality, truth, and knowledge. To this we can add the will to unconditional connectivity.

2. Globalization is a concept that is profoundly tied up with economic, cultural, and political power. The word originates from a vocabulary that has nothing to do with particularity and nothing to do with art. Our concern to communicate our work on a worldwide basis, and to carry this through without falling into the trap of such (pre)determinations, means that we need other concepts and other orientations. Poets and philosophers, like Édouard Glissant from Martinique, may be able to provide them rather than political or ideological strategists. Glissant operates with the concept of *mondialité* in contradistinction to *mondialisation*, which characterizes globalization as uniformity. Jacques Derrida also regarded the concept of *mondialité* very highly. *Mondialité* describes a quality of worldwide relationships, which are not defined in terms of their rational purposiveness, but as the "poetry of

relations." Art and theory that are created with the aid of advanced ideas and media could in this sense become "*mondiale*" theory and practice.

3. In case of doubt and with the options available, a risky decision in favor of the possible is more appropriate than a pragmatic decision in favor of reality. The need to make decisions has intensified. Modern science, technology, and art have expended their energies for over 400 years on making the invisible visible and the imperceptible perceptible. Through translating nature into binary data this process is now far advanced in rendering social relations, including their fine structures, systemic. The more that the technological world is programmed to make the impossible possible — namely, to make it function — the more worthwhile it is to attempt confronting the possible with its own impossibilities. This would be an open program as an alternative to establishing cybernetics as a cultural and social technology.

4. In the most advanced societies — advanced meaning societies with industries and services based on technology — we live in a permanent testing situation. Our environment is set up as a test department, which was also the name of a great band (Test Dept) in the 1980s from Glasgow, Scotland. Ideas and concepts that have barely seen the light of day are subjected to trials to test their viability on the market. By contrast, in elaborate artistic processes the experiment takes precedence over the test. Experiments have a high degree of freedom, including the possibility of failure. Tests, on the other hand, are tied to clearly defined purposes and pre-ordained objectives that have to be met. Tests serve to create products. In a test, input and expected output are connected as closely as possible.

5. In the early modern era the attraction of the alchemist's laboratory was not primarily to fabricate shining gold. Rather, the fascination was that they were places where it was possible to gather profound experience of active processes of changing something less than perfect into something more perfect. This process essentially consisted of research. And the transformation of the transformers was just as important as the transformation of matter.

6. Theory and practice of the arts that are realized by media, among other things, should not waste its energy on renovating and restoring the world, but rather on the never-ending experiment, which is never in vain, to create a better world than the one that exists. Because the media-based arts are all time-based arts, which are realized in a space–time continuum, one thing is of prime importance: to give back to those who will look at and enjoy the works some of the time that life has stolen from them (Godard).

7. The enormous amount of effort and energy, which is required to occupy the center of technological and cultural power, is not worth it. Movements at the periphery have greater freedom, give more enjoyment, and hold more surprises in store. Such movements do not preclude the occasional excursion through the center to reach other places on the periphery. On the contrary: living permanently on the periphery is only to be recommended if one knows the center's special qualities well and if one has an idea of how it works. Only then can one really enjoy the movements at the periphery.

8. In more ways than one, at the very least, dual identities are a basic requirement for activists in the field of interdependencies of the arts, the apparatuses, and the

theories associated with them. In economic terms this means to master the tactics of the guerrilla, and to know how the businessman thinks and acts (Pessoa). For those who have to deal with complex apparatuses it is not enough to be a poet and a thinker. In the long term they will need experience in arranging and organizing. Lazy attitudes have no place in the theory and practice of arts that are realized through media.

9. Imagination and mathematics have never been irreconcilable opposites and will not be so in the future. One can use them as two different, complementary possibilities of understanding, analyzing, or — via a third — constructing the world. The highest levels of pure mathematics are only accessible through imagination. And vice versa, imagination does well to not needlessly discard computing and calculating. And in any case, in their respective autonomies, they are inviolable.

10. One does not necessarily have to be an engineer or a programmer to produce exciting and inspirational things and processes through devices. It is, however, a great advantage to know how engineers and programmers think and work. Without respect for the work and working methods of others, complex projects are not possible.

11. For artists who have decided to rigorously engage with advanced technology, it is not sufficient to be merely an operator or a magician. An experimental approach to the world demands acts of intervention as well as actors who are prepared to follow a hands-on approach. The best is: magical operator or operative magician. It is high time to cease regarding what Walter Benjamin formulated over seventy years ago for "The Work of Art in the Age of Mechanical Reproduction" as an antagonism for art processes in the age of their limitless simulability.

12. The social and political macrocosm, just like the microcosm of the individual brain, is determined by great tension, which time and again threatens to pull one or the other apart. One does not have to be a psychiatrist or a psychoanalyst to engage with the theory and practice of art generated by advanced ideas and technologies. However, it is good to know in what ways they act within the stress field consisting of the regulating systems of censorship and the open regions of the imagination. (This is why the psychiatrist and philosopher Hinderk Emrich became one of my most important teachers).

13. The dream is the most powerful mental machine; we cannot regulate them but we can profit from them enormously. Cultivation of one's own dreams is just as important as constant practice at organizing everyday life. We should leave care of others' dreams to others. The activity of interpreting dreams and the activity of controlling dreams are closely related. That is the reason why we mistrust people who want to know what we have dreamed so that they can interpret them.

14. Art produced by advanced ideas and technologies does not necessarily have to increase the mysteriousness of the world. Nor does it necessarily have to increase the amount of what is obvious or self-evident. There is quite enough of both already, without any help from artists and theorists.

15. The difficult balancing act for the visual arts is to enable expression of the invisible using the resources of the visible. This also applies to the acoustic world and the world of poetry: to make what is tonally not imaginable accessible to hearing, and to formulate what is not expressible in language in a formal arrangement that has the greatest possible degree of freedom. The most

important task is to sensibilize, or maintain people's sensibility, for the Other, for that which is not identical to us, for that which is as a principle and in its essence alien, utilizing the means and instruments of aesthetics. This task of art will not change regardless of what media we use to express ourselves.

16. When the various levels of artificial reality (analog instruments, recording devices, computers, programs, digital tools) are mixed together so tightly in aesthetic productions that they become indistinguishable, the necessity of signalizing the technical structure of the various levels — as the classic avant-garde did — recedes into the background. At last all of the design parameters can be brought together in a relationship that plays out in freedom.

17. Perpetually dancing on plateaus that rest on volcanoes misleads people into professional dilettantism and, currently, to veneration of the passionate amateur as the guiding model of aesthetic activity. The courage to ascend vertical heights helps to avoid constantly slipping on the seductively smooth plateaus. However, we need both of these movements, the vertical and the horizontal — as well as an elegant finish to the jump off the cross formed by these two lines. (In remembrance of Dietmar Kamper).

18. The idea that one should save everything that one does or thinks in real-time on the Net is obscene (lifelogging). It is the endeavor to extend a limited lifespan equipped with a limited memory into eternity. The Long Now project, the artificial prolongation of a moment to at least 10,000 years, is equally obscene. In this way, the overtaxed ego of the modern age attempts to save itself for the future. An artificial paradise for the duration can

only be artificial and is a close relative of the prolonged moment induced by drugs that slow down the perception of time. Against this we propose rediscovering the ability to enjoy the present, for example, as a practiced culture of experiment.

19. To avoid an existence that is too caught up within time and is therefore paranoid, and to avoid being too little within time and therefore thinking one is at home on the rings of Saturn in melancholy and bitterness, it is helpful as a principle to cultivate the conscious split. We organize, learn, debate, and amuse ourselves in technological networks. We enthuse, think, enjoy, believe, and trust in autonomous, separate situations, each on his/her own and sometimes with other individuals. This amounts to a balancing act: in a single lifetime we have to learn to exist *online* and be *offline*. If we don't succeed in this, we shall become mere appendages of the world that we have created, merely its technical functions. We should not allow cybernetics, the science of optimal control and predictability of complex events, this triumph.

20. As the young Wittgenstein wrote in *Tractatus logico philosophicus*, subjectivity is an activity at the limit. This has not changed. Not even after the sovereign individual subject of the European modern age has been declared in various ways as dead. On the contrary, only the boundaries have shifted. The fact that such limits exist has not been eliminated.

21. Like heaven and hell, the Internet has no location. Body and mind, however, can only be in one place at a time. To prevent further sacralization of the networks it is useful to develop a profane relationship to them. This can only be done from somewhere located outside of them. Restaurants and taverns have a different quality

of public sphere than marketplaces, concert halls, and stadiums.

22. The Internet is one of the non-locations where physical and mental being squanders itself. The subjects, however strong or weak they are conceived to be, should not give up their willingness to squander gratuitously. However, it is time to think about who profits by this squandering.

23. The greatest impossibility that one can work on at the moment concerns the relations of individuals with each other and, as a consequence, the relations between the many. For Bataille, friendship was a deeply felt alienness in the world that one shares with others. Michel de Montaigne defined friendship, following Aristotle, as a constellation where one soul lives in two different bodies so that neither giving nor taking is an issue. "For table-talk, I prefer the pleasant and witty before the learned and the grave; in bed, beauty before goodness; in common discourse the ablest speaker, whether or not there be sincerity in the case."[195] Relationships between friends are characterized by the absence of any such determination of aims and intent. This absence is not a lack but a reflection of the greatest possible richness of experience. From this impossible point, sociality as a positive experience, as a sensation, is still conceivable — then as now.

---

195   De Montaigne (2005), p. 16.

Select Bibliography of Literature Used and Literature Cited

Adorno, Theodor W., and Max Horkheimer (1968), Kulturindustrie. Aufklärung als Massenbetrug, in: *Dialektik der Aufklärung, Philosophische Fragmente*, Amsterdam; English edition: (2002), *Dialectic of Enlightenment*, ed. G. Schmid Noerr, trans. E. Jephcott, Stanford University Press.

--- in conversation with Karl-Heinz Stockhausen (2008), spring 1960, recorded by the radio broadcaster *Hessischer Rundfunk HR2*, released 22.8.2008.

Agamben, Giorgio (1999a), Nie soll der Mensch so viel aushalten müssen, wie er aushalten kann, in: *Drucksache N.F. 1 Paul Virilio*, Berlin.

--- (1999b), *Remnants of Auschwitz. The Witness and the Archive*, trans. Daniel Heller-Roazen, New York: Zone Books.

--- (2002), *Homo sacer. Die souveräne Macht und das nackte Leben*, Frankfurt a. M.

--- (2003a), *Die kommende Gemeinschaft*, Berlin; (1993) *The Coming Community*, trans. Michael Hardt, Minneapolis: University of Minnesota Press.

--- (2003b), *Das Offene. Der Mensch und das Tier*, Frankfurt a. M.

--- (2005), *Profanierungen*, Frankfurt a. M.; *Profanations* (2007), trans. Jeff Fort, New York: Zone Books.

--- (2008), *Was ist ein Dispositiv?*, Zurich, Berlin; (2009) *What Is an Apparatus?*, trans David Kishik and Stefan Pedetella, Stanford CA: Stanford University Press.

--- (2009), *Signatura rerum. Über die Methode*, Frankfurt a. M.

--- (2010), *Nacktheiten*, Frankfurt a. M.

Almanacco Letterario Bompiani 1962 (1962), Milan.

Almanacco Letterario Bompiani 1963 (1963), Milan.

Anders, Günther (1980), *Die Antiquiertheit des Menschen, Vol. 1: Über die Seele im Zeitalter der zweiten industriellen Revolution*, Munich.

Badiou, Alain, Jacques Rancière (1996), *Politik der Wahrheit*, Vienna, Berlin.

Baecker, Dirk (2007), *Studien zur nächsten Gesellschaft*, Frankfurt a. M.

Balestrini, Nanni (2008), Attività combinatorie. A partire dal *Tristano* di Nanni Balestrini, in: *Il Verri*, no. 38, Special Issue on Nanni Balestrini, October 2008.

--- (2010), *Tristano. No. 7852 von 109027350432000 möglichen Romanen*, Frankfurt a. M.

Bartels, Klaus (2000), Erinnern, Vergessen, Entinnern. Das Gedächtnis des Internet, in: *Lab – Jahrbuch 2000 für Künste und Apparate,* ed. Thomas Hensel, Hans Ulrich Reck, and Siegfried Zielinski, Cologne.

Barthes, Roland (2010), *Mythologies,* édition illustrée, Paris ; English edition : (1972), *Mythologies,* trans Annette Lavers, London, Paladin.

Bast, Gerald, and Brigitte Felderer (eds.) (2010), *Art and Now. Über die Zukunft künstlerischer Produktivitätsstrategien,* Vienna.

Bataille, Georges (2000), Die innere Erfahrung nebst Methode der Meditation und Postskriptum von 1953, *Atheologische Summe (La somme athéologique)* vol. 1, Munich.

--- (2002), Die Freundschaft und Das Halleluja, *Atheologische Summe (La somme athéologique)* vol. 2, Munich; *The Unfinished System Of Non-knowledge* (2001), ed. and introduction by Stuart Kendall, trans. Michelle Kendall and Stuart Kendall, Minneapolis MN: University of Minnesota Press.

Baudry, Jean-Louis (1975), Le dispositif: Approches métapsychologiques de l'impression de réalité, in: *Communications* no. 23 "Psychanalyse et cinéma," pp. 56–72.

--- (1993), Ideologische Effekte erzeugt vom Basisapparat, in: *Eikon,* no. 5, pp. 34–43.

Baumgärtel, Tilman, Büro Friedrich (2002), [plug in] (ed.), *Install.exe – Jodi,* Basel.

Bellmer, Hans (1962), *Die Puppe,* Berlin.

--- (1975), Hans Bellmer, *Obliques,* Special Issue, Paris.

Benjamin, Walter (2002), *Medienästhetische Schriften,* ed. Detlef Schöttker, Frankfurt a. M.

Bense, Max (1960), *Programmierung des Schönen. Allgemeine Texttheorie und Textästhetik,* Baden-Baden, Krefeld.

--- (1965), Projekte generativer Ästhetik, in: M. Bense and Elisabeth Walther (eds.), *computer-grafik,* Edition Rot, no. 19, Stuttgart, pp. 11–13.

--- (1968), Estetika i programiranje/Ästhetik und Programmierung, in: *bit international I,* Galerije grada Zagreba, Zagreb.

--- (1998), Technische Existenz, in: M. Bense, *Ausgewählte Schriften, vol. 3, Ästhetik und Texttheorie,* Stuttgart, Weimar.

Beuys, Joseph (1996), *Konzert Joseph Beuys, Coyote III, Nam June Paik, Piano Duet,* Berlin.

Black, Edwin (2001), *IBM and the Holocaust. The Strategic Alliance between Nazi Germany and America's Most Powerful Corporation,* New York.

Blumenberg, Hans (2009), *Geistesgeschichte der Technik,* Frankfurt a. M.

Borrelli, Arianna (2008), Aspects of the Astrolabe. *Architectonica ratio in tenth and eleventh-century Europe*, in: *Sudhoffs Archiv*, no. 57, Stuttgart.

Brecht, Bertolt (1967), *Gesammelte Werke, Vol. 16, Schriften zum Theater 2*, Frankfurt a. M.; English edition: (1964), *Brecht on Theatre. The Development of an Aesthetic*, ed. and trans. John Willett, Methuen: London.

Brzeziński, Zbigniew (1970), *Between Two Ages. America's Role in the Technetronic Era*, Viking Press, New York.

Buber, Martin (2009), *Das dialogische Prinzip*, Gütersloh.

Burroughs, William, S. (1970), *Die elektronische Revolution*, Bonn.

Caillois, Roger (n.d.), *Die Spiele und die Menschen – Maske und Rausch*, Munich, Vienna; English edition: (1961), *Man, Play, and Games*, Urbana, IL.

Campanelli, Vito (2010), *Web Aesthetics: How Digital Media Affect Culture and Society*, Rotterdam.

Cesarano, Giorgio (1983), *Der erotische Aufstand*, Berlin.

Chapman, Jake (2003), *Meatphysics*, London.

--- (2005), and Dinos Chapman, *Hell, Sixty-five Million Years BC; Sex, Death, Insult to Injury; The Chapman Family Collection*, ed. Eckhard Schneider, Bregenz.

--- (2007), and Dinos Chapman, *Jake and Dinos Chapman*, New Art Up-Close 3, London.

--- (2008), *The Marriage of Reason and Squalor*, London.

--- (n.d.), Jake and Dinos, *Disasters of War*, n.p.

Chopin, Henri (2006), *graphpoemachines. sculture magnetiche e dattilopoemi / magnetic sculptures and typewriterpoems*, Sordevolo.

Cohen-Séat, Gilbert (1963), La civiltà dell'immagine, in: *Almanacco Letterario Bompiani 1963*, Milan.

Communications (1975), no. 23 "Psychanalyse et cinéma," Paris.

Dahlmüller, Götz, Wulf D. Hund, and Helmut Kommer (1974), *Politische Fernsehfibel: Materialien zur Klassenkommunikation, Strategien für Zuschauer*, Reinbek.

De Landa, Manuel (1997), *Meshworks, Hierarchies and Interfaces*, online: http://www.t0.or.at/delanda/meshwork.htm.

Deleuze, Gilles (1989), *Das Bewegungs-Bild. Kino I*, Frankfurt a. M.

--- (1990), *Das Zeit-Bild. Kino II*, Frankfurt a. M.

Derrida, Jacques (2000), *Grammatologie*, Frankfurt a. M.

--- (2001), *Die unbedingte Universität*, Frankfurt a. M.

Diederichs, Helmut H. (1973), *Konzentration in den Massenmedien. Systematischer Überblick zur Situation in der BRD*, Munich.

Dröge, Franz (1972), *Wissen ohne Bewußtsein*, Frankfurt a. M.

Dwoskin, Stephen (1975), *Film Is: The International Free Cinema*, London.

Ellul, Jacques (1973), *Propaganda. The Formation of Mens Attitudes*, New York.

Enzensberger, Hans Magnus (1976), Von der Unaufhaltsamkeit des Kleinbürgertums. Eine soziologische Grille, in: *Kursbuch 45*, Berlin.

--- (2000), *Einladung zu einem Poesie-Automaten*, Frankfurt a. M.

Fargier, Jean-Paul (1992), Die letzte Analogie vor dem Digitalen, in: *Video: Apparat/Medium, Kunst, Kultur*, ed. Siegfried Zielinski, Frankfurt a. M.

Fierz-David, Hans Eduard (1952), *Die Entwicklungsgeschichte der Chemie*, Basel.

Figuier, Louis (1868), *Les Merveilles de la science ou description populaire des inventions modernes. [1], Machine à vapeur, bateaux à vapeur, locomotive et chemins de fer, locomobiles, machine électrique, paratonnerres, pile de Volta, électro-magnétisme*, Paris.

Flusser, Vilém (1983), *Für eine Philosophie der Photographie*, Göttingen; English edition: (2000) *Towards a Philosophy of Photography*, London: Reaktion Books.

--- (2000), Von den Möglichkeiten einer Leibkarte, in: *Lab: Jahrbuch 2000 für Künste und Apparate*, published by the Academy of Media Arts Cologne (KHM) and the Friends of the KHM, Cologne.

--- (2008), *Kommunikologie weiter denken: Die Bochumer Vorlesungen*, ed. Silvia Wagnermaier and Siegfried Zielinski, Frankfurt a. M.

--- (2010), *We Shall Survive in the Memories of Others*, DVD, ed. C3 Budapest and the Vilém Flusser Archive Berlin, Cologne.

Foucault, Michel (1974), *Die Ordnung der Dinge. Eine Archäologie der Humanwissenschaften*, Frankfurt a. M.

--- (1978), *Dispositive der Macht: Über Sexualität, Wissen und Wahrheit*, Berlin.

Franke, Herbert W., and Gottfried Jäger (1973), *Apparative Kunst: Vom Kaleidoskop zum Computer*, Cologne.

Fuller, Matthew (2003), *Behind The Blip. Essays on the Culture of Software*, New York.

Galloway, Alexander R., 2008, The Unworkable Interface, in: *New Literary History* vol. 39, no. 4.

--- and Eugene Thacker (2007), *The Exploit. A Theory of Networks*, Minneapolis, London.

Galloway, Anne (2008), *A Brief History of the Future of Urban Computing and Locative Media*, PhD diss., Carleton University Ottawa, www.purselipsquarejaw.org/dissertation.html, 10.4.2011.

Georgiadis, Sokratis (1989), Giedions Versuch einer ästhetischen Theorie der Moderne, in: *Sigfried Giedion 1888–1968. Der Entwurf einer modernen Tradition*, Zurich, pp. 17–29.

Giedion, Sigfried (1948), *Mechanization Takes Command*, Oxford.

Glaesemer, Jürgen (1987), *Die Gleichzeitigkeit des Anderen. Materialien zu einer Ausstellung*, Stuttgart, Teufen.

Grafe, Frieda (1976), Ein anderer Eindruck vom Begriff meines Körpers. Friederike Pezold: Video, Zeichnungen und Fotos, in: *Filmkritik*, vol. 20, no. 231.

Graham, Beryl, and Sarah Cook (2010), *Rethinking Curating. Art after New Media*, Cambridge.

Grawert-May, Erik (1980), *Zur Entstehung von Polizei- und Liebeskunst. Versuch einer anderen Geschichte des Auges*, Tübingen.

Gysin, Brion (1986), *Calligraphies, Permutations, Cut ups*, Paris.

--- (2010), *Dream Machine*, ed. Laura Hoptman, London.

Habermas, Jürgen (1984), *The Theory of Communicative Action, vol. 1, Reason and the Rationalization of Society*, trans. Thomas McCarthy, Boston, MA: Beacon Press.

Hadler, Florian (2010), Virus, iPhone, Dispositiv. Potential und Grenzen einer Metapher, in: Ästhetik und Kommunikation no. 149/150.

--- (2011), *Denken nach den Medien*, Diploma thesis, University of the Arts Berlin.

Hartwig, Wolfgang (1955), *Physik als Kunst: Über die philosophischen Gedanken Johann Wilhelm Ritters*, PhD diss., Freiburg i. B.

Heath, Stephen (1997), Der kinematographische Apparat. Technologie als historische und kulturelle Form, in: R. Riesinger (ed.), (2003), *Der kinematographische Apparat. Geschichte und Gegenwart einer Debatte*, Nodus, Münster.

Hegel, Georg, Wilhelm Friedrich (1983), *Enzyklopädie der philosophischen Wissenschaften im Grundrisse, Part 2: Die Naturphilosophie mit den mündlichen Zusätzen*, Collected Works, vol. 9, Frankfurt a. M.; English edition: (1970) *Hegel's Philosophy of Nature*, ed. and trans. M.J. Petry, vol. 2, London: George Allen & Unwin.

--- (1986), *Grundlinien der Philosophie des Rechts*, Collected Works, vol. 7, Frankfurt a. M.

Hendricks, Jon (1988), *Fluxus Codex*, Detroit, New York.

Hübener, Wolfgang (1986), *Der dreifache Tod des modernen Subjekts*, manuscript from the seminar "Das unterwürfige Subjekt. Stationen neuzeitlicher Selbstentmächtigungsemphase," Philosophy institute, Free University Berlin, winter semester 1986/1987; see also: homepage.ruhr-uni-bochum.de/michael.renemann/Huebener_Tod_des_Subjekts.pdf

269

Interfacing Realities (1997), by Knowbotic Research, William J. Mitchell, Stephen Perrella, Stacey Spiegel, Siegfried Zielinski, Rotterdam.

Irren-Offensive, Die Zeitschrift von Ver-rückten gegen Psychiatrie (1999), no. 8, Berlin.

Jones, Joe (1990), *Music Machines from the Sixties until Now*, Berlin.

Kamper, Dietmar (1978), Maske, Schminke, Mimikry. Über Strategien der Nicht-Identität, in: *Make Up*, ed. U. Brüning, U. Hiersch, J. Kraft, and U. Raulf, Werdorf.

--- (1989), Das Auge: Zur Geschichte der audiovisuellen Technologie. Narziss, Echo, Anthropodizee, Theodizee. D. Kamper in conversation with Bion Steinborn and Christine Eichel-Streiber, in: *Filmfaust*, no.74.

Kittler, Friedrich (1984), *Aufschreibesysteme 1800/1900*, Munich.

--- (1986), *Grammophon – Film – Typewriter*, Berlin; English edition: (1999), *Gramophone, Film, Typewriter*, trans. Geoffrey Winthrop-Young and Michael Wutz, Stanford.

Klassenmedium Fernsehen (1973), published an edited by the Neue Gesellschaft für Bildende Kunst, Arbeitsgruppe Massenmedien (Knut Hickethier, Peter Jim Kruse, Erwin und Karin Reiss, Barbara Scholtyssek, Irene Tietze-Lusk, and Ernst Volland), Berlin.

Kleinrock, Leonard (1961), *Information Flow in Large Communication Nets*, Proposal for a Ph.D. Thesis, Boston, MA, 31 May 1961, www. lk.cs.ucla.edu/LK/Bib/REPORT/PhD/, 26.12. 2010.

Knilli, Friedrich (ed.) (1971a), *Die Unterhaltung der deutschen Fernsehfamilie. Ideologiekritische Kurzanalysen von Serien*, Munich.

--- (1971b), Erwin Reiss, and Karin Reiss (illustrations), *Einführung in die Film- und Fernsehanalyse. Ein ABC für Zuschauer*, Steinbach.

--- (1982), and Siegfried Zielinski (eds.), *"Holocaust" zur Unterhaltung. Anatomie eines internationalen Bestsellers*, Berlin.

Kolbe, Jürgen (ed.) (1973), *Neue Ansichten einer künftigen Germanistik*, Munich.

Konkursbuch. Zeitschrift für Vernunftkritik (1980), no. 5, Tübingen.

--- (1981), no. 7, Tübingen.

Kostelanetz, Richard (ed.) (1973), *John Cage*, Cologne.

Krafft-Ebing, Richard von (1886), *Psychopathia sexualis: Eine klinisch-forensische Studie*, Stuttgart.

Krauss, Rolf H., Manfred Schmalriede, and Michael Schwarz (eds.) (1983), *Kunst mit Fotografie*, Berlin.

Lacan, Jacques (1975), Das Spiegelstadium als Bildner der Ichfunktion wie sie uns in der psychoanalytischen Erfahrung erscheint. Report at the 16th International Congress of Psychoanalysis, Zurich, 17 July 1949, in: *Schriften I.*, Frankfurt a. M.

Lasswell, Harold Dwight (1971), *Propaganda Technique in World War I.*, Cambridge, MA, London.

Lévi-Strauss, Claude (1981), *Die elementaren Strukturen der Verwandtschaft*, Frankfurt a. M; English edition: (1969), *The Elementary Structures of Kinship*, ed. Rodney Needham, trans. J.H. Bell, J.R. von Sturmer, and Rodney Needham.

Lévy, Pierre (1987), *La machine univers. Création, cognition et culture informatique*, Paris.

--- (1990), *Les technologies de l'intelligence*, Paris.

--- (1997), *L'intelligence collective. Pour une anthropologie du cyberspace*, Paris.

--- (2001), *Cyberculture*, trans. Robert Bononno, Minneapolis, University of Minnesota Press.

Levine, Rick, Christopher Locke, Doc Searls, and David Weinberger (2000), *The Cluetrain Manifesto*, New York.

Lewallen, Constance M. (2001), *The Dream of the Audience: Theresa Hak Kyung Cha, 1951–1982*, Berkeley, Los Angeles, London.

Link, David (2006), There Must Be an Angel. On the Beginnings of the Arithmetics of Rays, in: *Variantology 2. On Deep Time Relations of Arts, Sciences and Technologies*, Cologne.

--- (2007), *Poesiemaschinen/Maschinenpoesie. Zur Frühgeschichte computerisierter Texterzeugung und generativer Systeme*, Munich.

--- (2010), Scrambling T-R-U-T-H: Rotating Letters as a Form of Thought, in: *Variantology 4*, Cologne.

Linke, Detlef, B. (2001), *Kunst und Gehirn. Die Eroberung des Unsichtbaren*, Reinbek.

Lombardi, Mark (2002), *Global Networks*, New York.

Lovink, Geert (2002), *Dark Fiber. Tracking Critical Internet Culture*, Cambridge, MA: MIT Press. German edition: *Dark Fiber. Auf den Spuren einer kritischen Internetkultur*, Bonn.

Lyotard, Jean-François (1985a), *Immaterialität und Postmoderne*, Berlin; English edition, *The Postmodern Condition*, Manchester University Press, 1984.

--- (1985b), *Les immatériaux: Album et inventaire*, exhib. cat., Les Immatériaux exhibition, from 28 March to 15 July, Centre Georges Pompidou, Paris.

Mackay, Charles (1995) [1841], *Extraordinary Popular Delusions and the Madness of Crowds*, Ware, Herts.: Wordsworth Editions; (1992), *Aus den Annalen des Wahns*, Frankfurt a. M.

Manovich, Lev (2001), *The Language of New Media*, Cambridge.

--- (2008), *Software Takes Command*, lab.softwarestudies.com/2008/11/softbook.html, November 20, 2008.

271

Massen/Medien/Politik (1976), Special Issue AS 10 of the journal *Das Argument*, with articles by J.J. Berns, B. Hoffmann, H. Holzer, E. Jürgens, D. Kramer, E. Reiss, J. Rocchi, A. Soppe, C. Unger, G. Würzberg, and S. Zielinski, Berlin.

McLuhan, Marshall (1951), *The Mechanical Bride: Folklore of Industrial Man*, Boston.

McQuail, Denis, and Sven Windahl (1981), *Communication Models for the Study of Mass Communications*, London, New York.

Metz, Christian (1966), La grande syntagmatique du film narratif, in: *Communications*, no. 8.

--- (1968), Probleme der Denotation im Spielfilm, in: *SPITZ*, no. 27.

--- (1973), *Sprache und Film*, Frankfurt a. M.

--- (1975), Le signifiant imaginaire, in: *Communications*, no. 23 "Psychanalyse et cinéma," pp. 3–55.

--- (2000), *Der imaginäre Signifikant. Psychoanalyse und Kino*, afterword by Robert Riesinger, Münster.

Moles, Abraham A. (1962), *Erstes Manifest der permutationellen Kunst*, Edition Rot, no. 8, Stuttgart.

--- (1971), *Informationstheorie und ästhetische Wahrnehmung*, Cologne.

--- (1988), Zur Philosophiefiktion bei Vilém Flusser, in: *Kulturrevolution*, ed. Alex Demirović and Walter Prigge, no. 17/18.

Montaigne, Michel de (2005), *Von der Freundschaft*, Munich.

--- The Essays of Montaigne, Complete, by Michel de Montaigne, Translated by Charles Cotton, Edited by William Carew Hazlitt, 1877, Chapter XXVII—Of Friendship.

Müller, Heiner (1981), Mich interessiert der Fall Althusser, in: *Alternative: Zeitschrift für Literatur und Diskussion, Louis Althusser. Frühe Schriften zu Kunst und Literatur*, no. 137, Berlin.

Nancy, Jean-Luc (1999), *Die Musen*, Stuttgart.

Nietzsche, Friedrich (1882), §324. In media vita, in: *Die fröhliche Wissenschaft, vol. 1*, Chemnitz; English edition: Aphorism §324. In media vita, in: *The Gay Science*, ed. Bernard Williams, Cambridge, Cambridge University Press, 2001.

Novalis' ausgewählte Werke (n.d.), ed. Wilhelm Bölsche, Leipzig, here vol. 1.

Paik, Nam June (1977), *Nam June Paik Werke 1946–1976, Musik-Fluxus-Video*, Kölnischer Kunstverein, Cologne.

--- (1984), *Art for 25 Millionen People: Bonjour, Monsieur Orwell; Kunst und Satelliten in der Zukunft*, DAAD-Galerie, Berlin.

--- (1989), *Eine Kerze, One Candle*, Frankfurt a. M.

--- (2004), *Global Groove 2004*, Ostfildern-Ruit.

Panizza, Oskar (1898), *Psichopatia criminalis. Anleitung um die vom Gericht für notwendig erkanten Geisteskrankheiten psichjatrisch zu eruïeren und wissenschaftlich festzustellen*, Zurich.

Parolini, Giuditta (2008), Olivetti Elea 9003: Between Scientific Research and Computer Business, in: *History of Computing and Education 3 (HCE3), World Computer Congress Milano 2008*, ed. John Impagliazzo, New York.

Peters, John Durham (1999), *Speaking into the Air. A History of the Idea of Communication*, Chicago, London.

Petroski, Henry (1990), *The Pencil: A History of Design and Circumstance*, New York.

--- (1994), *Messer, Gabel, Reißverschluss. Die Evolution der Gebrauchsgegenstände*, Basel, Boston, Berlin.

Pfeiffer, K. Ludwig (1999), *Das Mediale und das Imaginäre. Dimensionen kulturanthropologischer Medientheorie*, Frankfurt a. M.

Presas I Puig, Albert (2004), *Numbers, Proportions, Harmonies, and Practical Geometry in Ancient Art*, Berlin.

Prokop, Dieter (ed.) (1972–), *Massenkommunikationsforschung, 3 vols.: 1: Produktion, 2: Konsumtion, 3: Produktanalysen*, Frankfurt a. M.

Queneau, Raymond (2010), *Cent Mille Milliards de Poèmes*, Paris.

Rancière, Jaques (2005), *Die Politik der Bilder*, Zurich, Berlin.

--- (2006), *Die Aufteilung des Sinnlichen. Die Politik der Kunst und ihre Paradoxien*, ed. and introduction Maria Muhle, Berlin.

--- (2008), Ist Kunst widerständig?, Berlin.

Rheinberger, Hans-Jörg (2001), *Experimentalsysteme und epistemische Dinge. Eine Geschichte der Protheinsynthese im Reagenzglas*, Göttingen.

--- (2007), Über die Kunst, das Unbekannte zu erforschen, in: *Say It Isn't So*, ed. Peter Friese et al., Bremen.

Ritter, Johann Wilhelm (1984), Die Physik als Kunst. Ein Versuch, die Tendenz der Physik aus ihrer Geschichte zu deuten, in: *Ritters Fragmente aus dem Nachlasse eines jungen Physikers: Ein Taschenbuch für Freunde der Natur*, ed. Steffen and Birgit Dietzsch, Hanau; *Key Texts of Johann Wilhelm Ritter (1776–1810) on the Science and Art of Nature*, (2010), trans. and essays by Jocelyn Holland, Leiden, Boston, MA: Brill.

Dick Raaymakers: A Monograph (2008), ed. Arjen Mulder and Joke Brouwer, Rotterdam.

Robbe-Grillet, Alain (1961), *L'année dernière a Marienbad: ciné roman*, Paris.

Röller, Nils (2002), *Medientheorie im epistemischen Übergang: Hermann Weyls Philosophie der Mathematik und Naturwissenschaften und Ernst Cassirers Philosophie der symbolischen Formen im Wechselverhältnis*, Weimar.

273

--- (2011), *Empfindungskörper: Zur indirekten Erfahrung*, International Flusser-Lecture, Cologne.

Ronell, Avital (1989) *The Telephone Book*, Lincoln, NE: University of Nebraska Press; German edition (2001) *Das Telefonbuch: Technik, Schizophrenie, Elektrische Rede*, Berlin.

--- (2005), *The Test Drive*, Urbana, IL, Chicago.

Ropohl, Günter (1979), *Eine Systemtheorie der Technik. Zur Grundlegung der allgemeinen Technologie*, Munich, Vienna.

Sabri, Mahmoud (n.d. [1973]), *Quantum Realism: An Art of the Techno-nuclear Age*, n.p. [Iraq].

Schade, Sigrid (1989), Hans Bellmer: Die Posen der Puppe, in: *Kairos*, nos. 1, 2.

Schillinger, Joseph (2003), *The Mathematical Basis of the Arts, Part 1: Science and Esthetics*, New York.

Schiwy, Günther (1985), *Der französische Strukturalismus. Mode, Methode, Ideologie*, Reinbek.

Schmidgen, Henning (1997), *Das Unbewußte der Maschinen: Konzeptionen des Psychischen bei Guattari, Deleuze und Lacan*, Munich.

--- (2004), Peter Geimer, and Sven Dierig (eds.), *Kultur im Experiment*, Berlin.

Schrödinger, Erwin (1996) [1954], *Nature and the Greeks*, Cambridge.

Serres, Michel (1991), *Hermes I. Kommunikation*, Berlin.

Shannon, Claude E. (1948), A Mathematical Theory of Communication, in: *Bell System Technical Journal*, vol. 27, pp. 379–423, 623–656.

Simondon, Gilbert (1958), *Du mode d'existence des objets techniques*, Paris, Editions Aubier; *On the Mode of Existence of Technological Objects*, trans. Ninian Mellamphy, London: University of Western Ontario, 1980; *Die Existenzweise technischer Objekte*, trans. Michael Cuntz, Zurich 2012.

Telekommunikationsbericht (1976), published by the Kommission für den Ausbau des technischen Kommunikationssystems (KtK) on behalf of the Bundesministerium für das Post- und Fernmeldewesen, Bonn-Bad Godesberg.

Textsemiotik als Ideologiekritik (1977), ed. Peter Zima, Frankfurt a. M.

Turing, Alan M. (1948), Intelligent Machinery, Report for the National Physical Laboratory, reprinted in: *Machine Intelligence 5* (1969), ed. B. Meltzer and D. Michie, Edinburgh, pp. 3–23.

--- (1987), *Intelligence Service. Schriften*, ed. Bernhard Dotzler and Friedrich Kittler, Berlin.

Vattimo, Gianni (2005), *Jenseits vom Subjekt*, Vienna.

Video End (1976), ed. Pool Pfirsich [Horst Gerhard Haberl, Richard Kriesche, Karl Neubacher], Graz.

Virilio, Paul (1980), Die Dromoskopie oder das Licht der Geschwind-igkeit, in: *Konkursbuch*, no. 5, Tübingen.

--- (1986), *Krieg und Kino: Logistik der Wahrnehmung*, Munich.

--- (2002), *Unknown Quantity*, London.

--- (2007), *The Original Accident*, Cambridge.

Virno, Paolo, and Michael Hardt (eds.) (1996), *Radical Thought in Italy: A Potential Politics*, Minneapolis, London.

von Neumann, John (1928), Zur Theorie der Gesellschaftsspiele, in: *Mathematische Annalen* 100, 295–320; English trans.: On the Theory of Games of Strategy, trans. Sonya Bargmann, in: Contributions to the Theory of Games, vol. IV, *Annals of Mathematics Studies 40* (1959), ed. A.W. Tucker and R.D. Luce, pp. 13–42, Princeton University Press. The foundational English text of games theory, however, is: John von Neumann and Oskar Morgenstern, *Theory of Games and Economic Behavior* (1944), Princeton Univ. Press.

Vostell: Happening & Leben (1970), Luchterhand-Druck 8, Neuwied-Berlin.

Vostell: Leben=Kunst=Leben (1993), published by Kunstgalerie Gera, Leipzig.

Wege elektronischer Musik (1991), brochure of the Rheinisches Musikfest concert series, held 10–31 May 1991, Cologne.

Weibel, Peter (1992), Video als Raumkunst: Arbeitsnotizen, in: Siegfried Zielinski, ed., (1992a), *Video*, Frankfurt a. M.

Weingart, P. (1976), Die historische Funktion der Technik aus der Sicht der Soziologie, in: *Technikgeschichte*, no. 43.

Wiener, Norbert (1948), *Cybernetics, or Control and Communications in the Animal and the Machine*, New York, John Wiley.

Wiener, Oswald (1969), *Die Verbesserung von Mitteleuropa*, Reinbek.

Williams, Raymond [1974] (2003), *Television: Technology and Cultural Form*, London: Routledge Classics.

Wittgenstein, Ludwig (1970), *Das blaue Buch*, Frankfurt a. M.

--- (1975) *Wittgenstein's Lectures on the Foundations of Mathematics, Cambridge 1939*, ed. Cora Diamond, Hassocks, Sussex: Harvester Press; (1978), *Vorlesungen über die Grundlagen der Mathematik*, Schriften 7, Frankfurt am Main.

Youngblood, Gene (1970), *Expanded Cinema*, with an introduction by R. Buckminster Fuller, London.

Zielinski, Siegfried (1982), and Til T. Radevagen, Video-Software. Annäherungsversuche an einen neuen Markt, in: *Media Perspektiven*, no. 3.

--- (1992a), (ed.), *Video: Apparat/Medium, Kunst, Kultur. Ein internationaler Reader*, Frankfurt a. M.

--- (1992b), and Nils Röller, "Cogito ergo Video." Ein Textversuch zu Godards *Histoire(s) du cinéma*, in: Österreichisches Jahrbuch für Filmtheorie, vol. 3, ed. Gottfried Schlemmer et al., Vienna.

--- (1992c), Expanded Reality, in: *Cyberspace,* ed. Florian Rötzer and Peter Weibel, Munich.

--- (1993), Die 2 EJMs der Reihenphotographie. Zu einigen ihrer Differenzen in der Annäherung an den Körper vermittels aufzeichnender Apparate, in: *EIKON*, no.7/8.

--- (1999), *Audiovisions: Cinema and Television as Entr'actes in History,* trans. G. Custance, Amsterdam.

--- (2005), Theologici electrici, Einige Passagen, in: *Theologie und Politik. Walter Benjamin und ein Paradigma der Moderne,* ed. Bernd Witte and Mauro Ponzi, Berlin (2006 also published in an Italian version, Turin).

--- (2006), *Deep Time of the Media – Towards an Archaeology of Hearing and Seeing by Technical Means,* trans. G. Custance, Cambridge MA, London, MIT Press.

--- (2010) [1985], *Zur Geschichte des Videorecorders,* Potsdam (new revised edition).

--- (2010) God is electric, my soul is electric, nature is electric / Gott ist elektrisch, meine Seele ist elektrisch, die Natur ist elektrisch. For Paul DeMarinis, engl trans. G. Custance. Catalog, DAAD, Berlin (German / English).

--- (2005–2011), (ed.), *Variantology. On Deep Time Relations Between Arts, Sciences, Technologies,* 5 vols, ed. with Silvia Wagnermaier (vol. 1), David Link (vol. 2), Eckhard Fürlus (vols. 3–5), Cologne.

--- (2011), Thinking About Art After the Media: Research as Practiced Culture of Experiment, trans. G. Custance, in: *The Routledge Companion to Research in the Arts,* ed. Michael Biggs and Henrik Karlsson, London, New York.

--- (2013) Designing & Revealing: Some Aspects of a Genealogy of Projection, trans. G. Custance in: M. Blassnigg (ed.), *Light, Image, Imagination: The Spectrum Beyond Reality and Illusion.* Amsterdam

Univocal Publishing
123 North 3rd Street, #202
Minneapolis, MN 55401
www.univocalpublishing.com

ISBN 9781937561161